# Clusters of Creativity

# Clusters of Creativity

Enduring Lessons on Innovation and
Entrepreneurship from Silicon Valley and
Europe's Silicon Fen

Rob Koepp

JOHN WILEY & SONS, LTD

Email (for orders and customer service enquiries): cs-books@wiley.co.uk
Visit our Home Page on www.wileyeurope.com or www.wiley.com

*Other Wiley Editorial Offices*

John Wiley & Sons Inc., 111 River Street, Hoboken, NJ 07030, USA

Jossey-Bass, 989 Market Street, San Francisco, CA 94103-1741, USA

Wiley-VCH Verlag GmbH, Boschstr. 12, D-69469 Weinheim, Germany

John Wiley & Sons Australia Ltd, 33 Park Road, Milton, Queensland 4064, Australia

John Wiley & Sons (Asia) Pte Ltd, 2 Clementi Loop #02-01, Jin Xing Distripark, Singapore 129809

John Wiley & Sons Canada Ltd, 22 Worcester Road, Etobicoke, Ontario, Canada M9W 1L1

**British Library Cataloguing in Publication Data**

A catalogue record for this book is available from the British Library

ISBN 0-471-49604-9

Project management by Originator, Gt Yarmouth, Norfolk (typeset in 12/15pt Garamond)
Printed and bound in Great Britain by Antony Rowe Ltd, Chippenham, Wiltshire
This book is printed on acid-free paper responsibly manufactured from sustainable forestry
in which at least two trees are planted for each one used for paper production.

To Pete Snetzinger
*for encouraging visions*

and to Mom and Dad
*for helping to make them a reality*

PROMETHEUS: Ay, man thro' me ceased to know his death.
CHORUS: What cure couldst thou discover for this curse?
PROMETHEUS: Blind hopes I sent to nestle in man's heart.
CHORUS: This was a goodly gift thou gavest them.
PROMETHEUS: Yet more I gave them, even the boon of fire.
CHORUS: What? radiant fire, to things ephemeral?
PROMETHEUS: Yea—many an art too shall they learn thereby!

Aeschylus, *The Prometheus Bound* [1]

# Contents

# Contents

# Acknowledgments

Like the regions and enterprises this book examines, *Clusters of Creativity* has itself benefited from facilitation contributed by a great many individuals.

First among these is Charles Hampden-Turner. The chance to work with Charles at Cambridge University's Judge Institute of Management Studies was invaluable to the development of my own thinking about managing in divergent geographic settings. I took much encouragement from the success of Charles' recent research on cross-cultural management when I set out to explore the applicability of the lessons offered by locations such as Silicon Valley and Silicon Fen. I owe a large debt to Charles' discoveries about global management practices as his writings opened my mind to an approach that eschews cultural bias in order to gain a more nuanced and practical understanding of diverse strategies and leadership styles.

I also have Charles to thank for introducing me to Diane Taylor at John Wiley & Sons. Diane has been an exceptionally supportive editor and her faith in the book has provided a tremendous boost to my writing it. Diane and her assistants, Anne Flynn and Lorna Skinner, have provided much appreciated assistance and direction as the book has taken shape.

Richard Barker, Andrew Brown, Andy Cosh, and Chong Choi are among the others at the Judge Institute who provided helpful discussions and commentary about the book at various stages. David King, Alan Munro, Steve Young, Andy Hopper, Maurice Wilkes, and Shôn Ffowcs Williams—senior faculty members of science and engineering departments of the university who have participated in the Cambridge

Phenomenon in various ways—graciously shared their experiences with me. Library staff of various Cambridge University departments, Sharon Hicks at the Judge Institute library in particular, helped to make my data mining efforts all the more efficient and effective.

Bill Wicksteed of SQW (formerly Segal Quince Wicksteed) and Roger Quince (of the biotechnology science park Granta Park but a founder of Segal Quince Wicksteed) separately provided many helpful opinions based on their long-running research and observations of the Cambridge Phenomenon.

Elsewhere in Cambridge, there were many others who provided assistance at various levels. Philip Shaw, a serial entrepreneur with long-standing and far-reaching ties to Cambridge's commercial and academic circles, offered valuable perspectives and good leads. Judi Coe and Suzy Howes at the Cambridge Network offered useful introductions and kindly arranged for my attendance at many of their organization's events. Caroline Swift at the Cambridge Hi-tech Association of Small Enterprises was similarly helpful. Bruce Fell, a fellow alumnus of Cambridge MBA8, subjected himself to uncountable hours of verbal and emailed debate concerning editorial, stylistic, and factual aspects of the manuscript. His prodding arguments and counter-arguments, offered in the sort of meticulous detail at which Bruce excels, while not always accepted, were always appreciated and invaluably contributed to clarifying the positions I take within the following pages of this book.

Among the many I am grateful to in Silicon Valley, my especial thanks go to Robert Patterson at the law firm Squire Sanders. Bob, who has been active in Silicon Valley's thriving legal community since 1972, unhesitatingly shared his knowledge and experiences and made special arrangements for my attendance at a variety of functions and events to which I would have otherwise not had access. I am grateful to Scott Wilson of Venture Management Associates for providing both enlightening conversation and the introduction to Bob. For the introduction to Scott, thanks go to Rosemary Macedo at the investment management firm of Bailard, Biehl & Kaiser. Rosy assisted in numerous other ways too, not the least of which included providing me with a place to stay during my commutes back to the Valley and organizing social get-togethers with her friends and fellow members of the cluster's Caltech mafia.

Within Silicon Valley's academic circles, my thinking benefited especially from interviews and conversations with members of the Stanford community, notably President and Professor John Hennessy, Professor Emeritus and former Vice President Bill Miller, and James Gibbons, Professor and Dean Emeritus of Electrical Engineering. I am also grateful for enlightening discussions with other distinguished members of Stanford's faculty: Henry Rowen, Tim Lenoir, Margaruette Gong Hancock, and long-time friend Haun Saussy. I very much enjoyed ongoing discussions with Martin Kenney at his dual offices in Berkeley and Cambridge. University library staff at Stanford and Berkeley provided helpful assistance, especially Henry Lowood and others at Stanford's university archives department. Doug Henton of Collaborative Economics and Steve Levy of the Center for Continuing Study of the California Economy shared valuable insights concerning many aspects of Silicon Valley's economic structure and relevant public policy issues.

While preparing this book, I also conducted research trips to New York's "Silicon Alley" and the "Silicon Island" of Taiwan. Although in the end I elected not to feature either of these clusters, preliminary investigations in those locations nevertheless benefited the final written product as they enhanced my understanding of the global phenomenon of Siliconia. Special thanks to Marc Feigen of Katzenbach Partners whose firm kindly provided funding for my trip to Silicon Alley and for him arranging visits for me to various Alley firms. In Taiwan, my research efforts were aided by C. Y. Chang, President of National Chiao Tung University; Wei-An Chang, Professor at National Tsing Hua University; Dung-sheng Chen, Professor at National Taiwan University; Teresa Yang, Deputy Secretary General of the Taiwan Venture Capital Association; Y. C. Li, President of Fortune Consulting Group; Hubert Chen, Manager at the Electronics Research & Service Organization of the Industrial Technology Research Institute; and Rear Admiral Ming-Chao Hsu (Ret.), Vice President of Tai E Trading.

In that much of the research was itinerant, occasional difficulties with my well-traveled notebook computer were especially hard felt. IT problems were put aright on different occasions by Paul Nguyen, an old friend, and Björn Weidner, a new one. But for their efforts to rescue my data from an often low-performing piece of high-technology, this book would have not only been much delayed but the sanity of the author perhaps stretched beyond the breaking point.

I also want to thank all those who gave their time to be interviewed for this book. From casual conversations in cafés and building hallways to formal discussions in laboratories and meeting rooms, the insights volunteered by people immeasurably broadened my understanding of the book's subject matter. Those whose quoted remarks appear in the text represent just some of the individuals who kindly agreed to participate in both on and off-the-record interviews.

I began working in Silicon Valley in 1992 as a salesman and marketer of surface mount technology and semiconductor manufacturing equipment. The job exposed me to many aspects of the cluster's industrial functioning and the people I met along the way and the lessons I gained from them planted the seeds for this book, although of course neither they nor I realized it at the time. Even though they did not directly (or, perhaps more accurately, consciously) contribute to the research that went into *Clusters of Creativity*, I do thank them for having been a major part of its inspiration.

In a book such as this, where so many people have contributed in so many ways, it is important to stress that any errors or omissions in the writing effort and final product are mine and mine alone. An omission which I readily admit to is the time spent away from Rwo-mei, my wife, and our two children, Michelle and Robbie, during the progress of the book. Their understanding and support for allowing me to focus on this project made all the difference. I look forward to making up for times sacrificed.

# Introduction: The Hidden Lessons of "Siliconia"                    1

## THE SILICON VALLEYS OF THE WORLD

If names are anything to judge by, the imitative, often tenuous, styling of high-technology clusters around the world shows just how eager people are to claim their own version of Silicon Valley. Among the mountainous pinnacles of Austria now protrudes a Silicon Alps. A swath of Silicon Tundra can be found in the frigid latitudes of Canada. An industrial oasis known as Silicon Wadi graces the arid landscape of Israel. A Silicon Fen stretches over the green lowlands of England. The dykes of the Netherlands protect a Silicon Polder. The high-tech product workhorse of the world, Taiwan, is known as Silicon Island. Areas lacking the identifiable geology for siliconization simply localize the Silicon Valley title: Bangalore is called the Silicon Valley of India; Singapore and Penang vie for acknowledgment as the Silicon Valley of East Asia. A website that has made an electronic sport of identifying global "Siliconia"—clusters of technology-based industry that carry nicknames with the word "Silicon" or other technical-sounding designators—registers over 100 locations.[2]

Although the US is already home to the original Silicon Valley, throughout its lands as well you can find ample attempts, if made only in name, to claim a slice of Siliconia. Witness the existence of a Silicon Bayou, Silicon Glacier, Silicon Gulch, Silicon Hills, Silicon Hollow, Silicon Mesa, Silicon Prairie, Silicon Sandbar, and even a Silicon Swamp. The heated competition in the US for names is so intense, and the range of easily associated geographic features sufficiently limited, that disputed rights to Siliconia nomenclatures have spawned lawsuits.[3]

Perhaps the ultimate complement to *the* Valley—an area not so long ago looked down on by the more cosmopolitan regions of America as an agricultural backwater—is that the *haute monde* of Manhattan now calls its concentration of Web design firms Silicon Alley. This uptown New York techno-district boasts one of the closest mimics to the original Silicon Valley name and provides a telling metaphor for just how far the Valley has "made it," becoming a part of the world's popular imagination and a location of great cachet within the planet's corporate topography.

As Ethernet inventor Bob Metcalfe famously put it, "Silicon Valley is the only place on earth not trying to figure out how to become Silicon Valley."[4] Exaggeration aside, the observation captures the pervasive eagerness to cultivate hotbeds of high-tech enterprise and the alluring yet elusive nature of Silicon Valley's magic. The accomplishments of Silicon Valley easily inspire the popular imagination: the rags-to-riches success stories, revolutionizing breakthroughs, gee-whiz gadgetry, explosive business growth, headline-grabbing corporate feats, and, most of all, extraordinary economic wealth generated by the cluster make it the ultimate technopolis in a Global Economy (a term frequently used as if interchangeable with the concept of a "New Economy") that progresses in large measure according to the creation and innovative application of advancing technologies.

Attendant to this spreading zeal for recreating Silicon Valley, a real problem surfaces in that the forces associated with the Valley's stunning accomplishments frequently blur into the stuff of hype and legend—a situation helped in no small measure by the powers of imagination and self-promotion for which Silicon Valley and its wider territory, the San Francisco Bay Area, are famous. The news media, business commentators, and academics often play supporting roles, providing as much fawning lionization as meaningful analysis in their interpretations of forces that have built up the Valley as a utopia of *techné*. In this and many other regards, something plentiful Silicon Valley typically lacks is a sense of context. The Valley may be a world apart but it is still very much of this world. A melting pot of people and ideas, the cluster has since its beginnings thrived as a magnet, not an island. The Silicon moniker has stuck for several decades but belies the origins of a vibrant, changing regional economy; one whose dynamism stretches back to a time before the arrival of the semiconductor industry, one that has also moved far beyond the genuinely "silicon" activities of chip- and computer-related manufacturing. The constancy of the nickname that has launched more than 100 derivations gives a false sense of permanence to a cluster whose enterprises thrive on the powers of reinvention. Silicon Valley is more an economy of concepts than products, more of entrepreneurship than technology *per se*. The Valley is most celebrated— and subsequently suffers from the excesses of overconfidence—during high-tech booms, the dotcom bubble that swelled during the final years of the 20th century being but a recent example. Yet one of the greatest strengths Silicon Valley entrepreneurs repeatedly demonstrate is the ability to lead their economy out of its downturns, to seize new opportunities in the face of general decline. The area's enduring strengths are in many ways best appreciated (and frequently overlooked) when the cluster is challenged, not when it is riding at the peak of the latest technology wave.

The same sort of balanced, contextual appreciation would also benefit an understanding of other high-tech clusters. Lurking within the names of all those "Siliconia" geographies popping up around the world is the implicit notion that these are just distanced (or knock-off) versions of the original Silicon Valley, distinguished mainly by physical features— fen, island, wadi, glen, beach . . . whatever. The Silicon name associations might make for good marketing or pass for catchy headlining of an area's advanced capabilities, but they gloss over the endogenous forces that contribute to the particular management creativity that drives these divergent locations. There is also the issue of popular theories on the nature and significance of Silicon Valley and other high-tech regional economies. These tend to exhibit two extremes of bias. On the one hand, there are arguments that the emergence and success of Silicon Valley is accidental, a kind of freak of economic nature. The bottom-line message here is that Silicon Valley and similar clusters are really not so special after all. As economic geographies purportedly created by the luck of "first-mover advantages" and anonymous "cumulative processes" that follow a destined "path-dependent" trajectory, the sheer ingenuity and dedication that various leaders have committed to guiding the development and direction of these clusters receives little more than passing, if any, consideration. From the opposite angle, contentions are made that Silicon Valley effectively has all the answers. One popular body of thought argues that the region has produced a superior, if not altogether infallible, culturally based "system" of networks that will guide business activity so that the cluster is able to defy the mortality that inheres industry- and product-based life cycles. The implication of this way of thinking is that Silicon Valley is so superlative a location that it has found a way to beat out observed realities of managerial capitalism. Accordingly, the Siliconia of other regions are admonished to adhere to the allegedly unfailing wisdom of Silicon Valley's networking culture and implement a radical, new model for enterprises and industries.

## SILICON VALLEY IN CONTEXT

*Clusters of Creativity* constitutes an attempt to look beyond such exaggerations and obfuscations. It offers readers a more balanced, appropriately nuanced, practical, and internationally relevant set of perspectives for understanding what Silicon Valley and similar phenomena represent. In order to devote enough in-depth analysis while keeping the book of reasonable scope and length, it focuses on two outstanding locations of Siliconia: the original Silicon Valley and Europe's "Silicon Fen," the high-tech cluster radiating out from Cambridge, England. The triumphalism, mystique, uncritical adulation, and simple mischaracterizations that surround Silicon Valley and Silicon Fen, the Valley's closest foreign counterpart, tend to work against deriving widely applicable insights into the powers that sustain the clusters. Although local conditions very much influence the ongoing development of these exemplary regions of the world's modern economy, their underlying significance is not wrapped up in enigmas (or, if one prefers, "accidents") of geography, history, culture, technological discovery, or industrial networks. The progress of the clusters can only be understood if one gets behind how they and the enterprises that populate them have been managed, specifically regarding how management practices facilitate the cluster's lifeblood of innovation and entrepreneurship—two pillars of economic behavior that are universal to all forms of economic existence, not just the particular sectors of advanced technology with which the Siliconia are so readily associated.

The inclusion of Silicon Fen in this book also does more than add international balance. The Cambridge cluster qualifies as the most innovative and entrepreneurial silicon landscape outside of the US. It is known of well enough in Britain, somewhat in Europe, and only sporadically heard of elsewhere in the world—this is despite Cambridge's unsurpassed importance in the history of modern science and its position as the birthplace of so much of the human knowledge that underpins high technology in the world today. A comparative analysis of how and why Silicon Fen exists and the reasons that, in spite of its manifold advantages, this location of Siliconia has obtained less recognition (a function of its having built up less economic mass) than Silicon Valley helps put in perspective the factors that really matter in the workings of a vibrant industrial cluster.

*Clusters of Creativity* furthermore highlights not only instances of best practice but also illuminates instances of managerial failure. Looking at where things go right as well as where things go wrong provides for a more holistic and useful understanding of how these clusters do (and do not) work. Shedding light on shortcomings also helps dispel some of the mythology built up around Siliconia, making the comparative analyses that much more informative, not to mention objective and relevant to the world at large.

In terms of how the book is organized, *Clusters of Creativity* pursues a parallel structure for examining the lessons of Silicon Valley and Silicon Fen. In two separate sections, each location is explored through a brief introductory chapter followed by three principal chapters. The first of the three principal chapters examines the studied cluster's history and evolution; the second, its present-day dynamics; the third, the innovators and methods of innovation that fuel its creative vibrancy. A concluding chapter in each section reflects on the major issues and opportunities the cluster faces for continued growth. The text is filled with analyses of a variety of enterprises, exploring the contributing roles played by high-tech businesses and also those by peripherally supportive, low-tech commercial enterprises and institutions such as universities and government bodies. This approach helps provide for a more balanced appreciation of the clusters' separate functioning.

By deviating from popular theories that assert ill-defined mysterious forces lie at the heart of successful regional economies, this book demonstrates the ways in which matters of choice and management practice determine the direction and accomplishments of the areas studied. Through its focus on the role of decision-making and action, *Clusters of Creativity* serves mainly as an exploration of organizational strategies and leadership. I hope it will provide a useful set of perspectives for a wide range of readers: from practitioners to academics, from the generally curious to those wanting to know more about the types of leaders who make creative organizations and regions possible in order to augment their own efforts as agents for positive change.

In attempting to accommodate a wide range of interests, the book is written in a style intended to be accessible to the general reader. It makes its observations and critical analyses using as much plain talk as possible and does not shirk from repeatedly critiquing popular thinking that cloaks the deeper significances of the subjects it studies. The next two sections of this introductory chapter deal with the key theoretical concepts that the book either argues against or supports. For those less interested in theoretical constructs and wanting to embark directly on the explorations of Silicon Valley and Silicon Fen, they should skip the following two sections of this chapter (which begin below) and go directly to Chapter 2 (which starts on page 19). For those seeking more information on the theories this book challenges or accepts, the following sections on "Breaking with Accepted Orthodoxy" and

"Clusters and Enterprise" provide a sense of the relevant conceptual frameworks.

## BREAKING WITH ACCEPTED ORTHODOXY

Being a book about leaders and their roles in fostering and channeling the forces of innovation and entrepreneurship, *Clusters of Creativity* breaks with a disturbing aspect of fashionable thinking about Silicon Valley that discounts—if not outright dismisses—the role of management and human decision-making. As stated earlier, this work takes issue with two bodies of widely received thought in particular: explanations that attribute Silicon Valley's functioning to the powers of historical accidents and those that credit the omnipotence of a Silicon Valley system, or culture, of networks. There are variations on the "accidental" and "networks" themes but the reasoning articulated by two leading academic theorists stands out in particular. Because these theories offer the clearest articulations of popular schools of thought, the book occasionally refers back to them in order to contrast its analyses with these paradigms of conventional wisdom. Criticisms are raised not to put down the theories' advocates or their ideas but are voiced in the spirit of a constructive but pointedly argued debate on matters central to understanding the importance of clusters in modern society and business.[5]

### Accidents or Actions?

Princeton University economist Paul Krugman, probably the most vocal and visible economic pundit alive, is a spokesman for what is called "new trade theory" or "new international economics." A fundamental line of reasoning promoted by this school of thought is the concept of "increasing returns." The notion of increasing returns attempts to describe the workings of a variety of economic phenomena, and does so in many regards quite brilliantly. One of the areas where concept strays from providing meaningful insight, however, is when it is used to make the rather unenlightening claim that regions and the industries and companies based in them emerge from the occurrence of accidents and then grow simply through a fated "path-dependent" steam-rollering of "cumulative processes." Some economists seize on such aspects of increasing returns theory to show that a place like Silicon Valley is really not so special after all. Krugman in particular argues that the cluster is simply an over-promoted location based more on hoopla than substance. Somewhat ironically, this basic line of reasoning has found a receptive audience among Valley technologists and thinkers— not because of its depreciation for the way Silicon Valley works, but because the logic of the theory can also be used to explain the "unfairness" of how inferior technologies have succeeded in the marketplace. The classic example is Microsoft Windows—a product that, like the company that produces it, a significant number of individuals (especially those in Silicon Valley) truly love to hate. Windows is but one of several well-known but dubious examples of technologies that increasing returns theorists claim have accidentally locked in certain markets. The implied consequences of this interpretation of economic reality has actually been invoked by Silicon Valley interest groups to spur the US Department of Justice to prosecute Microsoft for anti-competitive behavior. Though an unproven theory, such thinking has not only entered Silicon Valley's state of mind but become an underpinning justification for new directions in federal government policy.

In regards to understanding the significance of clusters, although there are different ways to apply the reasoning of increasing returns theory, for Krugman (the theory's highest profile advocate) the important lesson is that localization of industry is a matter of happenstance. According to this interpretation, clusters are born and develop because an "accident" leads "to the establishment of the industry in a particular location" after which time "cumulative processes" will "take over" the industry's growth.[6] What these "cumulative processes" are exactly is never fully explained. What is clear, however, is that if regional economies are appreciated merely as the inevitable outcome of historical accidents, they lose much, if not all, of their value as places for understand-ing how and why they and their enterprises are managed in a particular manner—no need to bother with the details of management practices if it is history and the ripple effect of "cumulative processes" that dictate a cluster's economic success. Not surprisingly, Krugman is therefore particularly dismissive of Silicon Valley, a location that he argues "is not at all unique, either in time or space, but is simply a glitzy version of a traditional phenomenon."[7]

Krugman's interpretation of high-technology clusters seems framed by the irrelevant (even if true) conclusion that the origins of Silicon Valley or Route 128 (the technology district surrounding Boston and Cambridge, Massachusetts) are "on the whole … less romantic" than the beginnings of Old Economy manufacturing centers like Motown (Detroit) or Iron City (Pittsburgh). He furthermore observes that "[i]n general the new high technology clusters were the product less of intrepid individuals than of visionary bureaucrats (if that is not an oxymoron)." A summary by Krugman of Silicon Valley's evolution builds on similarly irrelevant (and to varying degrees, erroneous) descriptions:

> Silicon Valley was created largely through the initiative of Fred Terman, the vice-president of Stanford University. Through his initiative the university provided an initial stake for Hewlett-Packard, which became the nucleus of the Valley. It also established the famous research park on university land, on which Hewlett-Packard, then many other firms, began operations. There was a noticeable cumulative process operating through the university itself: the revenues from the research park helped to finance Stanford's ascent to world-class status in science and engineering, and the university's rise helped make Silicon Valley an attractive place for high-tech business.[8]

Krugman's observation of Silicon Valley and other clusters leads him to posit: "The important point is that the logic of localization remains similar. … small historical events start a cumulative process in which the presence of a large number of firms and workers acts as an incentive for still more firms and workers to congregate at a particular location."[9] It is a surprisingly limited observation, one whose reasoning is rooted in a sense of historical determinism. The only significance this type of analysis can derive from a place like Silicon Valley is that the cluster simply manifests the inevitable; that the Siliconia of today are created by "cumulative processes" that begin randomly as "small events" or "accidents." Mention of "incentive" at least implies that some consideration is given to the role of human agency but individual efforts are relegated to a status beneath that of those mysterious, and totally unexamined, "cumulative processes" that "take over" a cluster's development. In general, the powers of choice and agency are either blithely ignored or deemed bizarre, which is why someone like Stanford's Fred Terman (whose strategies and management practices are absolutely key to understanding Silicon Valley's origins) is treated as an abnormality, an incongruously "visionary" bureaucrat.

The assumption that the success of a regional economy somehow results from happenstance is the greatest misconception made by this line of thinking. Attributing key characteristics of an economy to matters of chance utterly ignores the complexity of forces at play. After all, any propagative occurrence in life (starting with one's own birth) can be classified as "accidental." What matters is not the "accident" itself but *how growth and development is guided thereafter*. We should be alerted by the ease with which one can label crucial occurrences in the formation of a Siliconia location as resulting from random events that somehow unleash the regenerative mechanisms necessary to create a flourishing concentration of enterprise. Clusters do not manage themselves, they are managed.[10] As the later pages of this book will detail, what is crucial to a cluster's development is not happenstance but rather how people respond to or, perhaps more accurately, create opportunities. Cambridge's cluster has surprising similarities to its Northern California counterpart: at the same time that Silicon Valley was gestating and growing, Cambridge had the benefits of its own visionary bureaucrat, a university-affiliated science park, a flourishing high-tech industrial base, a large pool of knowledge-workers (whose record of discovery and genuinely original innovations actually exceeded that of Silicon Valley's). The region was altogether massive in the drawing power that increasing returns theory claims would generate the kind of economic mass Silicon Valley has acquired. Yet Silicon Fen never drew in as many firms and workers as Silicon Valley did. Europe's version of Silicon Valley has nothing like the economic weight built up by its American cousin and has evolved in an entirely dissimilar manner. Neither "small events" nor "accidents" explain the difference, but the nature and effectiveness of management that has divergently responded to opportunities for growth does. What is so extraordinary—and not merely "glitzy"—about these two locales of Siliconia is the multitude ways in which individuals have reacted to prevailing circumstances (which by no means have been always favorable) to build up the exceptionally creative but economically unalike environments that they have. Managerial thinking and behavior, not chance, lies at the heart of the phenomenon.[11]

### Networks or Individuals?

Like assumptions about the deterministic powers of history and its "cumulative processes," assumptions about the workings of Silicon Valley's fabled body of networks also subordinate the importance of human agency to the concept of a mysteriously operating external force. It is not hard to see why some variation of a network's *über alles* perspective frequently informs interpretations of Silicon Valley. The area's skilled workers tend to cultivate social and professional affiliations throughout the cluster. They usually have friends and acquaintances in a wide number of local companies and the turnover rate for employees at high-tech firms is high. Workers will recognize a competitor as not only being staffed by friends but view it as a potential future employer. These human linkages widen the scope of personal economic opportunities and support a live-and-let-live attitude amidst an environment otherwise characterized by cut-throat competition and high-charged capitalism. Enterprises of many different kinds are also often bound together, sometimes through strategic intent. For example, Silicon Valley's leading venture capital firm, Kleiner Perkins, tries to foster synergies between the companies it invests in according to a modified version of Japan's intensely interlocked *keiretsu*-style of corporate linkages. At a more basic level, local companies will often simply elect to become intertwined because of advantages in integrating their supply chains. These aspects of work life in the Valley provide a strong sense that the cluster is a collection of virtual businesses that operate almost as if they were without boundaries between one another. The interlacing helps keep alive the feeling that there is more a unified Silicon Valley Inc. than a landscape of corporately separate firms and independently acting individuals.

It is important not to confuse the nature of causality in appreciating the role of networks, however. This book shows how networks—both of the human and technical kind—are a by-product of the innovative and entrepreneurial drives of individuals in Silicon Valley. The work that people in the cluster have done with the whole concept of networked interactivity, and in particular their contributions to building up Internet- and Web-based technologies and commerce, is exceptional and impressive. But just as the euphoria that surrounded Internet businesses exaggerated the value of e-commerce enterprises to ridiculous extremes (an aspect of the Silicon Valley dynamic that is explored in Chapter 4), so too has accepted wisdom on the powers of Silicon Valley's human- and industrial-based networks exaggerated their powers as well. The classic example of such thinking comes from the body of theories advanced by the University of California at Berkeley's AnnaLee Saxenian in her magnum opus, *Regional Advantage: Culture and Competition in Silicon Valley and Route 128.*[12]

A key premise of *Regional Advantage* is that "[i]n Silicon Valley, the region and its networks, rather than individual firms" function as "the locus of economic activity."[13] According to this viewpoint, with "a network-based industrial system like that in Silicon Valley, the region— if not all the firms in the region—is organized to adapt continuously to fast-changing markets and technologies."[14] The powers of this "industrial system" are said to be so great that the region is somehow capable of pursuing "multiple technical opportunities through spontaneous regroupings of skill, technology and capital."[15] This truly amazing, if not utterly incredible, ability of Silicon Valley for spontaneously reconfiguring its base of skills, technology, and capital allegedly confers a type of immortal omnipotence, making the local economy immune to such marketplace fundamentals as the turbulence created by product life cycles.[16]

In such ways and others, the *Regional Advantage* conceptualization of Silicon Valley suffers principally from its overstatements of the value and usages of networks. Networks can greatly aid the work of the innovative and the entrepreneurial but no evidence has ever surfaced that they have come to replace people or firms as the actual "locus of economic activity." Nor does anything suggest that even sectors as tightly networked as those found in Silicon Valley have found ways to reorganize instantly and automatically their resources according to changing market conditions. One need go no further than the tech-sector-driven recession unleashed in 2000—the world's real Y2K disaster—to see that the Valley is not so "protean," as the book describes the cluster, as to be immune from suffering downturns in market cycles. Yet *Regional Advantage* concludes by admonishing managers in the private and public sectors hoping to emulate Silicon Valley's success to abandon an "outdated conception of the firm."[17] The solution offered up is radical and (literally) ill-defined: a call for leaders to adopt a model of organization whereby companies are so tightly networked that their individual boundaries become simultaneously "turned inside out" and "blurred."[18] Taken as a whole, the body of concepts being advanced makes a profound assault on the competitive integrity and individualistic thinking that is key to innovative and entrepreneurially managed enterprise.[19]

These sorts of claims are cause for concern because they so heavily inform general thinking about Silicon Valley. *Regional Advantage* is required reading in business schools and university departments where regional economics and policy are studied. *Encyclopaedia Britannica* cites the book as one of only two recommended for reading on the subject of Silicon Valley. As with many of Krugman's mass-market works, Saxenian's *Regional Advantage* can even be found in airport bookstores, an indication that its wisdom spreads far beyond those with merely an academic interest in the subject of clusters and business—a strange situation considering how far the book goes in seeking to overturn basic principles of business management. Also strange is the way the book seeks to make the case for the notion of superior and inferior cultures—Silicon Valley is alleged to be blessed with a culture that is "better" than what is described as Route 128's autarkic-minded Puritan value system.

So it is with the concepts espoused by *Regional Advantage* as well that *Clusters of Creativity* breaks with what has become a dominant logic concerning the deeper meanings of Silicon Valley and other clusters to which it is compared. Throughout the following pages, people, not networks (nor even technology, for that matter), are shown to be the prime movers in high-technology clusters. This book's attempt at global balance furthermore eschews any effort to promote a particular culture or value system. The people living and working in the English fenlands—which, incidentally, are the geographic wellspring of American Puritanism—may have developed a smaller cluster than Silicon Valley's but it is impossible to argue that they have not succeeded in developing a version of Siliconia to which they have dedicated themselves. Hopefully *Clusters of Creativity* will in some measure help put to rest the biased notion that a people's belief systems or lifestyle decisions automatically disqualify them from enjoying the benefits of a vibrant, sustainable regional economy. So long as beliefs and lifestyles respect the integrity and nurture the creative capacity of the individual, the sort of entrepreneurial phenomenon that Silicon Valley represents is possible anywhere.

## CLUSTERS AND ENTERPRISE

The rise of Siliconia across the globe has been accompanied by a growing interest in the subject of industrial clusters. A basic definition describes a cluster as "a collection of related companies located in a small geographic area."[20] This book searches out a larger significance, seeing clusters not just as a collection of companies but rather as a concentration of "enterprises" (organized activity of all sorts, including that of various types of commercial firm, educational institution, research group, and government body) that are notable for more than being simply related to one another but in the various ways they actually interact. A cluster becomes especially interesting when it goes beyond representing a place to which enterprises have colocated and functions as a collection of intermingling enterprises whose leaders make use of local resources to manage their organizations better.

In economic literature, interest in how enterprise locates collectively in a particular area goes back at least to the writing of the Prussian landholder, Johann Heinrich von Thünen who in his book, *The Isolated State (Der isolierte Staat*, 1826) analyzed how concentrations of agrarian production operate.[21] Alfred Marshall, a founder of the English neo-classical school of economics and pioneer of microeconomic theory, in his *Principles of Economics* (1890) became the first economist to write in-depth about clusters (which he referred to as "industrial districts") as they relate to manufacturing in the modern age of capital.[22] Recent interest in clusters and in Silicon Valley, the best known industrial district on the planet today, has been stoked by the work of academics like Krugman and Saxenian and also the writing of Harvard Business School's Michael Porter who highlights the importance of clusters in his treatise on global strategy, *The Competitive Advantage of Nations* (1989).[23] In later years, Porter has updated and expanded his conceptualization of clusters to claim that they are the basis for "the new economics of competition," broadly impacting businesses at many levels:

> Clusters affect competitiveness within countries as well as across national borders. Therefore, they lead to new agendas for all business executives—not just those who compete globally. More broadly, clusters represent a new way of thinking about location, challenging much of the conventional wisdom about how companies should be configured, how institutions such as universities can contribute to competitive success, and how governments can promote economic development and prosperity.[24]

Within the pages of this book, clusters are viewed as important entities in their own right. Nevertheless, like networks, they are recognized as essentially the by-products of the more directed efforts that go into creating (and recreating) enterprise. Much of the currently vogue thinking about Silicon Valley and clusters in general has assumed that their economic structures assure a degree of success for the companies that inhabit them—either by the power of historical destiny, a spontaneously reacting networked system, or some other all-powerful mechanism that ensures a kind of "unstoppable" growth. Clusters in fact guarantee absolutely nothing so far as performance and growth are concerned. They are not somehow "recession proof"—a fact of life the aftermath of the year 2000's crashing of technology stock serves as but the latest potent reminder. But *effectively managed* clusters can perform outstandingly well based on how they facilitate the kind of entrepreneurship and innovation that keeps existing firms vibrantly operating and spurs the formation of new companies. It is this aspect of clusters that can provide a region with genuine economic staying power. It is also key to understanding how places like Silicon Valley and Silicon Fen exist and work as they do.

This book views the cornerstone of a cluster to be its innovators, its entrepreneurs, and the means by which they drive enterprise creation and growth. Some of the more informative descriptions of the nature and interrelation of all three elements come from Joseph Schumpeter (1883–1950), an economist who spent much of his career studying the role of innovation and entrepreneurship in society. In an article published close to the end of his life, and long before the world awoke to the wonders of a place called Silicon Valley, Schumpeter observed:

> The mechanisms of economic change in capitalist society pivot on entrepreneurial activity. . . . the entrepreneur and his function are not difficult to conceptualize: the defining characteristic is simply the doing of new things or the doing of things that are already being done in a new way (innovation). It is natural, and in fact an advantage, that such a definition does not draw any sharp line between what is and what is not "enterprise." For actual life itself knows no such sharp division, though it shows up the type well enough. It should be observed at once that the "new thing" need not be spectacular or of historical importance. It need not be Bessemer steel or the explosion

motor. It can be the Deerfoot sausage. To see the phenomenon even in the humblest levels of the business world is quite essential though it may be difficult to find the humble entrepreneurs historically.[25]

In the vein that Schumpeter describes, *Clusters of Creativity* takes an inclusive view of its key terms. Here, the concept of enterprise encompasses both commercial entities and those of government, academia, and other organized activity. This inclusive perspective helps underscore how the management of a wide variety of organizations, not only that of commercial firms, shapes a cluster. Along these lines, attention is also turned to the innovators and entrepreneurs working in all types of enterprise, making it less extraordinary-seeming that individuals who would otherwise qualify as "visionary bureaucrats" play the key roles that they do. Entrepreneurs are not only seen to be company founders, but, where appropriate, those employees (even *bona fide* bureaucrats!) who seize the initiative to bring about change in an enterprise or the region in which it operates. Schumpeter's contention that entrepreneurship and innovation are inherently similar turns out, in fact, to describe accurately how these forces work in Silicon Valley and Silicon Fen. In this book, the subtle interplays and overlaps of innovation and entrepreneurship infuses much of the writing.

At its core, *Clusters of Creativity* is about management and its consequences. It is written especially for those with an interest in the entrepreneurial leadership of enterprise and in how managers drive the development of economic clusters. The book intentionally avoids any attempt to specify a formula or produce a checklist about how to create the next Silicon Valley or Silicon Fen. The magic of Siliconia cannot be prescribed—if anything, a great threat to the vitality of a cluster are managers who embrace formulaic thinking, inflexible strategies, or other forms of groupthink. This is not to imply that enterprises or enterprise clusters exist without structure or that the entrepreneurship and innovation occurring within them are simply unplanned *ad hoc* activities; quite the opposite. This book shows structure and planning to be critically important. But methods have to match prevailing circumstances; there is no predetermined framework that will suit all needs. What is crucially important is that leaders maintain a sense of perspective, one rooted in critical thinking, not the dictates of a particular formula. *Clusters of Creativity* strives to promote a nuanced, multifaceted, and discriminating appraisal of the lessons offered by two exemplary locations of Siliconia. The objective is to stimulate thought and understanding, not dole out prepackaged answers.

As earlier noted, locations such as Silicon Valley and Silicon Fen should be seen fundamentally not so much as high-tech regions, but as entrepreneurial regions that happen to have high-technology sectors defining their main industrial activities. Thus, even when the narrative turns to items like microprocessors and electron microscopy, we should not lose sight that the same forces at work could produce, in Schumpeter's words, "Deerfoot sausage." After all, high technology is nothing really "new" despite all the talk of a "New" technology-driven global economy. Ever since our early ancestors started making use of simple implements hewn from rocks, sticks, and bones, humans have been applying whatever scientific knowledge they possessed to progress the frontiers of their economic existence. The rub is more in the application of the knowledge than the knowledge itself. Karl Marx famously lamented: "The philosophers have only interpreted the world, in various ways; the point is to change it."[26] Where Marxists have dreamed to tread (or actually trudged only to bequeath legacies of destruction and despair), the entrepreneurs and innovators of our world are now taking us. More than envisioning "new things," they make them a working reality. They are sure to continue transforming the world for many years to come.

# Introduction 2

For people not native to the area—a category that applies not only to visitors but the Valley's numerous current residents made up of transplanted Americans and the 35% of Silicon Valley's population that is foreign born—the Valley is often first glimpsed from the window of an airplane.[27] Flying in to the area is relatively easy: two well-serviced international airports, situated in San Francisco and San Jose, are separated only by about 40 miles and positioned at what are more or less the northern and southern tips of the cluster's geographic heartland. As the plane enters its descent, on a clear day you will get a scenic view of the Santa Cruz Mountains in the west, the foothills of the Diablo Range in the east, and the San Francisco Bay towards the north: features that roughly frame a planar expanse that is the Santa Clara Valley, what today the world commonly knows of as Silicon Valley. The area is blessed with attractive geology and a favorable climate—aspects of the natural environment that Valley inhabitants will frequently cite as non-economic incentives for wanting to live there. Yet geography and weather can hardly be thought of as distinguishing advantages for the cluster. Locations throughout the US and the rest of the world have natural settings that are at least as inviting as those offered by this patch of land. The bird's eye view of Silicon Valley reveals the most when attention is directed not to the natural environment but the man-made, physical evidence of the efforts that have gone in to attracting and accommodating infusions of people and firms. It is this artificial geography, the patchwork of asphalt and cement nestled between the salt water and earthen slopes, that physically contains and connects the Valley's mass of economic activity and distinguishes the cluster far more than its native ecosystem.

The expanse of suburban sprawl that constitutes Silicon Valley is home to more than 8,000 high-technology firms.[28] Operating in a region that provides more than half-a-million jobs associated with high-tech industries, companies in the Valley's leading technology sectors of computers, semiconductors, and software pay average salaries in excess of $150,000.[29] Though these represent remarkably high wage levels, indications are that employers get their money's worth. For years Silicon Valley's average value-add per employee has exceeded that of the US. The Valley's value-add per employee reached a new high in 2000 of over $120,000, double that for the US as a whole—an indication that the cluster has a professional labor force that is either (or in some combination) working unusually productively or working unusually hard.[30]

Before the plane touches down, if you gaze northward beyond Silicon Valley's blocks of bedroom communities, technology parks, and college and corporate campuses, you might also spot the skyline of San Francisco's financial district or the heavy loading equipment at the port of Oakland. (Many enterprises located in these cities also, despite being outside the suburbia typically associated with the Valley, see themselves as part of the cluster.) Although the suburban high-tech industrial environment of the Valley is distinct from these cityscapes to the north, the Valley immensely benefits by proximity to the metropolises. In turn, both the suburban Valley and the northern urban centers along the San Francisco Bay all share in the advantage of being part of a much wider regional economy: the nine-county Bay Area, home to nearly 7 million people.[31] The Valley itself draws in more than 200,000 commuters from communities outside its official boundaries (Figure 2.1).[32] The macro-region, moreover, provides a substantial economic base upon which Valley enterprises operate. If it were its own country, the Bay Area's gross domestic product would be larger than Sweden's.[33] With San Francisco's concentration of traditional financial institutions and Silicon Valley's mother lode of venture capital, the Bay Area serves as the financial hub of the Western US and the epicenter of America's venture

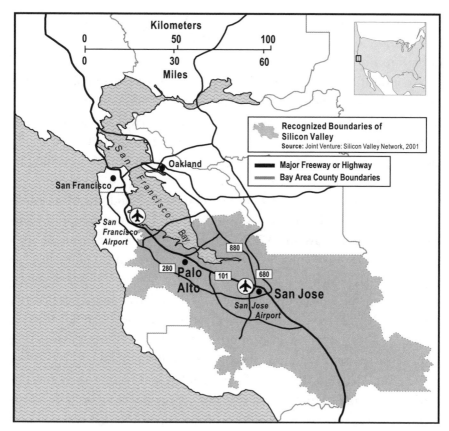

**Figure 2.1** Silicon Valley and the San Francisco Bay Area.
(Data from Joint Venture: Silicon Valley Network, used with kind permission)

capital industry, which itself is the largest in the world. The airborne view of the wider territory also serves as a reminder that, for all its allegedly special apartness, Silicon Valley does not exist in isolation, but instead draws on resources beyond what the cluster's generally accepted parameters suggest. At the same time, as the coming chapters will show, Silicon Valley was never ensured to do well because of its Bay Area location. Wealth, technology, and people never just poured into the once sleepy agricultural lands of the Santa Clara Valley to create the supercluster of today's New Economy. Specific, highly involved efforts were made to build up the area and its companies. Without such efforts and the ongoing execution of growth-oriented strategies, the region would still be more characterized by fruit orchards than its present-day sprawl of high-tech.

An indication of the results of the work that has gone in to creating a "land of chips and money" can be observed with the comparative topography provided by bar charts in Figure 2.2. Stacked up against other major high-tech clusters in the US, Silicon Valley turns out to be not "a valley" but "a mountain," towering above its counterparts according to such measures as high-tech workforce concentration, technology exports, fastest growing technology companies, and major research centers. A business journalist visiting from the telecommunications and bioscience complex around Washington, D. C. once felt inspired, after having come originally intent to defend the prestige of his home turf, to express jaw-slackened awe at the sheer scale of Silicon Valley's development: seeing the cluster up close he conceded defeat and described the Valley as the "Tigress and Euphrates of technology"—an apt turn of phrase for a cluster whose disproportionate high-tech output makes it in some sense the cradle of modern economic civilization.[34]

The superlative qualities of Silicon Valley lead many to see it as the end-all of Siliconia, if not the entire history of regional economic development. Yet contentions of absolute regional superiority get easily blown out of proportion. A book like *Regional Advantage*, for example, argues that the high-tech workers in Boston's Route 128 are at fault for forgoing the obsessive work styles of their Silicon Valley counterparts. Bostonians allegedly create regional *dis*advantage by committing the sin of going "home after work" instead of socializing with co-workers. When they do get together, Bostonians are further faulted for failing to keep work the topic of conversation by instead focusing their private banter on such apparently irrelevant topics as "politics, religion, sex and business of all types."[35] These sorts of polarized good/bad judgments about personal preferences and norms of social behavior are of dubious relevance at best. Even if accepted at face value, such attempts to claim there is a superior Silicon Valley work culture overlook important issues, the major one being that people who obsess about work may

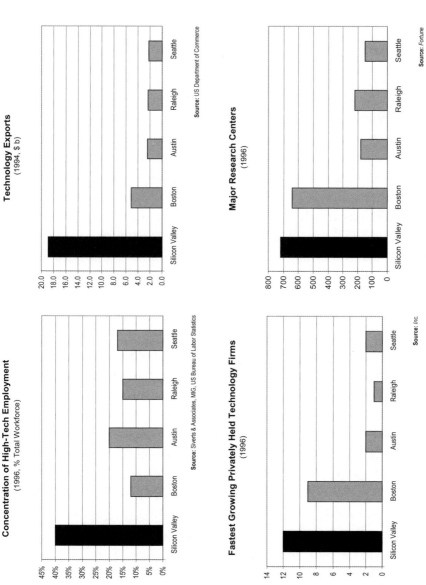

**Figure 2.2** Indicators of Silicon Valley Superior Performance.

(Data from Joint Venture: Silicon Valley Network, *Joint Venture's Comparative Analysis* (San Jose, 1997), used with kind permission)

well create higher economic output, but it is questionable if they create a higher quality of life. In terms of comparative lifestyles, Bostonians are not likely to look towards Silicon Valley and wish their communities suffered from more congestion or that their homes were less affordable or that public education for their children was less well funded. As easy as it is to show Silicon Valley slam-dunking other regions, one can also point to metrics that show Silicon Valley in last place (Figure 2.3).

An important point repeatedly overlooked in attempts to portray the socio-economic make-up of a region (or a country for that matter) as either superior or inferior is the issue of choice. There is a long list of critical decisions and actions made in shaping a territory's development. Silicon Valley grows according to the quality of efforts to attract, foster, and—most importantly—manage high-tech enterprise. The region flourishes economically because of the decisions entrepreneurs and managers take concerning the establishment, support, and direction of new organizations. Their work contributes to the cluster's tremendous economic mass, the creation of exciting new technologies, and a remarkably supportive business environment. But other choices have meant that during the last few decades matters such as poor performing public schools, a ridiculously tight housing market, and other issues relevant to the area's standard of living have been neglected. In more recent years, Silicon Valley businesses have proven themselves fairly inept at anticipating the consequences of looming problems such as California's seriously flawed energy deregulation and the swelling of a hyper-inflated dotcom bubble—two major crises to which Silicon Valley also disproportionately contributed. Despite the cluster's obvious superlatives, it does not offer a model deserving of unadulterated emulation. It is best appreciated with an appropriately admiring, but intellectually critical, approach.

On balance, Silicon Valley remains an exceptionally inspiring location for those with the skills and vision to take advantage of what it offers. It is a remarkably robust cluster, one whose entrepreneurs repeatedly show themselves able to seek out and build on new opportunities, helping the region to recover from whatever downturns it experiences. "The only place on earth not trying to figure out how to become Silicon Valley"

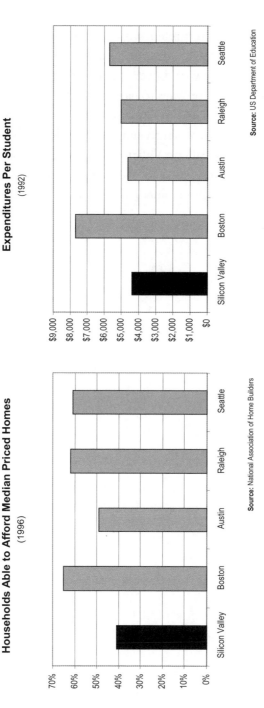

**Households Able to Afford Median Priced Homes**
(1996)

**Source:** National Association of Home Builders

**Expenditures Per Student**
(1992)

**Source:** US Department of Education

**Figure 2.3** Indicators of Silicon Valley Inferior Performance.
(Data from Joint Venture: Silicon Valley Network, used with kind permission)

can be meaningfully interpreted without resorting to the extremes of idolization or dismissing its significance as an abnormal fluke of history. With the nations of the world ever eager to claim yet another locale of Siliconia, and the quest for ways to harness the regenerative powers of innovation and entrepreneurship likewise rising in urgency, the lessons of Silicon Valley grow increasingly important. Hopefully the following chapters, which look at Silicon Valley's evolution, dynamics, and innovative capacity, do some justice to the task of distilling the managerial wisdom offered by the pre-eminent cluster of creative enterprises in the world today.

# From Semi-desert to Silicon Valley

The sheer wealth and prosperity that Silicon Valley currently enjoys can make it seem as though the area and its companies were simply destined for success. Author and *Newsweek* correspondent David Kaplan writes that Silicon Valley's origins are "intrinsic to the character of California—the state's DNA. The techno-entrepreneurial revolution belongs here as much as palm trees and sunshine. For 150 years, ever since the Gold Rush, every California story has begun with a dream."[36]

Kaplan's remarks touch on much of the pop mythology associated with the origins of Silicon Valley. One often hears talk about how the natural environment, dreams, or the "luck" of watershed historical events like the Gold Rush (or its mid-20th century equivalent: the funding bonanza provided by World War II and Cold War military spending) have somehow fated, as if by genetic design, the emergence of Silicon Valley. What such thinking overlooks is the extent to which committed, entrepreneurial efforts went into transforming an area once better known as "the prune capital of America" into the world's capital of high-tech. Silicon Valley exists (and exists in its particular form) because of the nature of the actions people have taken and continue to take in shaping the cluster. As this chapter will explore, Silicon Valley has not evolved according to quirks of history, the dictates of natural geography, the strength of its networks, nor the romanticism of the dreams nestling in the hearts of its residents. Nothing was predetermined in the cluster's development; there was no glide path toward success. Though suffering through some notable failures, entrepreneurial, innovative behavior matched by responsive, forward-thinking management practice have been the hallmarks of the cluster's genesis and evolution.

## OPPORTUNITIES SEIZED AND SQUANDERED

California's mid-19th century Gold Rush—that formative event that helped transform its loosely administered lands into the "Golden State" of the US—is one of several natural resource-related matters closely tied to California's identity. Whether it is the value of its gold and oil deposits or the beauty of its weather and geology, the abundance of favorable natural assets can give the false impression that the state's prosperity and development was in some measure ensured. But California has never been alone in enjoying favorable natural conditions. And as testified by the ways so many countries or regions mismanage the economic windfalls of their natural endowments, simply having access to the wealth bequeathed by nature is not the same as finding ways to maximize benefits from it.

The aftermath of the Gold Rush testifies to this reality. California's pioneer entrepreneurs, the gold prospectors, are celebrated as the economic founders of the state: latter-day Argonauts who with rugged individualism prospered by the grace of hard work and good fortune. Yet the real legacy of wealth-creation that California's pioneer capitalists left for later generations to expand upon was their demonstration of how ingenuity—not only working hard but working smart—and effective means of organization went much further than a hearty work ethos and simple opportunism. At the start of the Gold Rush in 1848, mining would earn for the lone prospector an average of $20 per day— equivalent to about $400 per day in 2000. The easy pickings did not last long, though. By 1851, earnings from individual prospecting brought in $8 or less. By 1856, a day's take had dropped to an average of just $3.[37] As high-grade gold drawn from shallow gravels became scarcer, those who decided to continue to prospect had a basic choice. They could remain as small-scale operators facing declining returns for their labor or could try to organize themselves into more substantial enterprises capable of extracting gold from further beneath the earth's surface. It was among those who chose to organize their operations better that most notably succeeded, creating firms that used their capital to employ technologically intensive mining methods. More importantly for the wider region surrounding extraction sites, as these businesses grew they pushed up demand for sophisticated hydraulic mining equipment, encouraging experimentation with mechanical adaptations and more fundamentally original technologies. San Francisco, whose port and other logistic advantages made it well suited for locating industry that served the mines of California's Sierra Nevada mountains, arose as what we would today call a "cluster" for the production of advanced mining equipment. Industrialists who built up foundries, machine shops, and leading-edge equipment manufacturers transformed the city into the first base in the Western US for technologically intensive manufacturing.[38]

Northern California's mining operations and the manufacturing industry created to support them helped set a stage for further technological advance. Curiously though, while San Francisco's industries of advanced technology flourished, little of this activity spilled into the region now known as Silicon Valley. At the time the lands of Santa Clara Valley were thoroughly agrarian, a region that local boosters would as late as the mid-20th century be advertizing as the "Valley of Heart's Delight" to celebrate its cornucopian fruit and nut orchards. While San Francisco noticeably progressed, the Valley essentially remained an economic backwater. The situation only began to change when residents of the area themselves organized attempts to modernize and industrialize the region. Although many individuals and enterprises engaged in such attempts, the most noteworthy series of efforts came from people affiliated with a uniquely forward-thinking center of higher education: Leland Stanford Junior University.

Founded in 1891 on an enormous 8,800-acre horse-trotting ranch in a dusty town along the San Francisco Peninsula called Palo Alto, the university was dedicated as a memorial to the son of the ranch owners, Leland and Jane Stanford. Funding for this extravagant tribute was made possible by Leland Senior's scandalously corrupt practices as president of the Central Pacific Railroad. (Considering the circumstances of the university's founding financial endowment, one critic dryly suggested that above the gated entrance to the campus should run the in-scription: "With Apologies to God.")[39] In sharp contrast to the origins of its money, the university's educational mandate was as principled as it was novel. To their credit, the Stanfords expressly intended to establish a university that would differ from an Ivory Tower, conceiving an insti-tution whose purpose was "to qualify its students for personal success, and direct usefulness in life."[40] The university boasted an exceptionally progressive agenda. Stanford charged no tuition, admitted both men and women, was without religious affiliation, and, apart from English, required no mandatory courses for undergraduates. *Die Luft der Freiheit weht* ("the wind of freedom blows") was the institution's motto selected by its first president, David Starr Jordan. A natural science professor who had formerly presided over the University of Indiana, Jordan took the practical aspects of a Stanford education to heart, declaring that a Stanford graduate "should be one who knows something and can carry his knowledge into action."[41]

At around the time of the university's establishment, one of the more intriguing opportunities for putting knowledge into action concerned the task of electrifying the Bay Area. By the last decade of the 19th century, advances in the application of electricity presented tremendous possibilities for modernizing public infrastructure. Bay Area businessmen and engineers recognized electrification as a step forward, not only as a means to advance the region but as a way to redirect and expand the tech-nology, know-how, and facilities that had grown up around hydraulic mining, by then an industry in decline. They also recognized that they lacked a means for the long-distance delivery of electricity from the mining industry's hydropower facilities located far off in the rugged terrain of California's Sierra Nevada Mountains. They turned to local academics for assistance, and found the electrical engineering faculty at Stanford to be particularly enthusiastic supporters. Stanford professors and research students who participated in subsequent joint university–industry research projects on long-distance electricity transmission would discover that collaboration with the private sector provided great mutual benefits, helping to upgrade the region's infrastructure while contributing to the development of Stanford's electrical engineering program.

The special university–industry collaboration begun by this section of Stanford's academic community added another legacy of economic activity that others would later build upon in creating an electronics industry cluster. But the time lag between these tentative steps and the actions that decisively contributed to the formation of Silicon Valley is a long one. In the Santa Clara Valley of the early 20th century, local technology companies did form, and several went on to become substantial enterprises. Still, despite a promising head start, the Valley at the time failed to build up and sustain a critical mass of technology-intensive industry. Its firms were not managed in a way that maintained their competitive edge and the region itself was not managed in a way that it retained talented individuals or high-caliber commercial operations.

The difficulties of the situation can be appreciated in considering the birth, development, and disappearance of Stanford's first major high-tech spin-out: Federal Telegraph. Founded in 1909 by Australian immigrant and Stanford electrical engineering graduate Cyril Elwell, Federal was a maker of wireless telegraph systems, very much a cutting-edge technology for its time. Stanford President Jordan was the company's first investor (he put in $500) and, following his lead, other Stanford faculty and local businessmen also invested. With sizable R&D and manufacturing operations in Palo Alto, for the next 20 years Federal was the Valley's first and only big-name manufacturer of advanced electronics. Throughout the wider region, it also populated the Bay Area with several spin-outs, the largest of these being Magnavox, a company that—after later relocating outside of California—became even better known than its progenitor.

If historical events and cumulative momentum had the sort of powers often ascribed to them, the birth of Federal Telegraph should have signaled the birth of Silicon Valley. Yet it did not. The establishment and growth of Federal was undeniably important historically. This significance of the past, however, was overshadowed by failures of its present: Federal's inability to expand its market position, its researchers failure to capitalize on technology breakthroughs, it and the region's failure to retain top-quality individuals, and, ultimately, the failure to even retain in the Valley the presence of Federal itself. The missteps associated with Federal's best known personage, the world-famous inventor Lee de Forest, illustrate the sorts of problems that plagued the Valley's earliest attempt at developing a concentration of major high-tech businesses.

Dr. de Forest, a quixotic and long-suffering scientist who coveted recognition as "the father of radio," joined Federal in 1911 and spent the two years of his career there in the company's Palo Alto research facilities. He devoted most of his time to experimenting with his best known invention, a three-element vacuum tube called the audion—a device as central to the complex electronic equipment of its day as semiconductors would become to the information technologies of the latter half of the 20th century. When experimenting at Federal in the summer of 1912, de Forest once inadvertently created a self-regenerating feedback circuit: a technology that, properly controlled, could oscillate an audion's signal output. The underlying potential of what de Forest had stumbled upon was tremendous—"something just as important as his original discovery of the triode audion," as one scholar has noted— and if correctly applied would take the versatility and power of existing vacuum tube technology to new heights.[42] With a grasp of the logic behind the circuit, de Forest and his Federal colleagues would have had in their hands the latest, greatest "new thing" in electronics.

Unfortunately, nobody involved *did* grasp the implications of the discovery. No one associated with conducting or overseeing the research bothered to file a patent. No one, either through work within the company or through any effort to create a spin-off enterprise, attempted to commercialize the breakthrough. As a de Forest biographer notes, what today we would call the "killer application" of regenerative circuitry completely escaped the inventor and his colleagues:

> De Forest understood so little of the potential of regeneration that he failed to copy the notes of his supposedly crucial August 1912 experiment, failed to

explain regeneration technically, failed to make use of its oscillating feature, and as late as 1915 stated in print that oscillation did not depend on regeneration.[43]

De Forest not only overlooked the potential of the technology his experimenting had produced, he furthermore saw no compelling reasons for staying with Federal or remaining in the area at all. He left both behind in 1913 to join a new venture, one established to devise a means for adding sound to motion pictures, that had formed in New York. As for the monumental invention whose implications he had utterly failed to grasp, not long after de Forest's departure from Federal a graduate student at New York's Columbia University, Edwin Howard Armstrong, made a similar but more substantial innovation in regenerative circuitry. Crucially, the young inventor *recognized* the significance of his findings and filed and won a patent for his version of the circuit. It was through Armstrong's patent that de Forest later realized the ramifications of his previous experimenting in Palo Alto. Initiating a high-profile court battle *ex post facto*, de Forest eventually won (in what is commonly regarded as one of the most egregious breakdowns in intellectual property rights protection in the US) legal rights to the circuit. Federal's former employee could thus claim as a point of law to having "discovered" regenerative circuitry. Yet apart from its symbolic value, which observers of Silicon Valley history tend to overplay, de Forest's presence in Palo Alto and his later court victory meant little, if anything, for the industrial development of the cluster.[44] By the time de Forest won legal claim to the circuit, he was no longer present in the area and his previous employer, Federal, had become a waning power in the region's industrial firmament. As a commercial product, regenerative circuit technology was principally developed by large firms on the US East Coast. Around Palo Alto, no thriving bastion of high-tech, no "Regenerative Circuit" Valley, ever emerged.

Emblematic of how poor the Valley was in retaining high-tech talent at the time, the same year that de Forest resigned from Federal, the company's founder, Cyril Elwell, left Federal as well to pursue more promising opportunities in Europe. The region in those years was simply not an appealing location to which ambitious technopreneurs would locate. The land's "DNA" and visions of grandeur harbored by de Forest and others were unable to spark the "techno-entrepreneurial revolution" for which Silicon Valley would later become synonymous. In 1931, Federal's Palo Alto operations shut down permanently after the company was bought out by ITT and relocated to New Jersey. The closing of the Federal lab coincided with the initial phase of severe deterioration in the region's overall economic fortunes during the Great Depression. Though a few small engineering operations would continue to soldier on, the Santa Clara Valley's tentative beginnings as a world-class technology hub were effectively at an end.

## THE TERMAN TURNAROUND

The consequences of de Forest and his Federal colleagues failure to recognize and act on the potential of regenerative circuitry underscores the point that dreams or mere vision are of far less value than perceptiveness and commitment in sustaining an enterprise. That top technical and managerial talent like de Forest and Elwell—and high-potential companies like Federal and Magnavox—would also so easily abandon the Bay Area further indicates that it would take more than the Valley's pleasant climate, a well-regarded university, modern infrastructure, and technological breakthroughs to develop a thriving high-tech cluster. Better skilled managers—more precisely, better *managerially skilled innovators and entrepreneurs*—would be needed, people who could perceive as well as respond to opportunities and effectively marshal the resources necessary to capitalize on them. The abilities of commercial managers would ultimately determine how far the transformation of turning the world's prune capital into its Tigress and Euphrates of technology would run. The effort to get high-caliber individuals simply to locate to the area would precede any creation and growth of major business enterprise. In other words, entrepreneurial attempts to manage the resources of region would constitute the first steps in the metamorphosis of the

Valley. Though not alone in acting as a leading entrepreneur who dedicated himself in this capacity, the person who stands out most for managing regional conditions to facilitate commercial entrepreneurship is Fred Terman, Stanford's so-called "visionary bureaucrat."

Even a brief examination of Terman's life and work reveals that the dismissive label attached to him is a gross mischaracterization of his contribution to the dynamics of Silicon Valley. Terman's importance to the cluster is not so much that he was simply a "visionary" but that he was a committed actor; that he did more than articulate platitudes about how things could be but actually seized the initiative and took responsibility to bring his visions to fruition. Branding a person like Terman a "bureaucrat" also overlooks how his attitude and actions were at their core entrepreneurial. His clearing the way for many key enterprises in Silicon Valley constituted behavior that was in fact *anti*-bureaucratic. Terman worked to tear down entrenched mindsets and policies that stood against new forms of collaboration between Stanford, industry, and government. Within debates about the correct role of an American university, Terman undeniably represents a controversial figure (as some consider the activities of an academic entrepreneur to violate the proper calling of a career in higher education). But within a non-ideological examination of Silicon Valley's birth and evolution, Terman cannot be judged as anything other than a pivotal individual who was strategically purposeful in his thinking and constructively catalytic in his behavior.

Born in 1900 to Lewis Terman, a well-known Stanford psychology professor, Frederick Emmons Terman was very much a son of Stanford. Graduating from the university with a degree in chemistry in 1920, the younger Terman worked briefly at Federal Telegraph before earning Stanford's Master's-level electrical engineering, or "E. E." degree. After going on to earn a doctorate in electrical engineering from the Massachusetts Institute of Technology, Terman at first accepted a teaching position at the prestigious Cambridge, Massachusetts-based university. While visiting family back in California, however, he was stricken with a severe case of tuberculosis. During a slow and difficult recuperation, he began assuming part-time teaching duties at Stanford and in the end decided to stay and help rebuild what had become its struggling and grossly underfunded electrical engineering department. Stanford may thus by one measure perhaps be considered "lucky" to have acquired Terman as an employee (this line of reasoning, however, further demands that one overlook all the efforts that went into creating Stanford as an institution that was able to attract Terman and his family to the university in the first place). Even if seeing Terman's presence as sheer fortuitousness, it is still patently obvious that neither "luck" nor "accidents" had anything to do with what Terman subsequently accomplished. From his appointment as Assistant Professor in 1927 until his retirement as Provost in 1965, Terman uniquely contributed to the strengthening of Stanford's engineering and science programs. His work at improving the university's academic standing, building up a viable local job market for Stanford graduates, and realizing his larger aspirations for regional economic development laid many critical foundations that continue to support today's Silicon Valley.

In spite of promising beginnings as one of the university's strongest programs, electrical engineering at Stanford had by the 1920s become particularly limited. The department was at the time employing a lone senior professor and had not managed to acquire its own research lab until 1926. The new laboratory itself represented something of a mixed blessing. It was made possible because of financial support the department had earned from closely collaborating with local power companies. It was accordingly dedicated to research on high-voltage electricity. As the first high-voltage lab in the American West and the only two-million-volt university laboratory in America, it was in its own way state of the art.[45] The problem was it was a dying art. Research on electrical power reflected the department's origins of 35 years before, not the new directions in electronics or "radio engineering" as the field was then called. By turning down the chance to teach at MIT, the most prominent and best technically equipped university for scientific study in America, Terman was forgoing a tremendous opportunity and accepting a set of daunting challenges.

Conditions and morale for the electrical engineering department, and the university as a whole, were only to worsen. Within a few years of Terman's appointment, the impact of the Great Depression and the policies US President Franklin Roosevelt implemented to address it were reverberating throughout the campus.[46] Stanford's most famous alumnus and the dominant force on its Board of Trustees was Herbert Hoover, the outgoing holder of the Oval Office—a man whose reputation was in tatters and political philosophy thoroughly rejected. He and Stanford President Ray Lyman Wilbur (who had taken a leave of absence to serve as Secretary of the Interior in the Hoover administration), returned to Palo Alto in 1933 to witness first-hand how badly the financial health of the university had plummeted. Stanford had been primarily relying on the philanthropy of wealthy individuals and research foundations to meet the costs of its operations, sources of funding that dried up in the aftermath of the 1929 stock market crash. In the eyes of Stanford's ideologically conservative leadership, the situation was exacerbated by the growing perception that the status of their privately funded and fiercely independent university was in decline just as the federal government began to assume a larger role in American higher education.

The contravening rise in the prestige and resources of Stanford's local academic rival, the California state-funded University of California at Berkeley, particularly galled Stanford's administrators. Especially annoying were the strides UC Berkeley was making in scientific research and Stanford's inability to keep pace. By 1924 Berkeley had completed construction of Le Conte Hall, the first physics building at an American public university. Throughout the depression era Berkeley's star physicist, Ernest Lawrence, kept a steady stream of private and public money flowing into his multidisciplinary Radiation Laboratory. Expanding the laboratory after his 1931 invention of the cyclotron (a revolutionary particle accelerator the press took to calling a "proton merry-go-round"), Lawrence led Berkeley to the cutting-edge of nuclear physics. Meanwhile, 50 miles across the San Francisco Bay in Palo Alto, Stanford found itself so cash-strapped that on two occasions the university actually had to turn away gifts of equipment for building its own cyclotron. The university administration felt it could do little other than meekly apologize for lacking the resources to assemble and operate the equipment on offer.[47]

In the case of Stanford's electrical engineering resources, the state of deterioration was darkly comical as Terman recalled in an interview many years later:

> You can't realize how tight things were. I just really got the electronics program going and then 1929 hit; from then on there were 12 purely static years. In fact, when my reputation was being made nationally, at the end of a seven-year period, I was getting less money from the University than I was at the beginning in salary, because salaries were frozen and there had been a ten percent cut and then they reduced it to a five percent cut. The old electronics laboratory had a leaky roof and they didn't repair the roof. What they did was to build some wooden trays lined with tar paper and caulked with tar, then put these trays underneath where the leaks were and they'd catch the water![48]

Despite working in appalling conditions, Terman was able to earn widespread respect for his research and the quality of Stanford's electronics curriculum. A major boost to the standing of both came with the 1932 publication of Terman's *Radio Engineering*, an immediate classic that was adopted as a standard university textbook throughout the US. To help alleviate the department's financial penury, Terman contributed a portion of the royalties from his book and donated some of his personal radio equipment to the dilapidated electronics lab. With his own money he also provided for a number of student loans, a major incentive for prospective students during the Depression.

Terman furthermore committed himself to the future careers of his department's graduates. Something the professor was not prepared to put up with, even in the depths of global economic stagnation, was for any Stanford E. E. degree holder to be unable to find work and he proactively utilized his extensive network of contacts in industry to help his graduates land jobs. The challenge was made all the greater because once-prominent local firms like Federal and Magnavox had already left the Bay Area. Surveying the landscape, he rued how the region had become "kind of a semi-desert" for technology business.[49] Small electronics and specialty engineering firms could still be found but Terman felt compelled to shepherd his graduates into positions elsewhere, feeling strongly that his "boys" deserved "better jobs than were available in most cases because we just didn't have the equivalent of a Bell Laboratories type of operation, the General Electric level of sophistication in engineering."[50]

Terman was appointed acting head of the Department of Electrical Engineering in 1937. In 1941, at the urging of a group of industry leaders, he ran for and was elected President of the Institute of Radio Engineers, the leading professional society in electronics. In the years leading up to the United States' entry into World War Two, Terman increasingly pushed Stanford to embrace more applied research and to strengthen the university's ties to industry. He realized that successful engineering programs at MIT and, closer to home, the California Institute of Technology ("Caltech", based in Pasadena in Southern California) owed the quality of their resources to corporate patronage. Following the outbreak of the war Terman was selected—through the influence of one of his admirers in the business world, he speculated—to run Harvard's Radio Research Laboratory, a highly strategic and exceptionally well-funded organization that developed radar countermeasure technology for the US military. Through his experience at Harvard, Terman saw up-close how valuable the patronage of government as well could be for developing cutting-edge scientific capabilities in a university.

Returning from Harvard after the war as Stanford's newly appointed Dean of Engineering, Terman quickly set to work to improve Stanford's level of government funding, which at the time was miniscule compared with the amount being received by other major US universities. The first financial infusion he organized was a contract from the US Navy to finance three projects for basic research in the fields of chemistry, physics, and electrical engineering. The money that went into physics supported research carried out by Felix Bloch, a vocal naysayer regarding government sponsorship of university science.[51] Ironically, for his government-funded work on nuclear magnetic resonance, Bloch subsequently shared the 1952 Nobel prize in physics and became Stanford's first-ever Nobel laureate. From the funding that went toward the electrical engineering project, Terman developed a series of follow-up initiatives that ultimately helped create two leading Stanford research facilities: Stanford's Electronics Research Laboratories (ERL) and the Stanford Linear Accelerator. The ERL in particular developed close ties with newly formed, locally based technology firms like Varian Associates and Hewlett-Packard (Terman closely associated himself with both companies). Along with their own R&D efforts, these firms were able to convert much of ERL's basic research into product applications that they then successfully marketed. Varian, Hewlett-Packard, and Stanford's aggressively expanding science and engineering programs became the new icons for a reborn high-technology base that was emerging in the Santa Clara Valley.

This was just as Terman had intended. He viewed Stanford's chances for revival as an academic powerhouse to be closely tied with the region's ability to incubate home-grown technology firms. Terman argued that the US West must move beyond a lingering dependence on natural resources and agriculture to engender a "strong and independent industry" based on "its own intellectual resources of science and technology."[52] The professor exhibited a patriotic fervor for the cause of regional economic development. He implored a staid Stanford administration to appreciate how "industrial activity that depends on imported brains and second-hand ideas cannot hope to be more than a vassal that pays tribute to its overlords, and is permanently condemned to an inferior competitive position."[53] Despite the original mission of the university and the electrical engineering program's legacy of positive interaction with industry, highbrow attitudes in many departments and among Stanford's deeply conservative overseers meant that collaboration with the public or private sectors was deemed a betrayal of the university's educational ideals. Stanford's wholehearted support for the high-tech industrialization of the Valley was by no means a foregone conclusion.

The evolving nature of the Stanford Industrial Park reflects aspects of this reality. Stanford's administration, still squeezed for cash, had conceived of a business park in 1951 as a means to generate revenue through leasing plots from a 40-acre section of the university's massive estate. Beyond that, little thought was given to a strategic role the park could play in the long-term development of Stanford and the region. Varian Associates, a pre-war Stanford Physics Department spin-out, was the first applicant and a logical tenant for the park as the company still worked closely with the university (Terman served as a director and other Stanford faculty were managers, consultants, and investors in the firm). The second lease, however, went to Kodak for a photo processing plant—an operation that hardly represented leading-edge technology or meaningful opportunities for collaboration with the university's departments. Terman was further dismayed to discover that an insurance company was being considered for admission as well.

Terman responded by imploring the university planning authority to take a more sophisticated view and only admit firms with relevance to the university's scientific research. He called for Stanford to utilize whatever chances it had to bolster targeted areas—"steeples of excellence" as he referred to them—where collaboration with outside sources would improve the university's academic capabilities. Owing to Terman's lobbying and personal efforts at tenant recruitment, instead of becoming an unremarkable mixed-use commercial development, the business park assumed the form of a unique real estate project dedicated to the high-tech sector and genuinely complementary to Stanford's research activities. The resulting Stanford Industrial Park (later renamed the Stanford Research Park) counted among its early tenants Varian, Hewlett-Packard, General Electric, and Lockheed Space and Missile Division. Within half-a-century of its founding, the park would emerge as a 700-acre development housing 150 high-tech companies, R&D operations, and professional services organizations—all integral components of a local high-tech economy that provide an environment whose support of Stanford (along with other nearby universities) has expanded and strengthened the academic resources of the Valley. What nearly became a small patch of university land originally intended simply to house "a little light industry" has—owing to Terman's vision,

persistence, and the continued pursuit of his management objectives—
since become a major institution that reinforces the dynamism of the
cluster.[54]

Terman is the outstanding individual among those who have contributed to the sustained clustering of high-tech enterprise in the Santa
Clara Valley. Considering the highly directed and unique contributions
Terman made, it would be easy, but wrong, to credit his work as having
created—or having started the cumulative processes or networked
system that created—Silicon Valley. Stanford's biggest academic entrepreneur laid vital groundwork (more of which will be described) and
put his university on a footing whereby highly synergistic cooperation
with government and industry would be supported as an integral part
of, not an exception to, its operating principles. This new form of
collaboration was major innovation in its own right. Yet sustained
economic growth for the region would require far more efforts, especially
in the commercial sectors. The great importance and, at the same time,
the profound limits of foundation-building work like Terman's can be
seen through the manner in which Silicon Valley's two largest firms,
Hewlett-Packard and Intel, were established and grew.

## THE "BIRTH" OF SILICON VALLEY

Despite the crucial support to the cluster offered by the Stanford
Industrial Park, the university's experimental real estate development
was founded long after the facility credited in both local lore and official
government history as the birthplace of Silicon Valley: a one-car garage
located at 367 Addison Avenue in Palo Alto. The car shed never
boasted the advantages that the park could offer a corporate tenant. It
was in no way "purpose built" and never constructed as part of an over-
arching plan to attract high-technology firms to the area. Yet the
modest timber-frame building is recognized as the launch pad of Silicon
Valley because it is where the cluster's largest and most respected technology company, Hewlett-Packard (HP), got its start in the Autumn of
1938. Of course, neither the Stanford Industrial Park nor the Addison

Avenue garage legitimately qualifies as the real birthplace of the cluster. Silicon Valley was born in the interplay of human actions, not a fixed location or moment in history. The creation and growth of HP tellingly illustrates this point.

Bill Hewlett and Dave Packard had thought about starting a business together ever since 1933 when, during their final undergraduate year at Stanford, they took a Master's-level radio engineering class taught by Fred Terman. True to Terman's vision for the region, his classes dealt with more than theory and experimentation; the professor actively encouraged his students to consider setting up technology businesses of their own as well. Disappointing to their academic mentor, the pair left the region to follow a well-beaten path to the East Coast—Hewlett to take his Master's degree at MIT and Packard to join General Electric Company in New York. They had little compelling reason to return to the Valley to further their careers, let alone fulfill earlier hopes to co-found a company. With his MIT degree in hand, in Depression-era America Hewlett found he "had exactly one job offer" and that was in Chicago.[55] Packard had a promising, if somewhat unchallenging, future ahead of him at GE, then a premier destination for electrical engineering talent. He also had plans to marry his college sweetheart and given the state of the economy was in no position to take any great risks with his means of livelihood.

Nevertheless, the company Hewlett-Packard was founded, and founded in what has since become Silicon Valley, and not somewhere in New York or Illinois because of the intervention of Fred Terman and the positive responses his actions elicited from his former students. The determined academic—who confessed to a "selfish interest" in getting "little companies" to form in the area "because now and then they might hire one of my fellows"—started making things happen not long after both men had left the Valley behind.[56] Once Hewlett had completed his studies at MIT, Terman steered him away from the Chicago job-offer and back to Palo Alto by arranging technical project work around the area and at the Stanford electronics laboratory. It was at the lab in 1938 that Hewlett invented what would become HP's first product: a variable frequency audio oscillator, a device particularly well suited for the testing of high-end sound equipment that was then being introduced to movie production. At the time, Packard was still with GE and Terman had been using periodic trips to back East to act "as a kind of go between for Packard and Hewlett" in the attempt to "coax Packard to come back."[57] For years nothing came of it but after Hewlett's invention Terman intensified his efforts to get Packard to return. He offered his former student a Stanford research fellowship that paid $500 and, as a further income supplement, found him swing-shift employment at Litton Engineering Laboratories, what was then one of the small Federal Telegraph spin-offs that had remained in the Valley.[58] An additional enticement Terman presented to Packard was the chance to earn a Stanford E. E. degree, something Packard had intended to do before the job opportunity at GE had changed his mind. Terman even sweetened the deal by proposing to grant course-equivalent credit for research Packard had already been conducting at work, meaning that Packard's residency requirement could be waived and his studies completed in only a year. Terman's inducements stoked Packard's desire to establish a company with Hewlett, making it hard to ignore the upsides of returning to Palo Alto.

Together again in California, Hewlett and Packard at first collaborated informally. Packard juggled research at Stanford and work at Litton with whatever tinkering he could squeeze in at the garage. Hewlett devoted himself to developing products and refining designs. After working this way for several months the two men decided to formally found Hewlett-Packard on New Year's Day 1939. They numbered their company's kick-off product, a device based on Hewlett's audio oscillator circuitry, the HP 200A—a product number chosen to give customers the impression that it was one in a long line of established HP equipment. The two turned to Terman to supply a list of potential customers whom they then wrote enclosing makeshift catalogs they cobbled together. Their marketing technique, while not very refined, was all the same highly effective. The 200A was an elegant yet simple oscillator with a lightweight design and offered exceptional value.

Priced at $54.40, it cost a customer only about 15% of what the closest competitor charged for a much bulkier device. The oscillator became the first in a wide array of successful HP products marketed on the principle of providing customers outstanding quality and value.

After being founded with $538 in start-up capital, HP earned back during its first year of operations almost ten times that amount in revenue and three times as much in profit. As the company grew, the founders made managing the organization a top priority, seeking out a leadership style that would foster an organization with a creative, motivated workforce. The set of management principles they developed over time became known as "The HP Way," a main feature of which was the expectation that administrators practice management-by-walking-around or "MBWA." Pure deskwork was frowned upon. HP managers were appraised on how close a rapport they kept with front-line workers and their ability to stay abreast of customer expectations. At the general employee level, workers were given objectives to meet and allowed a basic degree of latitude to reach them. Hewlett once famously broke a lock that he found some transgressor had placed on a company storeroom. The note he left behind sternly warned that the room not be kept off limits to anyone—a memorable demonstration of senior management's faith in the integrity and competence of the workforce. HP's inclusive culture was further reinforced at the bottom line. All staff participated in an employee incentive plan and after HP's stock was publicly traded they were eligible to receive stock options as well. Generous medical coverage, training, and education programs became other perks of employment.

Giving credence to Terman's belief in the mutual benefits that would come to academia through proactively collaborating with local industry, Hewlett and Packard became prominent supporters of Stanford, aiding the university's outreach efforts to attract more science-based industry to the area and contributing enormous benefactions to their alma mater. By the time of David Packard's death in 1996, Stanford officials estimate that the two alumni and their charitable foundations, mainly through anonymous gifts, had donated to Stanford University over $300m—an

amount, adjusted for inflation, that nearly equals the Stanford family's
founding grant.[59] In May 2001, following Bill Hewlett's death earlier in
the year, the charitable foundation he had established more than doubled
the nominal value of the contributions the two men had already bequeathed, giving an additional $400m to Stanford—at the time, the
largest single donation ever given to a university in US history.[60]

Though HP flourished as a technologically creative company, some of
the greatest innovations the firm made concern the quality of its management, both in terms of management style and the management decisions
enacted at key junctures in the firm's evolution. The HP Way, now celebrated as a model of progressive management doctrine, was at first seen
by the business community as too unorthodox and shunned, even
within the friendly circle of Stanford business studies academics. In
1942, when a 26-year-old Packard attended a Stanford conference on
wartime production, he debated with Stanford professor Paul Holden,
then one of the nation's leading authorities on industrial organization
and control:

> Somehow, we got into a discussion of the responsibilities of management.
> Holden made the point that management's responsibility is to its share-
> holders—that's the end of it. And I objected. I said, "I think you are absolutely
> wrong. Management has a responsibility to its employees, it has a responsibil-
> ity to its customers, it has a responsibility to the community at large." And
> they almost laughed me out of the room.[61]

Packard's sense of collective responsibility extended to his working with
other local companies in order to strengthen the competitiveness of the
region as a whole. During the war years he organized a group of
Northern Californian firms to join the West Coast Electronics Manufacturers Association, an industry coalition that lobbied for defense-
related manufacturing contracts. He later recruited a number of local
CEOs to join him in establishing the Silicon Valley Manufacturing
Group, an association which has since become the leading voice for the
business interests of Silicon Valley, representing 190 firms that directly
account for nearly 275,000 local jobs.[62]

HP's corporate successes are revealing in other ways. What had begun as a two-man garage start-up in 1938 was some six decades later a corporation of more than 88,000 worldwide staff, generating for their firm annual revenues of nearly $60b—statistics that, in both the categories of total employees and sales, make HP the single largest company in the Silicon Valley cluster.[63] Having set off as a manufacturer of measurement and testing equipment, the company was at the start of the 21st century describing itself as a "global provider of computing, Internet and intranet solutions, services and communications products."[64] HP is not the first high-tech firm from Santa Clara Valley to have hit the big time (that distinction would go to Federal Telegraph), but it is, from among the pre-World War Two generation of Valley high-tech enterprises, the only one to have had enough staying power to build large mass and remain a dominant force in its global markets. Another break from the proto phase of Silicon Valley: HP has stayed independent (i.e., not been bought out by another company) and remained headquartered in the Valley. Though sometimes criticized for being slow to make organizational adjustments, HP nevertheless has demonstrated repeatedly a capacity to adapt to changing market conditions and reorganize itself as required—a common characteristic of firms in the Valley that manage to succeed over the long term.

HP's first major transformation was initiated in 1957. By then, nearly 20 years since the company's founding, the firm had approximately 2,000 employees, 400 different products, and $30m in annual sales. The founders decided to drop the largely *ad hoc* structures that had characterized their company since its days as a start-up venture and moved toward shaping HP into a more formally organized corporate entity. The firm adopted a divisional structure, issued its first mission statement (an explicit codification of the HP Way), launched an IPO, and moved into the Stanford Industrial Park. In the aftermath of these changes, the company accommodated additional growth and new directions. Annual sales came to surpass $2b and employee numbers grew to 60,000 worldwide.

A second round of large-scale change began in 1966 when, as a way to enhance its core offering of test and measurement equipment, HP decided to start supplying computers for improved instrumentation control. This was followed in 1968 by HP's introduction of the world's first programmable scientific desktop calculator, a forerunner to the desktop computers that would proliferate in the next decade. From these early beginnings in computer technology, HP management drove the company to positions of market dominance in key computer sectors. Though far from a painless transition, by the 1980s HP had managed to position itself as a major force in the computer industry. Its line of successful computer products ranged from PCs to powerful workstations, complemented by a series of computer-related technologies such as laser and inkjet printers that came to set standards in their markets. In 1988, on the eve of its 50th anniversary, HP entered the Fortune 50. Sales crossed the $10b threshold. In another 10 years they would amount to five times that historic volume. Today HP is America's second largest computer/office equipment manufacturer after IBM—an accomplishment owed to the company's flexibility and perseverance in pursuing new opportunities.[65]

HP's latest round of changes occurred in 1999 when its board of directors decided to jettison the company's original instruments business (thus completing the full transformation of the firm) and focus only on computer-related products and services. (HP's instruments group was spun off as an independent concern, Agilent Technologies, which has 47,000 employees and $11b annual sales—an enterprise that on its own represents a tremendous record of growth for HP's original line of business.)[66] The board that year also appointed Carleton "Carly" Fiorina as HP's new CEO. Fiorina's appointment signaled several breaks with HP tradition: she lacked a technical degree (at Stanford she had majored as an undergraduate in medieval history and philosophy), came from outside the company (standing policy at HP had been to promote from within), and represented HP's first female chief executive officer. Assertive, charismatic, and having made her career in the service side of America's telecommunications industry, Fiorina was seen by many as the ideal person for bringing further change to a company that, for all its growth and new directions over the years, was feared to be in danger of becoming a lethargic behemoth. At the same time, Fiorina's lack of in-depth knowledge of HP's core businesses and familiarity with the company's established value system have made her a target for critics—of particular note, Bill Hewlett's son, Walter Hewlett—who claim her strategies are taking HP in the wrong directions and are destroying the HP Way, the very soul of the organization.

After orchestrating a controversial acquisition of Compaq Computers in 2002, Fiorina's reputation as CEO was a topic of hot debate in the Valley. The wisdom of her appointment and the innovations she has striven to introduce to HP will have to be left for future evaluation. What is irrefutable, however, is that the series of transformations that have made HP's growth possible have not been the result of the company coasting as if "path dependent" on its historical momentum. Nor has the company's leadership succeeded by adhering to the dominant logic of the Silicon Valley cluster or the industries in which HP operates. Throughout its evolution HP has distinguished itself as a maverick innovator. One of the most basic (almost tautological) yet frequently overlooked lessons from HP's growth is simply that the company has been managed; managed for better or worse but managed nonetheless. Its continued performance will rely not on mysterious external forces but how well those in charge are able to recognize and respond to opportunities to move the firm forward.

This core aspect of the "mystery" of HP's success, which applies as much to the company as it does to other Valley firms that have risen in its wake, is repeatedly ignored in common interpretations of the origins of both Hewlett-Packard and Silicon Valley as a whole. Notice, for example, the telltale line of reasoning from a BBC radio documentary on the phenomenon of clustering:

> There's an interesting element of pure chance . . . and that crops up again and again in economic geography. Silicon Valley, the most famously successful place on the planet, happens to be there because Dave Hewlett and Bill

Packard, the founders of computer company Hewlett Packard, were graduate students at nearby Stanford University. It's a typical piece of historical happenstance.[67]

"Pure chance" had nothing to do with the specific actions that laid the foundations of Silicon Valley and paved the way for the establishment of HP in Palo Alto. "Historical happenstance" likewise has played no role in determining HP's success over the years—the company has been reinvented so many times that it defies its own organizational history. HP is obviously only one company, but close scrutiny of other leading firms that have emerged since HP reveals that their success as well is not owed to accidents or historical destiny. One need go no further than the creation and development of the cluster's intense concentration of semi-conductor firms, the very industrial agglomeration that gave "Silicon Valley" its name, to recognize the centrality of innovative, entre-preneurial management in the Valley's economic development.

### Silicon in the Valley

The two words that would eventually inspire a hundred place name knock-offs came from a three-part series of articles written by semicon-ductor industry journalist, Don Hoefler. Hoefler had become amazed by what he saw as the "frantic" pace of semiconductor firm start-ups that had occurred in Santa Clara Valley during the late 1950s and throughout the 1960s.[68] Writing a series titled "Silicon Valley—U.S.A." that ran in *Electronic News* in 1971, Hoefler traced the stories of nearly two dozen in-tegrated circuit manufacturers (who used silicon as the core material for their products) that had clustered mainly in suburban towns just below Palo Alto along the 101 freeway. The articles describe a very changed Santa Clara Valley, a location that was now attracting and retaining a rapidly proliferating number of top high-tech firms and talent. The region's ability to hold on to these economic assets was in marked contrast to earlier eras where, before individuals like Terman and Packard provided workers and companies with incentives to stay, people would as soon set up a company in the Valley as they would

abandon the region. This degree of asset retention was all the more remarkable because competitive turbulence in the sector meant that
prominent semiconductor firms could quickly decline to wither into
obscurity or corporate oblivion altogether. Key employees at semiconductor firms, moreover, had a tendency to job-hop or split from
established companies to establish new ones. Thus, hanging on to talent
was key to sustaining a sizable local industry.

The biggest company to come out of this early concentration of semiconductor firms is Intel, an enterprise that is today not only the largest
semiconductor firm in the world but, after HP, the second largest
company in Silicon Valley. The nature of the events leading up to its
formation and the type of leadership that has characterized Intel's
success in the marketplace again testify to the importance of strategically
responsive, highly entrepreneurial management. An appreciation of
Intel's development also helps put in perspective the advantages and
limits of a supportive cluster environment. Intel's rise to prominence—
indeed, the emergence of a flourishing semiconductor cluster in the
Santa Clara Valley—contrasts with the fate of the Valley's first "silicon"
company, Shockley Semiconductor Laboratories. The intellectual
resources provided by institutions like Stanford, special support offered
by administrators like Fred Terman, access to venture capital,
ownership of leading-edge product technology, employees who were at
the top of their field—all these pluses were available to Shockley Semiconductor. Despite the company's "first-mover" and numerous other advantages, the firm was poorly managed and failed miserably. The nascent
cluster, though, would go on to survive and flourish. The support
mechanisms put in place meant that even such a major failure did not
devastate the area: the Valley's blossoming enterprise base did not
recede; the region did not revert to a "semi-desert" once again. Out of
the ashes of Shockley Semiconductor Laboratories instead arose still
more semiconductor firms, not all of which were successful but most of
which crucially remained in the local area.

Through viewing the market successes of Intel, the leading member of
Shockley Semiconductor's family of descendents, the point is again

brought home that a company's establishment and growth can be immensely *aided* by a supportive cluster. No matter how marvelous a cluster's support mechanisms may be, however, the success of the firms it contains is ultimately *determined* by the qualities of its management. Intel, just as with HP, has crucially benefited from the unique assistances afforded to enterprises and individuals in the Valley. Massively successful companies like HP and Intel nevertheless have had to innovate on their own, marshalling independent resources and utilizing separately conceived strategies that often go against the grain of prevailing logic. The firms have flourished owing to their managements' resourcefulness and strong sense of corporate self-preservation—a passion for commercial survival and growth that has spurred corporate leaders to initiate extraordinary transformations of their organizations in order to maximize marketplace opportunities.

To appreciate the context of Intel's birth and development requires an understanding of Shockley Semiconductor Laboratories and its founder, the Valley's semiconductor industry pioneer. Similar to Fred Terman in respect to upbringing, William Shockley spent the formative years of his youth influenced by the heady, academic atmosphere of the recently established Stanford University. Settling in Palo Alto with his family at around the start of the 20th century, Shockley's interest in technology was kindled by a neighboring Stanford physics professor who took him in as a kind of surrogate son. The Shockleys left Palo Alto in 1923 and Bill went on to take degrees at Caltech and MIT. In 1947, he headed the team at AT&T's famed Bell Laboratories in New Jersey that invented the semiconducting transistor, a truly revolutionary technology if there ever was one. The semiconductor would come to replace devices like de Forest's vacuum tube triode and serve as the central component in advanced electronics products. It would function as the *ne plus ultra* of widgets in the dawning age of Information Technology.

Feeling underappreciated at AT&T, in 1955 Shockley decided to raise some capital and strike out on his own. He originally planned to establish a semiconductor firm on the East Coast and used his personal network to approach potential backers throughout that region. He was able to establish a semiconductor operation at Raytheon, a famous MIT spin-out, for a short time but in the end they, and all the other East Coast organizations he went to, were unwilling to commit the $1m in financing Shockley sought. He eventually called a fellow Caltech alumnus, Arnold Beckman, founder of Beckman Instruments (BI) in Los Angeles (a company that at the time was roughly the size of Hewlett-Packard). After just one week of discussions in Southern California, Beckman agreed to finance Shockley but wanted the firm to locate around L. A. to be close to BI's headquarters. Shockley preferred his childhood hometown of Palo Alto. To his cause he enlisted the readily available assistance of Fred Terman who, in characteristic fashion, put in the effort to see that Shockley's company would establish itself in the Valley.[69]

Setting up in Palo Alto in 1956, Shockley Semiconductor Laboratories had all the advantages that could be reasonably desired. Terman, who was at the height of his influence as Stanford Provost, helped Shockley Semiconductor get established and located close to Stanford. The firm was a direct beneficiary of Terman's exertions at "steeple building." Terman also aided the company in identifying and recruiting some of the best semiconductor technologists from throughout the country. In addition to the talent brought in, the firm had with its leader Shockley an unquestionably brilliant physicist, the world's expert on semiconductors. The company was backed by ample, patient financing—not just from any venture capitalist, but from a successful technologist and fellow alumnus of Shockley's; a man who viscerally understood the challenges of running a high-tech enterprise. The company was operating in a promising new branch of high-end electronics. The military applications of the products alone meant that Cold War defense spending in the US would ensure a steady stream of customer demand. The company also had a substantial head start, a "first mover" advantage over other semiconductor firms that would later flock to the Valley. Despite having nearly every conceivable factor in its favor, however, after one year in operation the company was effectively finished. Enduring consistently poor performance, the company passed through three corporate owners before finally being closed in 1968 (a year that was, paradoxically, the same one in which Intel started). Even operating in a hot new industry, employing some of the best minds in the field, and benefiting from an unusually supportive cluster environment, Shockley Semiconductor Laboratories lacked effective management—and that made all the difference.

Prone to fits of paranoia, vindictiveness, and exhibiting a heavy-handed, capricious leadership style, Shockley may have been one of the least competent managers ever to start a company in the Valley. A great irony to his shortcoming was Shockley's conviction that he had actually formulated a scientifically infallible method for boosting organizational productivity. Shockley's carefully calculated management formulas only strengthened his false sense of managerial prowess and further alienated his high-caliber employees who eventually found his behavior completely insufferable. In the end, Shockley's meticulously crafted management techniques could do nothing to stop his handpicked crew from defecting *en masse* out of frustration for the way they had been treated. Securing funding from Fairchild Camera and Instruments in New York, eight of the defecting scientists and engineers left Silicon Valley's pioneer semiconductor firm to found Fairchild Semiconductor in Mountain View, only a few miles south of Shockley's Palo Alto facilities. After Fairchild was established, within a few years the Valley began to become populated with numerous "Fairchildren"—the Fairchild spin-offs whose creation and further offshoots gave name to Silicon Valley. The original eight Shockley defectors, labeled the "Traitorous Eight" by their old boss, had themselves all left Fairchild to go on to other ventures within about 10 years. The last of the eight to leave Fairchild were Robert Noyce and Gordon Moore, the founders of Intel.

The type of experienced talent the founding of Intel brought together is a testament to how far Silicon Valley had developed since the days of Hewlett and Packard's garage; how much cluster facilitators, entrepreneurs, and workers had turned the Valley "semi-desert" into an "oasis." Intel's co-founders were themselves not only well versed in business, during their time at Fairchild they had become trailblazers in the embryonic semiconductor industry. Within only a decade, Noyce (who served most of his tenure at Fairchild Semiconductor as its General Manager) took the organization from the level of a start-up to a multinational firm with 12,000 employees and $130m in sales. Apart from his skills as a manager, Noyce was an industry legend for having co-invented the integrated circuit, the first "killer app" for semiconductors that made their widespread use feasible. Moore had been Fairchild's head of R&D. He became known for his axiomatic observation, later reverently titled "Moore's Law," that the density of transistors on a semiconductor (and hence its power) will double every year while the price for semiconductors will conversely drop.[70] In addition to his astute market sensibility, Moore proved to be an able listener who possessed a quick grasp of perplexing engineering issues. Staff would approach him with problems that had frustrated them for weeks and find that he could help them realize a solution in a matter of hours.[71]

By the 1960s the Bay Area was also home to Arthur Rock, a transplanted New York venture capitalist who knew Noyce and Moore from having organized the financing that allowed them to establish Fairchild Semiconductor. After deciding to start Intel, the pair turned to Rock who in only two days put together $2.5m to fund their new venture. Rock was famous for contributing his time to help the managers of the high-tech firms he invested in stay motivated and focused on market issues. His approach to venture capital investment was to nurture people, not products. (A kind of "Rock's Law" for venture capital is that funding should be based on the quality of a start-up's management team, not the promise of the technology the company plans to offer.) Rock became Intel's chairman. Another key manager brought on board was Intel employee number four, Andrew Grove, who had joined with Noyce and Moore in their defection from Fairchild. As head of operations and later CEO, Grove was the prime force in the hands-on running of Intel for its first three decades.

The formation of a company like Intel, just one of the myriad new ventures to have sprung up in the Santa Clara Valley since the 1950s, in and of itself represented a major achievement for those who had consciously dedicated themselves to building up the area as a favored location for high-tech enterprise. Members of this group included not only entrepreneurially minded academics like Terman and community-minded industrialists like Packard, but also leaders from local government and the service sector (examples of which will be discussed in the final section of this chapter). The efforts of those trying to build up the local industrial base were further aided by the attitudes of managers of established companies in the Valley, who were relatively tolerant of new firms being launched by defecting employees. Such aspects of business life in Silicon Valley offered to entrepreneurs like Intel's founders additional enticements for setting up their own company—and to setting it up, moreover, in the local area (as opposed to other appealing high-tech regions at the time such as Los Angeles or Boston). Even with entrepreneurship made as easy as it could be in 1960s' Silicon Valley, however, actually managing Intel for growth would require a type of innovative management approach that was unrelated to the local environment or the past experiences of Intel's corporate leaders. In fact, if Intel had followed the trends or "networked wisdom" of local industry, or had been guided by the experience and traditional mindset of its managers, it would be far less a company today than it actually is.

Better prepared, better connected, and entering the marketplace at a better time than any local entrepreneurs who had come before them, Noyce and Moore had grand ambitions for their firm. They established Intel for the express purpose of designing and building memory chips, a hot product concept for semiconductors at the time. By the late 1960s integrated circuits were being used in computers to handle a variety of tasks but memory functions were still the province of a far more rudimentary technology: magnetic cores. Memories, as the new type of chips were styled, could replace the electromechanical functioning of cores and realize what many saw as the next great leap forward for semiconductor integrated circuitry. Intel rapidly pioneered a 64-bit Static Random Access Memory (SRAM) chip in 1969 and by the following year had invented a 1,024-bit Dynamic RAM (DRAM). Management viewed the company's technology breakthroughs and later market successes with memories as validation of Intel's original business model. Unremittingly, Intel championed memory devices as its main product offering for the next 15 years. As Andrew Grove described the mindset that took hold, for the people at Intel "memories *were* us."[72] This kind of guiding logic prevailed even when an Intel researcher created a far more significant technology, the microprocessor (which brought computing functions to the level of a single chip), in 1971. The enormous importance of this discovery was largely ignored by Intel senior management at the time.

Intel's single-mindedness built market share and profits but the product category of memory chips quickly matured. In a predicament faced at one time or another by virtually any manufacturer, by the mid-1980s Intel had to contend with the reality that its cash-cow product was past its prime. Memories were on the declining slope of a product life cycle curve, a situation exasperated by foreign competition, mainly originating in Japan, that operated with better manufacturing efficiencies and quality control. Intel's management watched as the formerly high-margin market for memories that they had trailblazed devolved into a "commodity market" where "high-quality, low-priced, mass-produced" Japanese products dominated.[73] Intel's earnings slipped into negative territory. Something had to be done or Silicon Valley's flagship silicon company would go the same way of Shockley Semiconductor. Intel management came to the conclusion that it basically had four options:

1  compete head-on with the Japanese as mass producers of memories;
2  effectively abandon large-scale manufacturing and focus on developing some new "avant-garde technology" that Japanese manufacturers could not compete against;
3  outflank the Japanese by manufacturing "special-purpose" memories; or
4  continue as a semiconductor manufacturer but as a maker of microprocessors, not memories.[74]

According to the thinking that dominated Intel at the time, the company should have pursued option one—the logic being that a memory company *is always* a memory company. Perpetuating this legacy would have been disastrous. Intel lacked the resources, internally and available to it in the cluster, to make competing against the Japanese in memories anything less than corporate suicide. On the other hand, if Intel had heeded the prevailing thinking of Silicon Valley at the time, it would have pursued options two or three. Many Valley semiconductor firms in the 1980s adopted just such strategies as a means to circumvent competing against better-positioned Asian manufacturers. The book *Regional Advantage*, the most widely accepted study on the workings of Silicon Valley, specifically lauds specialization strategies because they allow companies to plug into the allegedly product-life-cycle-defying "model of semiconductor production that built on the region's social and technical networks."[75] Going the "avant-garde" or "special purpose" routes was certainly feasible. But pursuing either path would also have gutted Intel permanently and turned it into a drastically scaled down niche player. The firm would not be the kind of powerhouse in semiconductors that it is today and the prominence of the Silicon Valley cluster in its namesake industry would be noticeably diminished if Intel had chosen to specialize.

Following neither the direction of its organizational past nor what were then prevalent trends of Silicon Valley's present, Intel's management made a gutsier (and more innovative) decision: it chose option four. As the "Intel Inside" label on most of the world's PCs today reflects, it did spectacularly well in this regard. Intel now is a bigger, far more influential semiconductor company than the memory chip competitors who once pummeled the company in the 1980s. With personal computers, for example, Intel occupies an 81.9% share of the market for microprocessors used as Central Processing Units (CPUs), the brains of today's PCs. Combined with the 17.0% market share of its nearby Valley rival, AMD (which moves in step with Intel's basic product strategy), the two Silicon Valley chip firms account for an astonishing 99% total share of this major global market.[76] With sales amounting to $33b and employees totaling 86,000 worldwide, Intel has successfully transitioned from a memories company into a provider of microprocessors and related technologies, allowing the company to forgo scaling down to the level of a specialist supplier and instead pursue a high-growth strategy.[77] It was by no means an easy transformation. Intel's previously blinkered thinking—which, it is worth noting, the company's complex network of local relationships did nothing to mitigate against—took a serious toll. Reorienting the company toward the overlooked earlier product development of the microprocessor was painful, psychologically for those at Intel who carried out the reorganization and in even more so for those who suffered the brunt of Intel shuttering factories and laying off thousands of personnel. Yet Intel's standing in Silicon Valley and beyond amply testifies to the merits of its decision in terms of the company's long-term market position and development as a corporation.

Looked at over an evolutionary horizon, Intel's successes are particularly impressive in light of how the company that brought Noyce and Moore to Silicon Valley, Shockley Semiconductor Laboratories, was such an enormous failure. Here again, historical momentum was proven to be of no consequence. Shockley's managerial failures did not set off a mindlessly snowballing bundle of processes whereby still more of the Valley's semiconductor businesses failed. Rather, perspicacious managers like Noyce and Moore moved beyond the mistakes of the past, seized the special opportunities that the Valley's maturing high-tech cluster afforded, and created more, and better managed, semiconductor enterprises. Like the barren industrial landscape that spurred Fred Terman to action, business difficulties, as much as triumphs, proved to be a stimulus for learning and action in the Valley's development as a high-tech cluster.

## ADDED FACILITATION AND STRUCTURE

As the varying performance of Shockley Semiconductor and Intel illustrate, special assistance (or even being in possession of the greatest of technologies) mean very little to a company lacking the insight and skill to capitalize on the opportunities put before it. Ultimately, the success of an enterprise is determined by those in charge. At the same time, viewed from the macro-perspective of the region's economy, it is clear that since the bleak days of the 1930s there was a profound qualitative change in the Valley's business environment. The cluster that emerged from the ravages of the Great Depression offered increasingly strong incentives for firms to set up and remain in the region. It moreover boasted special assets (human and institutional) that could enhance the performance of firms. The highly involved nature of the efforts made by people like Fred Terman and David Packard in bringing about this change has already been discussed. Although such pre-eminent leaders of the cluster clearly stand out, they and the organizations they directly influenced were far from alone in working to increase the attractiveness and synergism of the Valley. In considering the breadth and depth of efforts devoted to the economic transformation of the region, at least two additional figures deserve (if only brief) discussion: Anthony Hamann, former city manager of San Jose, and the commercial property developer, Thomas Ford. The work of these two individuals aptly illustrates how seemingly mundane activities can critically affect the opportunities a cluster offers its commercial enterprises.

## Dutch Hamann and His Sprawl Machine

A towering figure among those who led the build-up of the cluster's physical infrastructure is Anthony P. "Dutch" Hamann, City Manager of San Jose from 1950 to 1969. (San Jose, the county seat of Santa Clara County, is not only the Valley's largest city but serves as the political nexus of the cluster.) Hamann does not typically feature in books that address the how's and why's of Silicon Valley, a rather strange omission considering his enormous influence in shaping key features of the cluster.

Hamann came to power on the back of the ascendancy in Valley politics of a coalition of interests known as the Progress Committee. Formed in 1944, the Committee traces its roots back to the early 20th century when professional- and middle-class reformers battled against various corrupt political machines for control in San Jose over city and county affairs. The reformers scored an early victory in 1914 when they won enough seats on the San Jose City Council to rewrite the municipal charter and professionalize its system of governance. New statutes shifted executive authority to a nonpartisan, professional city manager. This position was very much conceptualized in the mold of a business enterprise, the city manager's relationship with the electorate designed to be analogous to that "borne by the general manager of a corporation to its stockholders."[78]

The progressives' primary economic objective was to diversify San Jose away from dependence on an unstable agriculture sector. Despite ascent to elected power, the progressives still had to battle entrenched elements of San Jose's political machines until the 1940s when the movement's leaders finally consolidated their political position. They then persuaded city and county governments to recruit advanced industries to the area. Boeing became an inward investment target as did IBM. The Boeing effort failed—one wonders what additional economic opportunities there might have been had Boeing chosen to establish a manufacturing presence in the region—but in 1943 IBM selected San Jose as the site of its first West Coast production facility. When progressive forces were able to secure the appointment of Dutch Hamann as San Jose's city manager seven years later, they had scored a victory that even their most pro-growth advocates probably were unable to fathom fully.

A graduate of the Jesuit-run Santa Clara University, Hamann had studied law. Prior to his stint in government, he held a string of jobs ranging from car parts salesman to oil company representative to university business manager. Hamann was, if anything, a master at selling the appeal of an aggressively expanding San Jose. By the time he retired in 1969, the city had grown from a population of about 100,000 occupying 17 square miles of municipal land to a population of 450,000 occupying 150 square miles. Hamann and his team of assistants, known as "Dutch's Panzer Division," oversaw some 1,400 annexations of neighboring communities. Orchards spread across 100,000 acres of Santa Clara Valley in 1940. By the early 1970s, they occupied barely 25,000 acres.[79] Although this kind of growth stirred controversy during Hamann's tenure (and is frequently rued in hindsight today), the man carried a popular mandate. He was elected to his position by the citizenry seven consecutive times after the post of city manager became open to contest. In Hamann era San Jose, the courting of high-tech business also reached new levels of aggressiveness and coordination:

> Between 1950 and 1965, the Chamber of Commerce spent a million dollars plugging San Jose, subsidized by the city and county governments. Arriving industry found a cooperative local government eager to provide the zoning and capital improvements needed. What industry wanted, it got. When IBM planned to expand south of the city, San Jose simply annexed the area for the corporation's convenience. Scenarios like this were repeated many times over as the city did everything it could to woo and accommodate industry.[80]

The drive to bring in high-tech business was accompanied by a concerted push for new home construction. Hamann additionally lobbied for government funding and supported bond acts to develop the region's road and airport infrastructure. These efforts, carried out in conjunction with similar initiatives by other local, state, and federal authorities, brought to the region an extensive automobile transport network. By the early 1960s the surface streets of the Valley and San Francisco Peninsula had been augmented by two multilane freeways, the 101 and 880, which both converged at San Jose. The 101 eventually became Silicon Valley's principal transportation artery around which the Fairchildren semiconductor spin-offs and later generations of high-tech enterprise would gravitate. The 1960s also saw the construction of a second outer ring of freeways, the 280 and 680, that ran along the Valley's eastern and western peripheries and also merged at a San Jose apex.

The lack of thoughtfulness behind the construction boom created the major downside to work and life in Silicon Valley today: the sprawl. Nevertheless, the initiatives of public sector officials like San Jose's "CEO" Dutch Hamann were crucial for providing the area with the physical foundations within which Silicon Valley's cluster of economic activity operates. Roads, houses, and strategic assistance for industry were vital in preparing the area for the large-scale business growth that is the hallmark of today's high-tech mecca. San Jose's special treatment of corporations like IBM might seem obsequious (and was perhaps by some standards ethically questionable), yet in terms of the economic opportunities brought to the area such moves proved especially wise. Recruiting and accommodating IBM made San Jose home to not only IBM's first West Coast manufacturing site but also the first research center to be established by the computer giant outside its New York base. Beyond the lab's basic presence providing the area with a heightened profile as a favorable location for high-tech businesses, IBM scientists in San Jose produced major inventions like the computer hard disk drive and relational database software. Both became the technological seeds for a local hard disk industry and for Silicon Valley's largest (and the world's second largest) software firm, Oracle.

## Leading the VCs to Storm Sand Hill

Another individual whose work illustrates, albeit more subtly, the importance of entrepreneurial facilitation is Thomas Ford, the person who laid the physical groundwork for Silicon Valley's mini-cluster of venture capital firms located along Sand Hill Road in Menlo Park.

Within the geography of present-day Silicon Valley (a time when the once heavy dominance of semiconductor firms has subsided), probably the most talked about concentration of commercial enterprise is Sand Hill Road's bastion of venture capital. It is the Wall Street of the Valley; the floodgate for billions of dollars in high-risk finance that flows regularly to Bay Area start-ups. Venture capital is a wellspring of lifeblood for the cluster today. As the examples of Federal, HP, Shockley Semiconductor, and Fairchild Semiconductor demonstrate, financial assistance for starting up a company in the Valley once typically came from personal acquaintances or corporate backers. It was not until the 1960s that a significantly large, local body of professional financiers emerged. The Bay Area's first generation of venture capitalists, however, were predominantly located in San Francisco's financial district. The Valley lacked its own financial hub until 1969 when property developer Thomas Ford broke ground at 3000 Sand Hill Road for four sedate-looking office complexes located across from a remote corner of the Stanford campus.

A consummate but low-key networker, Ford managed to draw into his offices Silicon Valley's most promising newly hatched venture capital firms (VCs) of the early 1970s: Kleiner & Perkins, Mayfield, Sequoia, and Institutional Venture Associates. Other VCs and associated professional service providers soon followed suit. Ford's networking was aided by his choice of location. His Sand Hill developments— following the success of the original four buildings Ford added another eight—are surrounded by a country club and sit adjacent to the pictur-esque and (in contrast to the 101) unclogged 280 freeway. Elite suburbs like Atherton and Woodside, home to many of the wealthy professionals who work at the Sand Hill complexes, are only a few minutes drive away. Apart from Ford's sense for geographic positioning, he was able to bank on the simple appeal of having venture capital firms bunched together at one location in the Valley. VCs benefited by being close to one another to keep abreast of investment activity, share information, and coordinate among themselves on deals requiring co-investment. Entrepreneurs also benefited by having a central location for shopping around their business plans. Enhancing the flow of interactivity, Ford went out of his way to put his tenants in touch with one another. William Del Biaggio III, founder of Sand Hill Capital, notes that Ford's properties flourished because the man himself "embodied the spirit of doing business. He's the one who created an environment of tearing down all the walls."[81]

By the time of Ford's death in 1998, within a half-mile radius of 3000 Sand Hill there were over 40 venture capital firms, nine law practices, seven investment advisory firms, six consultancies, five executive search firms, four investment banks, and three accountancies—all critical com-ponents in the tightly integrated supply chain of professional services that support high-tech businesses in the Valley. Firms not able to occupy a coveted Sand Hill address might establish themselves somewhere else close by but tend to find they miss out on the ease of intimate interaction Ford planned for and encouraged within his developments. "A lot of firms are locating in downtown Palo Alto," a veteran of Sand Hill once observed, "but they don't have the same sort of cluster and opportunity to meet colleagues the way you do here."[82]

The nature of Ford's work again underscores how the innovativeness and entrepreneurialism of individuals in the cluster extends far beyond those involved in starting and managing high-technology companies. The captains of high-tech industries are aided by the efforts of leaders operating in low-tech areas of the local economy. The origins and evolution of Silicon Valley have been crucially influenced by people who not only build companies but by those who facilitate enterprise formation and interactivity.

None of this is to say that facilitating support—no matter how extraordinary—explains the accomplishments of cluster businesses that operate in competitive markets. Successful Valley firms have distinguished themselves by an ability to think and act individually, regardless of where conventional wisdom in the Valley's tight-knit industrial communities might try to steer them. An ironic upshot of the cluster's intensely communitarian spirit is the tremendous independence and originality that its leading firms exhibit.

The next two chapters delve deeper into Silicon Valley's creative capacity, examining in detail the present-day dimensions of the cluster's dynamism and the characteristics of its innovators. Though the focus of attention shifts, the implications regarding the centrality of critically thoughtful and entrepreneurially responsive management remain unchanged.

# Valley Dynamism 4

With an economy that thrives on change, Silicon Valley presents a significant challenge for any attempt to identify its characteristic dynamics. Dominant industrial activity in the cluster evolves rapidly. During World War Two and the post-war eras, defense-related work was the major driver of growth. From the 1960s, as the area came to be known as "Silicon Valley," semiconductor firms helped expand the cluster and lead it in new directions as did computer and computer-related companies from the late 1970s. In the latter half of the 1990s, "New Economy" Internet-related business—and established Valley firms that rebranded themselves as leaders of the e-business world—arose as the key enterprises pushing the cluster forward. Depending on whatever industry or mix of industries is in ascendancy, the defining features of the cluster's dynamics will change accordingly.

To explore the most contemporary aspects of Silicon Valley's dynamism that can be adequately assessed, this chapter examines the origins and meaning of the Internet boom that the cluster's leader helped create and, for many in later years, also misjudged. While critically analyzing the fallacies and missteps committed during the heady days of dotcom mania, the chapter devotes attention to where perspicacious thinking and constructive action took place as well. It considers how the entrepreneurial mindset and structural preparedness of the cluster helped its innovators seize the opportunity to create and build upon Internet technologies when other high-tech communities were disinterested in what the Net represented. It also shows the great degree to which forward-thinking but solidly pragmatic entrepreneurialism still imbues the cluster with a fundamental resilience that outlasts both the troughs of economic hardship as well as the heights of irrational exuberance. As with the previous chapter, enterprises directly involved in Silicon Valley's high-tech output, along with those operating at the periphery of the technology sectors, are evaluated in order to offer an encompassing view of the cluster's vitality.

## HYPE AND SUBSTANCE

Writing in *The Silicon Valley Edge*, a book that went to press at around the peak of the year 2000's hyper-inflated stock market bubble in technology shares, Valley venture capital wunderkind Steve Jurvetson left for posterity the following snapshot of the prevailing mindset of the cluster at the time: " 'The Internet changes everything.' This is a Silicon Valley mantra. And the Internet is synonymous with entrepreneurship."[83] This syllogistic reasoning encapsulates the kind of misguided groupthink that had taken hold of 20th century *fin de siècle* Silicon Valley. The Internet is a powerful technology, but was never as powerful as its most vocal promoters claimed. That this passive, artificial device used to link together computers was ever considered equivalent to the all-too-human thinking and actions that entrepreneurship actually entails reflects just how far those who whipped up the froth of the Internet bubble lost touch with the cluster's entrepreneurial roots.

It is hard to be charitable in assessing the errors of logic that occurred while dotcom mania swept the Valley. Nevertheless, for all the craziness of the dotcom bubble, the follies of the boom need to be viewed with a sense of perspective. Internet euphoria took hold in large part because people in the Valley had so enthusiastically developed networked computer communications long before those in other regions awoke to the possibilities of the technology. Such ahead-of-its-time dedication to new opportunities, shared across a wide range of Valley enterprises and workers, remains a strongpoint of the cluster.

The cluster's history and pre-history did not "make" Silicon Valley but they do show how local entrepreneurs, at least the successful ones, have repeatedly distinguished themselves by seizing opportunity and

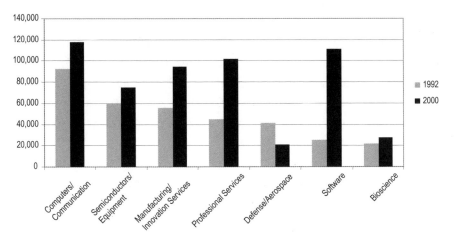

**Figure 4.1** Silicon Valley High-tech Employment, 1992–2000.
(Data from Collaborative Economics, used with kind permission)

finding creative solutions to adverse market conditions. This is a feature of the cluster's dynamics that one does not have to go back so many years to observe. As recently as 1992, Silicon Valley was wrenched by a severe economic downturn as California wallowed in its most painful recession since 1941. Santa Clara County's unemployment rate soared to 7.4%. With cutbacks in US military spending following the end of the Cold War, the Valley's defense and aerospace sector, the traditional backbone of the cluster, was hit especially hard. The predicament represented a change in fortunes for the Valley that had come full circle. In the 1940s, entrepreneurs found ways to take advantage of a surge in military spending to rekindle the Valley's high-tech economy. Fifty years later, however, the government was in retreat from the marketplace. As Figure 4.1 indicates, throughout the 1990s employment in the Valley's defense-related firms plummeted: workforce levels in that sector shrunk by about half between 1992 and 2000. The interesting thing about this decline is that overall impact on the cluster was negligible. In the years since World War Two, the majority of existing and new businesses in Silicon Valley moved away from defense-related work, resulting in the cluster's defense sector becoming one of the smallest by the time of the early 1990s recession. Thus, Silicon Valley was better positioned to weather the effects of defense spending cutbacks. As defense-related business further dropped off throughout the decade all other components of the Valley's high-tech economy conversely expanded. In the last eight years of the 1990s, total employment in Silicon Valley leapt by more than 200,000—a rise of 60%, adding to the high-tech labor pool 10 times as many workers as those who were lost to defense-sector lay-offs.

Ten years after the bottoming out of the early 1990s' recession, Silicon Valley again found itself enduring economic decline. How exactly, and in what sectors, Silicon Valley will arise from the latest downturn is unclear. Still it is possible, even before the smoke from the smoldering debris of dotcom mania has entirely cleared, to see what weaknesses of the cluster contributed to the irrationality of the boom and what strengths will help guide it forward. To appreciate the sheer robustness of the Valley's economic vitality requires differentiating between the hype and substance of its latest technology craze.

## NETTING THE FUTURE

Next to assertions that the Internet changes everything, probably the greatest myth about the Net (certainly one of the most persistent) is the pervasive belief that it originated as an impenetrable communications system, one supposedly dreamed up by US war planners who wanted to ensure that American missile sites would remain "on line" in the event of a nuclear attack. Although a nuke-proof telecommunications system was once proposed in the early 1960s, that idea never went beyond the drawing board.[84] The origins of what today we call the Internet instead stretch back to the ARPAnet, a communications network that was born in an initiative taken in 1966 by Robert Taylor, a civilian director in the US Department of Defense's Advanced Research Projects Agency (ARPA). Taylor's goal was far less ominous than ensuring the flow of command-and-control instructions in the event of nuclear Armageddon. He instead sought to link together the computers of ARPA-funded research centers at universities and other contractor sites, the idea being not to put missile silos online but scientists, engineers, and researchers.

The concept of Taylor's ARPAnet proposal was thus for peaceful purposes and relatively simple. It was also in very many ways quite extraordinary. Computers in the 1960s were monolithic behemoths. Fortresses of hulking circuit boards, entwined wires, and whirring reels of magnetic tape, they lacked the interconnectivity of common hardware and software platforms that characterize today's personal computers and workstations. Transferring data between divergent computer systems, let alone between systems over a wide area, was impossible. As a result the computing resources of America (and the world) stood isolated and underutilized. Taylor's proposal to link together disparate computers over a wide area was a concept other leading thinkers in computing science had hoped would one day come to pass but no one had yet found a way to push forward. It also turned out that the idea of a seamless computer network that so excited Taylor was, like William Shockley's business plan, an opportunity that would be shunned by key organizations in the East Coast but seized upon by those in Silicon Valley.

ARPA-sponsored research centers (also known as "investigators") based at locations outside the American West resisted Taylor's idea. Led by East Coast Ivy League universities, this group declined to participate in the network experiment from the very first gathering Taylor organized to introduce ARPAnet's goals. Their stance:

> ... revealed the lack of enthusiasm, if not downright hostility, to Taylor and [his MIT-trained assisting technical director] Roberts's proposal. Few ARPA principal investigators wanted to participate in the experiment. This attitude was especially pronounced among researchers from the East Coast universities, who saw no reason to link up with campuses in the West. They were like the upper-crust woman on Beacon Hill who, when told that long-distance telephone service to Texas was available, echoed Thoreau's famous line: "But what would I possibly have to say to anyone in Texas."[85]

In the end, only four investigators agreed to participate in the launch of the ARPAnet. Three of the participants were in California: UC Los

Angeles, UC Santa Barbara, and the Stanford Research Institute. The fourth, the University of Utah, hailed from a neighboring western state. The supreme irony of this configuration was that the critical hardware and software for the ARPAnet was conceptualized, designed, and physically created in the Eastern US, principally by people and organizations connected with Boston's Route 128 cluster. Owing to the varying reactions of those offered the chance to experiment with and further develop the network, however, the ARPAnet was essentially transferred to two states in the West. In Silicon Valley in particular it was then built upon and heavily commercialized.

A convenient but incomplete explanation to make for how Silicon Valley rather than Route 128 wound up assuming the lead in the subsequent development of the Internet would be to claim that cultural differences resulted in the Valley overtaking the East Coast cluster. Obviously, attitudinal differences played a major part in influencing which people recognized the opportunity the ARPAnet provided. The issue though was more of resource management and structural preparedness than of cultural bias. Computer science research and education at the East Coast's Ivy League universities, especially Harvard and MIT, was conducted in Ivory Tower enclaves. Their goals were to protect their well-endowed computing resources, not share them. On the other hand, in terms of "cultural openness," all four Western ARPA investigators—UCLA, UC Santa Barbara, the Stanford Research Institute, the University of Utah—were equal in their being receptive to the ARPAnet concept. They also equally shared the "first-mover advantage" of each being one of four nodes on the pioneer network that later evolved into the Internet. Only Silicon Valley, however, went on to dominate so decisively the field of networked computing. This accomplishment was not owing to the Valley's cultural style but to how members of the cluster intentionally worked to attract new technology opportunities and the methods employed by those who capitalized on them.

The arrival and subsequent development of Internet technologies in the Valley again speaks to the quality of physical and human resources that were being actively cultivated in the cluster from the 1930s onwards. The Stanford Research Institute (SRI, then a university–industry interface group within Stanford University but now an independent R&D think tank and consultancy) had been especially well positioned by its managers to participate in the ARPAnet experiment. SRI's leadership had worked closely with Fred Terman in his efforts to publicize the Valley as a major center for high-tech and the Institute had its own expanding computer science research program. Of especial benefit, SRI had hired the eclectically minded computer scientist Douglas Engelbart. Even before the ARPAnet had been proposed, Engelbart was already at work at SRI trying to create a new hypermedia system known as NLS, the "oNLine System." As he would later recall about first hearing of the ARPAnet at its inaugural project meeting: "I realized there was a ready made computer community. . . . It was just the thing I was looking for."[86]

The Stanford Industrial Park, which by the time of the ARPAnet's launch was being managed according to Terman's "steeples of excellence" framework, would serve as a further conduit to broaden work on Internet technologies begun at SRI. In 1970, just after SRI had become one of the original four nodes of the ARPAnet, Xerox decided to establish a presence at Stanford's high-tech business park and founded on a scenic hillside plot the Xerox Palo Alto Research Center, or PARC. Xerox, the world's largest producer of document-making equipment, created the center hoping it would allow the company to discern the competitive threats that emerging computer technologies would pose to Xerox's efforts to meet the office information needs of the future. The cutting-edge research activities being carried out by local universities and organizations such as SRI and IBM San Jose meant the Valley offered a unique environment to look out for new trends in computing. In the plans for Xerox PARC, the potential threat posed by networked computing was already in mind as the company hired Robert Taylor, who had recently stepped down as ARPAnet's overseer, to join the research center. Taylor subsequently recruited into PARC's ranks the computer-communications experts whom he had known from leading the development of the ARPAnet. Though Xerox later proved itself to be notoriously inept at taking action to profit on PARC's long litany of breakthroughs, under Taylor PARC became a highly prolific and deeply admired Silicon Valley institution, acting as a chief catalyst for the Valley's rise as the world leader in commercializing computer networking technologies.

The collection of talent that Taylor assembled at PARC made the facility a place akin, in spirit if not form, to Fairchild for its role in further seeding the Valley's commercial enterprise base. A former ARPAnet engineer from Harvard who joined PARC at its establishment, Bob Metcalfe (quipper of the line "Silicon Valley is the only place on earth not trying to figure out how to become Silicon Valley"), left PARC in 1979 to establish 3Com, the "computer, communication, and compatibility" company. 3Com went on to succeed in commercializing a local area network technology, the Ethernet, that Metcalfe had led the development of at PARC, making it the Valley's first major computer networking company. Important Valley firms like the computer maker Apple and software maker Adobe went on to hasten the development of personal computing and computer networking through the integration of key PARC inventions to their products. One of the most significant influences exerted by PARC was the way its network experiments inspired Berkeley graduate student Bill Joy to design Internet Protocol-enabled computer workstations. These workstations became the core product made by the company he co-founded in Palo Alto in 1982, Sun Microsystems. Sun, whose networking focus is exemplified in its trademarked slogan, "The Network Is The Computer," went on to produce hardware and software that was crucial to stimulating further growth of the Internet. (A company that in 2000 earned $19b in sales and employed 37,000 worldwide, Sun became Silicon Valley's fifth largest firm.) The Valley's third-largest firm, Cisco ($23b in sales, 34,000 employees), is even more directly connected with the Valley's rapid rise as a center of Internet technology.[87] Founded in 1984 by a husband-and-wife team of Stanford University computer system administrators, Cisco was the first company from the cluster to gain prominence by offering network routers, the very technology that links separate networks together, thus making an interconnected network of networks, or "Internet," possible. The importance of Cisco's technology and the size the company would grow to are indications of the disproportionate degree of networking capabilities built up by the cluster in only 15 years since SRI became a single point on the Pentagon's experimental computer network.

## THE SOLECTRON BEHIND THE CISCO

Projecting out approximately another 15 years from Cisco's founding, by the close of the 20th century the Valley had reached an apex point in its (and by then, the world's) enthusiasm for networked computing. Cisco, the shining emblem of the cluster's acquired prowess in Internet technologies and services, had become the Valley's newest Titan. Having maneuvered itself to the crest of an Internet-inspired stock market bubble, by April 2000 Cisco's market capitalization reached one-half-trillion-dollars, eclipsing that of America's contending technology stock heavyweight (and Silicon Valley's perceived arch nemesis): Microsoft.

The company's success, at least in this particular phase of Cisco's existence, was poorly handled, however. In fact, Cisco's management behavior at the time of the company's stratospheric market cap offers its own parable for how the Valley's once legitimate enthusiasm for computer networking had overstretched itself. It is important to look at such foibles critically but, also important and in certain regards more instructive, to look closely at those management practices that demonstrate greater longevity, that were in use before the mania and are outlasting it.

In the case of Cisco, without too much oversimplification, its stumble can be fairly easily summarized. A few months after the firm's historic market capitalization it had become clear that the good times in the Internet sector were not going to keep rolling. By the summer of 2000, the Nasdaq index was plunging along with the financial health of dotcoms and telecommunications businesses that formed the backbone of Cisco's customer base. Demand for Cisco equipment was plummeting and the company's parts suppliers and contract manufacturing partners were warning Cisco that it was facing imminent backlogs. Heedless of these signals and the telltale signs of a general market downturn, Cisco's senior management plowed forward, enamored with a vision of steadily increasing future sales. Their expectations were based primarily on an overconfidence accumulated from past experience and the data provided by a poorly configured internal order network (the latter a particularly ironic source of weakness considering Cisco's technical networking expertise). Company management stood by its overly optimistic projections and proceeded with aggressive parts purchasing and staff hiring up until the end of the year. Meanwhile, the company's inventories swelled as sales failed to materialize. Then in April 2001, barely a year after Cisco's historic stock market peak, reality hit. With the company's share price plunging to about one-fifth its earlier high, Cisco executives finally took corrective action, announcing they would write off $2.5b in inventory, incur $1.2b in restructuring charges, and lay off 8,500 employees (16% of the workforce).[88]

High-tech bubbles are nothing new to the Valley. Semiconductor memories, PCs, and hard-disk drives are just a few of the other sectors in the Valley that have ridden the cresting and falling of technology waves. No company can hold back the forces of business cycles. Well managed, however, a firm can at least stay on top of changes in the marketplace and prepare itself for the future. Cisco in 2000 presents an instance of a company that poorly handled its market cresting at the tail end of a technology boom. It was far from alone in its misjudgments, operating, after all, in an environment where the Internet was seen to "change everything." But though Cisco and many other local enterprises became wrapped up in the exuberance pervading Silicon Valley, there were those Valley firms not blinded by the buzz, whose leadership spent the heady years building company mass by being more creatively strategic than simply uncritically opportunistic. Such Valley companies can even be found in Cisco's own local supply chain network and were, in fact, vocally warning Cisco of its looming backlog problems. A closer look at one of these Cassandras, the contract manufacturer Solectron, reveals how adeptly managed companies remain a major feature in the Valley's landscape; that even during the height of technology crazes, independently resourceful leadership will take a company farther than simply trying to ride the crest of a swelling market tide.

Solectron is a major Valley company that remains largely unknown to the public at large because it produces nothing under its own label. As a contract manufacturer—or an "electronics manufacturing services" provider as it is officially categorized—Solectron operates production lines for brand-name firms like Cisco and other high-tech manufacturers throughout Silicon Valley and around the world. Despite its relative obscurity, Solectron is immensely important to the region's economy, not just for its manufacturing output (which helps an increasingly services- and software-oriented cluster stay connected to the physical production of high technology), but for its mass. With $19b in sales and 65,000 employees worldwide, Solectron is a larger company than far better known Valley firms such as Sun, Oracle, and Apple.[89]

Founded in 1977 by a former manager at the Silicon Valley game maker Atari, Solectron began life as a job shop that handled overflow work from local electronics manufacturers. The founder's long-term goal was to move the company (which he titled as an amalgam of "solar" and "electronics") away from contract assembly to become eventually a brand-name manufacturer of solar-powered devices. That dream came to naught as the company failed to turn a profit and fell heavily into debt. It was rescued by Winston Chen, a Taiwan-born physicist who had worked at IBM and used money from an inheritance to buy a 50% stake in the struggling firm. Taking control of the company's operations, he moved Solectron forward by implementing stringent quality-control production standards, intensifying workforce training, and installing advanced factory automation equipment. This high-end approach helped set Solectron apart in an industry typically viewed as one run on manually intensive labor. By 1984 sales had reached $50m and the company was ready to expand. In this instance, Silicon Valley's vaunted networks of venture capital were of no assistance. Unable to obtain local financing, Chen traveled to New York and secured $8m to realize his expansion plans. (The failure of local VCs to finance Solectron, an already important company that would grow to become a highly critical component of Silicon Valley's manufacturing base, serves as an important reminder: the real aid to a cluster's development is not so much the amount of local capital investment available or even the amounts doled out, but how well capital infusions are directed to deserving companies.)

In 1987 Chen recruited Koichi Nishimura, his former boss at IBM, to join Solectron as COO. Nishimura, a *nisei*, or second-generation Japanese American, shared with Chen a deep admiration for Japanese-style production methods. By 1991 Solectron had fully integrated Japanese-originated "5S" principles of manufacturing and won the coveted Malcolm Baldridge National Quality Award. (In 1999 Solectron again won the award, becoming the first manufacturer to be a two-time Malcolm Baldridge winner.) The 1991 honor provided a major boost to Solectron's standing in the marketplace, helping to dispel the image of low value-add conferred on it by its industry sector and placing the firm on the same pedestal occupied by such previous Baldridge Quality Award winners as Motorola, Xerox, and IBM.

Since 1992, Nishimura has managed Solectron as CEO. Under his stewardship the firm has transitioned from being a large but locally focused contract manufacturer to becoming a fully globalized manufacturing services provider offering turnkey production solutions. Much of this transformation was realized through Solectron's strategic acquisition of the manufacturing operations of key clients. Factories absorbed in this way total more than 30 sites and include those from such paragons of high-tech as IBM, HP, Texas Instruments, Philips, Mitsubishi Electric, and Sony. Instead of taking a hatchet-job approach to re-engineering operations and laying off workers, Solectron's policy with new acquisitions is actually to increase investment in facilities and human resources. The company keeps on previous plant managers who are given free reign in finding ways to adjust a factory's operations to integrate them within Solectron's existing structure. Even when facing tight labor markets, Solectron enjoys a strong rate of employee retention through offering skills training, worker empowerment, and incentive pay programs that benefit both managers and front-line staff alike. The company's stock-purchase program is estimated to have provided more than $1b worth of shares to employees, including part-time laborers.[90]

Solectron now leads the worldwide electronics manufacturing services industry. The company's sales are nearly twice that of its main competitor and the former industry leader, SCI Systems of Huntsville, Alabama.[91] As Solectron's warnings to Cisco show, the company places a premium on reliable market intelligence and stresses maintaining a close rapport with customers. It is constantly linked to clients electronically, not through overly complex, fault-prone system configurations but rather through a basic, easily monitored EDI (Electronic Data Interchange) system. Its most important information tool is even less complicated: a customer satisfaction index that is compiled from the weekly reports all Solectron factories must solicit from the companies they serve. If satisfaction problems are identified, managers of the groups responsible detail and carry out plans for improvement. In day-to-day operations, rank-and-file employees are also given the freedom to respond to developing issues without going through committees, thus addressing problems before they become crises.[92] Despite operating at what is considered the low end of the Valley's supply chain, Solectron maintains an empowered and entrepreneurial workforce.

Solectron's outstanding management methods have not made it immune to the effects of market downturns—in 2001, it too ended up cutting jobs and restructuring. All the same, indications are it entered the trough of that business cycle in tune with the realities it was facing. Until Solectron abandons the responsive management practices that have helped it stay ahead thus far, the company will be well positioned to take advantage of future opportunities. Solectron's performance in the late 1990s exemplifies how, although there will be firms that sacrifice prudent behavior and succumb to the intoxicating atmosphere of the cluster's booms, there remain vital companies like Solectron that grow through more sustainable strategies and behaviors.

## VALLEY LAW

A further measure of, and explanation for, the resilient vitality of the cluster comes from another beneath-the-surface—and, in this case, thoroughly low-tech—source: Silicon Valley's legal services sector.

The application and practice of law has been influencing the Valley's economic vibrancy since the early days of silicon. Fairchild Semiconductor had only been operating 18 months when it sued its former general manager who had taken 10 employees with him to found Rheem, the first of Silicon Valley's "Fairchildren." The plaintiff claimed that proprietary information had walked out the door with the 11 defectors. As Fairchild had orchestrated the same sort of activity with the Traitorous Eight's abandonment of Shockley, however, the company was amenable to reaching an out-of-court settlement, allowing Rheem to continue on in the Valley as the first of Fairchild's many offshoots.

This type of approach to asserting a firm's legal rights—where lawsuits (or the threat thereof) were used as a tool of competition but not pursued to a degree that gutted the local industrial base—helped give definition to the emerging dynamics of Silicon Valley. Don Hoefler, the reporter who first promoted the name "Silicon Valley," commented on a telling difference between Rheem's legal entanglements and those occurring at the same time involving Connecticut-based National Semiconductor:

> [National] had been formed in Danburry, Conn., in 1959, when Dr. Bernard Rothlein led a group out of Sperry Semiconductor. Sperry didn't take too kindly to that, and sued. This action, however, made Fairchild's suit against Rheem in the same year look like a church social. Sperry was going for the jugular, and found it.
>
> Sperry's Exhibit A in the court room was a large blow-up of its organization chart before Dr. Rothlein and his group left. Then the Sperry barrister slowly and dramatically placed large black squares, one by one, over each box which represented a defector. It was a hokey performance which probably would be laughed out of court in high-turnover California, but it did the job and brought National to its knees. [93]

The legal battle nearly bankrupted National. After being reinfused with cash, the company's leaders moved the firm to the more inviting business environment of Santa Clara County in 1967 where Charles Sporck, a high-profile manager of Fairchild's manufacturing operations, joined the company as its new CEO in the usual style: bringing with him an exodus of Fairchild employees and know-how. Surprisingly, National was spared a lawsuit altogether, with speculation that this was only possible because of an unofficial truce Sporck had wisely arranged. Sporck stayed on friendly relations with those he left behind, perhaps even allowing a situation whereby "a number of Fairchild's insiders made substantial capital gains in National stock, buying it a very depressed prices before the Sporck move was made public."[94] Whatever the exact reasons for National being able to avoid costly litigation, the point remains that, in marked contrast to experiences elsewhere, semiconductor spin-offs in the Valley were able to form in a largely tolerant legal climate.

As the industry matured and competition between semiconductor firms heated up, the give-and-take equilibrium became less forgiving. Big-ticket lawsuits against bands of defecting employees were filed by National in 1979 and by Intel two years later. Per the original pattern, these cases were settled out of court and seemingly brought more for the purpose of deterring future direct-competitor spin-offs than being part of a determined effort to stifle the establishment of new firms. Not all lawsuits have been so easily resolved, but, as the continued growth and start-up activity of Silicon Valley demonstrates, the forces of entrepreneurship have not been noticeably hampered either. As the cluster has further evolved, defecting employees have learned to be more observant of legal proprieties, relying on the advice of lawyers to ensure their departures do not cripple a new company before it has had a chance to be up and running. For established firms, the emphasis of legal strategy has moved increasingly to fending off greater competitive threats from enterprises based in locations outside the region: notably Japan, Taiwan, and other parts of the US. Silicon Valley's lobbying of the US government to prosecute the Seattle-based software giant

Microsoft for anti-competitive practices provides a revealing case in point.

In late 1994, in response to Microsoft's announced acquisition of the Silicon Valley financial software firm, Intuit, a group of Valley lawyers and economists gathered together to compose a detailed, highly critical white paper. The document, "Technological, Economic, and Legal Perspectives Regarding Microsoft's Business Strategy in Light of the Proposed Acquisition of Intuit, Inc.," challenged not only the planned takeover of Intuit, but the entire legality of Microsoft's behavior as the world's largest software company. The reasoning of the paper struck a deep chord with US Department of Justice lawyers and court judges who had been handling a series of anti-trust lawsuits against Microsoft. The economic concepts underpinning the white paper's arguments are particularly interesting because they were provided by two Stanford professors, one of them a leading voice for increasing returns theory, the economist Brian Arthur. Joel Klein, the attorney in charge of the US government's prosecution of Microsoft, was especially persuaded by Arthur's theories concerning how matters of "happenstance," "small events," "first-mover advantages," and the like can unjustly lock in markets; the theories provided a crucial "new synthesis" to support the Justice Department's case.[95] Armed with the certainty of this economic logic, the US government pursued its charges against Microsoft with increased vigor.

The government's "new synthesis" of reasoning marked a key turning point in Microsoft's courtroom battles. At the time, the Justice Department was beginning to adopt a conciliatory stance on pending litigation against the Seattle software maker. That all changed with the issuance of the white paper in whose wake Microsoft suffered two major legal setbacks in rapid succession. Microsoft's legal defeats eventually culminated with the ruling in 2000 that the company be split up. In June 2001, that ruling was overturned (and in September of that year government prosecutors dropped their case for corporate dismemberment altogether), but in the Silicon Valley order of things the particulars of this denouement have not mattered much. From the competitive perspective of the cluster, the steamrolling of Bill Gates Inc. was successfully curtailed, the Valley's business turf protected. Long before the Microsoft break-up order had been issued, members of the white paper team could congratulate themselves for having forced Microsoft to abandon its acquisition plans for Intuit. (Intuit employees are said to have erupted in cheers when they received word that the takeover attempt had been halted.) The white paper and follow-up efforts to it again demonstrated how supporters of the cluster could band together to address collective threats. Gary Reback, the Silicon Valley attorney who organized the drafting of the paper and subsequent efforts like it, became recognized as one of the most powerful lawyers in America and, to him surely an even greater complement, as the "biggest thorn" in the side of Microsoft.[96]

Any claim that Microsoft somehow "accidentally" locked in its markets and has succeeded by the cumulative momentum of happenstance is, of course, erroneous. (That is not to say Microsoft is not otherwise guilty of abusive monopoly behavior and did not deserve the verdicts rendered against it; nor is it to say it was guilty and did—that issue is suited for a separate discussion altogether.) Regardless of the dubious aspects of the economic arguments against Microsoft, what was spot on about Silicon Valley's pleas against the software company was the lawyering. Pulling together a masterfully compelling argument that effectively neutralized a perceived threat to the cluster, Reback and his team undeniably succeeded in their mission of justice for the Valley.

Looking after the interests of Silicon Valley's high-tech community has been a long-term preoccupation of the law firm where Reback served as partner, Wilson Sonsini Goodrich & Rosati.[97] Like other key events in the Valley, Wilson Sonsini's origins stretch back to the crucial foundation-building days of the 1950s. In 1957, John Wilson established a securities law practice in Redwood City. Three years later, he relocated several miles south to join with two Palo Alto-based lawyers, creating a new partnership that represented the first full-service law firm specially serving the area's growing collection of high-tech companies. In its first decade, Wilson's law firm signed up important local venture finance

groups like Davis & Rock, established its own venture investment
fund (a first for a US law practice), and launched an aggressive recruiting campaign that would bring in new blood like UC Berkeley
law school graduate, Larry Sonsini. By 1979, Sonsini was heading the
partnership and would lead it to draw national attention as the fastest
growing law firm in America. From barely measuring on the radar
screens of established San Francisco rivals, Wilson Sonsini rapidly
emerged as a major power in California law. It is now the second largest
law firm in the Bay Area and ranks in the top five of all California law
firms.[98]

While lawyers are for many among the more lamented necessary evils
of doing business in America—and they are a long way away from
being universally loved in Silicon Valley—reputable Valley law
practices are understandably appreciated for the catalytic roles they
perform. Wilson Sonsini pioneered the concept of a law firm doing
much more than merely dispensing legal advice. CEO Larry Sonsini
credits this aspect of his organization as key to its growth and also as a
main reason for why, even with a prestigious legal community based in
nearby San Francisco, Silicon Valley's once parochial law firms have
arisen as a major force in California and US law. Recalling how the Bay
Area legal scene has changed in the decades since he joined what was
then a small partnership in 1969, Sonsini remarks:

> San Francisco was the seat of the legal business up here. What we did in this
> firm is get involved in building companies in the technology industry. That
> is, we got involved in how to grow companies—how to build enterprises as
> opposed to just servicing certain legal problems that affect mature enterprises.
> And as the technology industry grew here that became the critical factor in
> our delivering a professional service. A professional service that's needed for
> a technology company comes really from someone who is part lawyer, part
> business person, part banker, part consultant. And so you need to bring to
> bear a different type of delivery of the service to do well here. The San
> Francisco firms just never quite adjusted to that. We became the dominant
> firm in the state by focusing on high-tech and by focusing on the needs of
> that industry.[99]

Wilson Sonsini's management had recognized early on that to be truly "full service" would require that its attorneys perform a variety of roles to meet the changing needs brought on by a client's growth. As Sonsini again explains:

> We think of the business of technology as three evolving circles. The first, the venture stage, is where you're really representing entrepreneurs. There, a lot of your judgment is very business start-up oriented. Then as these companies go public, you represent them in their maturing phase. When these companies become bigger, you're representing multi-billion dollar global corporations. And so the practice here has to be very diverse and very business oriented. Lawyers are being sought as much for their legal distinction as they are for their ability to guide businesses. [100]

Studies by sociologist Mark Suchman on the Silicon Valley legal community basically confirm Sonsini's interpretation of how successful legal services operate in the cluster. They also confirm Sonsini's position as the chief innovator of this approach to lawyering. Suchman identifies a variety of important roles fulfilled by local attorneys that are crucial to the cluster's interorganizational dynamics, including those of "dealmaker," "counselor," "gatekeeper," "proselytizer," and "matchmaker." One prominent attorney he interviewed made an observation that echoes much of the research findings:

> Business lawyers in this area—at least the ones who are quite successful—tend to be counselors in the broader sense. I think Larry Sonsini is the best example. Larry is a director of more and more companies, and I think it shows the fact that he's gone beyond just being a business lawyer into being something of a business advisor. [101]

A firm, of course, does not flourish only because of the actions of its leader. The hundreds of lawyers working at Wilson Sonsini have been recruited to contribute according to the firm's multi-phase strategic services model. The firm heavily emphasizes critical thinking, judgment, and interpersonal skills when hiring in to its ranks:

We're looking for people who can be creative and inventive, we're looking for people who really can relate well with others because so much in this entrepreneurial environment moves so fast. Decisions have to be made quickly. So you're looking for people who have skills in communication and who can, as I say, be creative and also very flexible in order to adapt.

The practice here . . . [is] very much focused on how to team build a client's organization: how to hire people, how to develop a business plan. You know, the unique part of the law in this business is that you really are molding an idea and a concept, and you're seeing that in the context of certain legal disciplines such as intellectual property but you're also bringing in a lot of judgment: how to work with people, how to put teams together, how to motivate a workforce with equity incentives.[102]

There are those who complain that Silicon Valley's top lawyers have become disproportionately important and are actually detrimental to the cluster's entrepreneurial environment. "I really do think he [Larry Sonsini] is the most powerful guy in Silicon Valley. I think people are concerned about that," rues one attorney at a Wilson Sonsini competitor.[103] Others, like Sun CEO Scott McNealy, conversely seem to regard the legal profession as little more than a nuisance; a sector that he does not even bother to include in what he sees as the real work of the Valley's high-tech community: "At least Silicon Valley makes something. Wall Street brokers, lawyers and career politicians have what I call nonjobs. They don't make anything other than money."[104] There are also indications that the hard-nosed but in the end conciliatory live-and-let-live legal ethos once embraced by Silicon Valley is slipping away. Luc Hatlestad—in an article pointedly titled "I'm Gonna Sue Your Ass!"—has observed that established Valley high-tech firms are adopting an "aggressive 'East Coast' style" and using their extensive patent portfolios to extort money from start-ups with the threat of frivolous lawsuits. Hatlestad also sees the authority of lawyers in Silicon Valley as having exceeded healthy boundaries: "Venture capitalists usually are regarded as the most powerful people in high tech, but nothing, whether a business deal or a potentially dicey interview with a reporter goes forward without the approval of a company's lawyers."[105]

Frivolous lawsuits are no doubt a growing problem but this is more a nationwide (if not worldwide) problem than one specific to Silicon Valley. As for a legal figure like Sonsini, while guardedly eyed by his firm's competitors, he appears to be genuinely admired among the mainstream of the Valley's entrepreneurs and business leaders. Sonsini was, for example, among several figures—including the founders of Adobe, Liquid Audio, and Phone.com—to be honored in 2000 as "local heroes" by the Bay Area's Software Development Forum in its annual Visionary Awards. Suchman's research has also concluded that as much as lawyers like Sonsini can be gatekeepers, they can also be crucial "gate openers" because their:

> ... hands-on advisory role often extends to mediating relations between start-up companies and venture capitalists. In the face of pack investing, Silicon Valley lawyers "package" and "steer" unorthodox clients so as to maximize the likelihood of locating start-up funds. In particular, entrepreneurs having trouble winning the favor of financial backers are drawn by the ability of lawyers such as Larry Sonsini to sell ideas to the tight-knit community of investors: "Sonsini can appear stark naked and talk a board of directors into believing he's wearing a tux," one grudging admirer says.[106]

Lawyers may not push the frontiers of high technology but in Silicon Valley the roles they play are both operationally and strategically vital. The type of lawyering that goes on in the Valley, although a frequently overlooked component of the cluster, helps shape Silicon Valley's dynamism and resilience. The formidable influence of lawyers also serves as a reminder that while information, services, and resources easily flow between companies—making the cluster as a whole at times seem like one giant "Silicon Valley, Inc."—firms are not so porous as to be without sentinels who guard a corporation's legal integrity against violations by defecting employees and other competitive threats. Law as practised in the Valley reinforces both entrepreneurial interests and established corporate boundaries. It offers a constant means of facilitating firm formation and growth that transcends the ups and downs of business cycles.

## MONEY WAVES AND WIPEOUTS

Lawyers wield considerable behind-the-scenes influence in Silicon Valley but, if there is any tribe of professionals who act as Masters of the Silicon Valley Universe, it is the venture capitalists (VCs). The days when the birth of companies like Federal Telegraph or HP had to be aided with almost charitable investments or inducements from supportive faculty mentors at Stanford are long past. In the years since watershed events like the major investment (and subsequent massive capital gains) that backed the Traitorous Eight who started Fairchild Semiconductor, Silicon Valley has come to represent a promised land for venture capital. The area once viewed as a high-tech wasteland only two generations ago is now prone to be viewed with unrestrained glee by technology financiers. As Valley star venture capitalist John Doerr has famously, and with characteristic overstatement, summed up the financial significance of the cluster and the role of VCs in it: "We are coconspirators in the largest legal creation of wealth in human history."[107]

Doerr and other leading members from the reigning generation of Valley venture capitalists epitomize much of the benefits and detriments for the cluster being awash in cash. The mere presence of multitudes of risk capitalists—both "formal" professional VCs (those who invest the money from funds they manage) like Doerr and "informal" VCs (also known as "business angels," those who invest their own wealth)—provides the region with an extraordinary capacity to support new and growing enterprises. Depending on how this capacity is utilized, however, the impact on the cluster's dynamism can be positive or negative. The role Valley venture capital played in fostering the dotcom bubble, and the misguided thinking that underpinned investment trends during the mania, illustrate how this is so.

John Doerr, for example, lists among his many feats his role as the principal VC behind Netscape, the commercial web browser company whose spectacular 1996 initial public offering (IPO) effectively spawned the "craze phase" of the Internet industry's development in Silicon Valley. Doerr was one of the initial proselytizers that "the Web changes everything." He and the Valley's venture capital community were immensely successful in getting others in the cluster, the US, and eventually the world to buy into the idea that Internet technologies and services enjoyed a kind of omnipotence. The seductiveness of the logic used was not only conceptual but seemed infallibly mathematic. In a cluster whose collective consciousness is dominated by the rationale of engineering and science, when it came to justifying the sloganeering of the dotcom bubble, investors could take solace in a kind of "new math" formula: $n^2 - n$. Known as Metcalfe's Law (in honor of yet another observation made by computer network engineer and 3Com founder, Bob Metcalfe), the mathematic notation attempts to quantify the value of interconnectivity.[108] With *n* representing the number of interconnected points in a given network, the reasoning behind the "law" is that something like a fax machine is on its own worthless as a communications tool; one fax machine has a network value of zero ($1^2 - 1 = 0$). Every machine added to a network as a connection point, the thinking goes, generates an exponential increase in value. With two fax machines in a network, value comes from having two channels for communication ($2^2 - 2 = 2$). Accordingly, three machines have a value of six; four machines, twelve; five machines, twenty *ad infinitum*. Whether linking together fax machines, telephones, or computers (or rather, *especially* computers), Metcalfe's Law was seen to prove that connectivity guaranteed an exponentially inflating value to a growing networked system.

In assessing and talking up the significance of Internet businesses, a key aspect of the formula that Silicon Valley's financial wizards overlooked was that Metcalfe's Law at best expresses only the potential value of a network. It is true that the more computers—or more precisely, the more computer users—have access to one another, the greater is the opportunity for data sharing and gaining the sundry benefits that come from enhanced information flow. But opportunity is only of value to those who use it. A network, no matter how many people it interconnects, offers little genuine commercial benefit unless the data on offer is actively managed to support the generation of revenue. Much of dotcom mania was fueled by the basic assumption

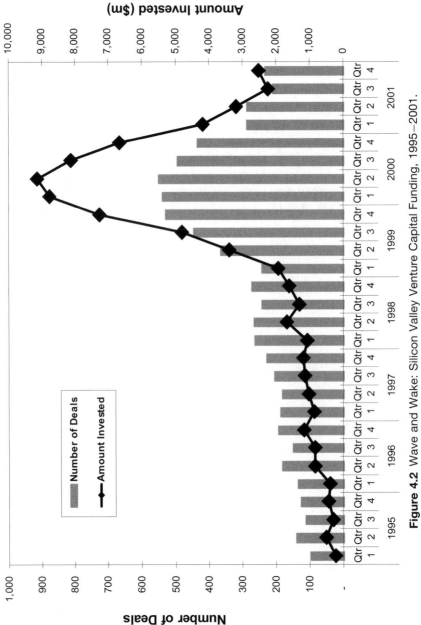

**Figure 4.2** Wave and Wake: Silicon Valley Venture Capital Funding, 1995–2001.
(Data from PricewaterhouseCoopers/Venture Economics/Venture Capital Association, used with kind permission)

(incorrectly inferred from the kind of logic inherent in Metcalfe's Law) that the Internet somehow had the power to create economic wealth automatically. It was as if the right WWW address alone meant that money would naturally pour into an e-business. Valley pundits like John Doerr traveled the globe with convincingly graphed PowerPoint presentations to proclaim that the age of e-commerce promised unabated, exponential growth for business. Doerr's presentation was fittingly titled "It's Possible That the Net Has Been *Under*-hyped." Another telltale axiom was his postulation that "It's not about Moore's Law anymore, but Metcalfe's Law."

That such outlandish thinking could become so widely embraced shows how the intense, almost insular, interactivity of the Valley has its pathological sides, experiencing times when overconfidence in the cluster's capabilities lead its members to do patently unintelligent things like shower poorly run dotcoms with money. Rafe Needleman, a commentator for the Silicon Valley-based venture capital magazine, *Red Herring*, captures a feel for the bizarre thinking of the investment climate with a September 1999 opinion piece:

> ... while, yes, there is some rationale to being exuberant ... lately things have been getting out of hand ... especially if you're building an Internet company. Oddball businesses get funded, go public, make zillionaires of their founders ... Peter Ziebelman, general partner at 21st Century Internet Venture Partners, calls it "venture under the influence"—VUI.[109]

There was indeed an intoxicating appeal to the money that could be made. *Business Week* famously reported that for 1996, the year venture capital set out on a massive upward trajectory (see Figure 4.2), on average "a Valley company went public every five days, minting 62 new millionaires every day."[110] With the money pouring in and bubbling up in the form of stellar IPOs and stratospheric stock valuations, the Valley, especially its mini-cluster of venture capital firms on Sand Hill Road, in many ways seemed more like Wall Street than Wall Street. As one well-known chronicler of modern-day financial manias attests, the whole thing had a strange quality of *déjà vu*:

> In the second part of the 1990s Silicon Valley had the same center-of-the-universe feel to it as Wall Street had in the mid-1980s. . . . [American finance] was turned on its head by new companies and new technologies and new social types created just south of San Francisco. The financial success of the people at the heart of the matter was unprecedented. It made 1980s Wall Street seem like the low-stakes poker table.[111]

The stampede mentality combined with the recursive logic of "networks change everything" to foster unsound investment practises. Valley investors not only put unwarranted faith in the power of the Internet but applied the same assumptions of infallibility to their own social and professional networks. Needleman provides another revealing scenario from an incident that occurred in early 2000, close to the pinnacle of the dotcom stock feeding frenzy:

> A successful venture capitalist I know is visiting me. He sees a press kit on my desk, from a company I met with a few days prior. "You know these guys?" he asks. "What do you think of them?"
>
> "Not impressed," I [reply]. "The product's pretty bad, and I don't get the strategy." Then I see his eyes begin to dart around, like a cornered animal. "Why?" I press. "You're not invested in them, are you?"
>
> "Let me see this . . ." he says, almost pushing me aside as he fires up their site on my PC. My chair is across the room so he's kneeling in front of my desk. "Oh no, this is terrible. I can't believe it. Oh no . . ." He's pretty worked up.
>
> "This is news to you?" I ask.
>
> As it turns out, the company in question is run by a friend of a friend, and he invested a small amount of his own money "socially." That is: Blind. Chances of him seeing a return on this money: About zero. Value of this lesson for all of us (especially him): Very high. Easy capital doesn't make every business a winner. Due diligence never goes out of style.[112]

The interaction described reinforces an important point about the dynamic structure of Silicon Valley: its networks can facilitate business like no other place on earth, but, unless they are used by critically thinking individuals, the facilitation can be as much for disaster as for success.

For a VC community that prides itself on its perceptiveness and intelligence, the swelling mania offered plenty of reason to pause and reflect on what was happening. But the crazed environment was more often seized upon as reason to crow. Marketing consultant and venture capitalist Geoffrey Moore, a major figure in Silicon Valley's pantheon of gurus, when writing about the euphoria taking hold, soaked in the atmosphere to enthuse rather presumptuously about a "Silicon Valley business model" that had evolved around the philosophy of "Ready, Fire, Aim!" Although admitting to being nervous about its potential long-term effects, Moore felt no hesitation in warning (with rather comical undertones of belligerence) that the rest of the world must step in line and follow the Valley's new way of doing business or suffer the consequences: "In business as in football, the West Coast offense is here to stay, and the East Coast establishment and other economies around the world must absorb it and respond to it, not reject it."[113] As Moore saw things, the wisdom of "Ready, Fire, Aim!" had, to Silicon Valley's credit, been embraced by all sectors of the economy, allowing the cluster to be fueled by a:

> ... breathlessness and urgency that lies at the very heart of the place and state of mind known as Silicon Valley. Pressing forward daily, hourly, this frenetic sense of speed and change permeates the entire technology industry ... Once it gets into the bloodstream, it doesn't leave. The venture capitalists have it. The entrepreneurs have it. The engineers have it. The service providers have it.[114]

Of course, the people who subordinated personal common sense to join in the collective mania eventually did "get it" when the Internet-fueled stock market bubble burst. The tech-heavy Nasdaq composite index fell below 2,000 on 12 March 2001, almost a year to the day that it had crossed a historic high of 5,000 on 9 March 2000. The flow of venture capital funding coming into the Valley assumed similar contours, like a tsunami wave that swelled beyond sustainable proportions to crash with devastating effect. Having reached a quarterly peak of $7b in the third quarter of 2000, by the first quarter of 2001 VC funding was down to less than half that amount and still had further to fall (Figure 4.2).

At first the drop in the capital markets was not met with great alarm. The initial consequences of the downturn had many positive features from the perspective of daily living. The frenzied pace of business slowed and people felt that they could at last catch their breath. Traffic congestion lessened and a modicum of sanity returned to the local housing market. The first set of lay-offs mainly affected dotcom yuppies who had come to Silicon Valley toward the end of the bubble in search of fast money. Not many long-time residents bemoaned the hard times visited on these recently unemployed. The running joke was that the newly laid off gave different meaning to ubiquitous dotcom era acronyms of B2B (business-to-business) and B2C (business-to-consumer) e-commerce—the buzzwords being rephrased to mean out-of-work dotcommers had been forced to go "back-to-banking" and "back-to-consulting" (or, expressed in regional terms, "back-to-Cleveland").

By early 2001, however, lowered earnings forecasts followed by lay-off announcements from leading Silicon Valley firms—companies like HP, Intel, and Cisco—made the situation considerably less humorous. Between January 2001 and January 2002, Santa Clara County's unemployment rate more than quadrupled, from 1.7% to 7.5%, back to its historic highs of only 10 years previous.[115] Even the perspicacious *Red Herring*, after over-expanding during the height of the Internet craze, found itself in May 2001 announcing a third round of lay-offs after being unsuccessful in selling itself to publishers from that despised stronghold of the East Coast establishment, New York City. The mindset of "Ready, Fire, Aim!" did not produce for Silicon Valley an invincible business model but it did create a good deal of self-inflicted wounds. This period of downturn in the cluster's fortunes is a potent demonstration of how open-minded enthusiasm for new technologies and business methods is only of benefit when such innovative fervor is guided by solid management. The dotcom bust also offers yet another refutation of that strangely persistent assumption that Silicon Valley's networking culture somehow gives it a regionally based advantage over other clusters.

What is particularly interesting in the recent spate of bad financing is that it represents a break from the "classic" methods of venture capital investing that funded the early growth of the cluster. Although Silicon Valley is a cluster that repeatedly breaks with its past, the classic-style venture capital that was once a hallmark of the cluster is a legacy that would be better perpetuated than forgotten.

Though not the cluster's first venture capitalist, the person who deserves much credit for establishing the Bay Area as a venture capital powerhouse is Arthur Rock. A New York born-and-raised, Harvard-educated, former Wall Street investment banker, Rock was introduced to the possibilities of funding high-technology enterprise in California when he received a proposal in 1956: a business plan for establishing a semiconductor manufacturer sent by Eugene Kleiner, spokesman for Shockley's Traitorous Eight. Excited by the potential of Kleiner and his team, Rock doggedly pursued more than two-dozen possible funders before finally managing to secure Fairchild Camera and Instruments as a backer for the enterprise. After brokering the deal, Rock stayed in contact with the newly formed Fairchild Semiconductor management team, watching from the other side of the continent as the founders grew rich and Fairchild Semiconductor expanded and subdivided with spin-outs, making the Santa Clara Valley alive with new high-tech activity. From his base in New York, Rock also helped arrange a private placement for Teledyne, a Los Angeles-based technology company that was founded in 1960. Following the success of these deals, Rock decided that he should change locations and headed to San Francisco. Reflecting on the reasons for his move, Rock would later recall: "The fact that we could do Fairchild and Teledyne from the East Coast indicated to me that there weren't enough people out [West] to do whatever there was to do."[116] Or, as he phrases things more bluntly: "The money wasn't there but the ideas were."[117] Rock and other investors from beyond the region descended on the Bay Area to address the imbalance.

In 1961, at Rock's instigation, one of his California acquaintances, Thomas "Tommy" Davis (whom Rock knew as vice president of the wealthy California Central Valley property developer, the Kern County Land Company), joined him in founding the venture capital limited partnership of Davis & Rock. The firm's $3.5m fund was contributed by wealthy individuals, mainly members of California's high-tech *nouveau riche*, including the satisfied beneficiaries of Rock's previous investment activities with Fairchild and Teledyne. There were other risk finance groups and individual investors operating in the region at the time but none had Rock's track record. Nor would any experience the success Davis & Rock attained. For the first investment their partnership considered, a stake in the minicomputer start-up Scientific Data Systems, Davis & Rock put in $257,000. When Xerox later purchased the firm for $1b, the pay-off was $60m, a 233-times return. The profile and success of deals like Scientific Data Systems made Davis & Rock a benchmark for other venture capital firms to follow.

John Wilson, a *Business Week* reporter who was one of the first people to chronicle the early Bay Area venture capital scene, noted the following "secret" to the Davis & Rock investment philosophy:

> First and foremost, they tried to back outstanding people—superior managers of high-technology ventures—without worrying too much about the details of the product and the marketing strategy. "I believe so strongly in people," says Rock, "that I think talking to the individuals is much more important than finding out too much about what they do." Rock disagrees with investors who put great weight on the technical breakthrough or the market opportunity in evaluating deals. "It takes good people not only to run a company but to figure out what will be dynamic and grow," he points out. Davis once summed up their philosophy in a speech modestly titled "How to Pick a Winner," in which he stated The Principle as, simply, "Back the right people."[118]

Davis & Rock's investment strategy, which emphasizes people over technology, contrasts markedly with what guided VC money in the 1990s. Plenty of rhetoric described the dotcom craze as inspired by humanistic goals: democratizing information, building online communities, increasing opportunities for entrepreneurs—and to a certain degree these were legitimate accomplishments of the spending spree. Yet dotcom mania's article of faith was that the artificial technologies of the Internet so essentially reordered the world as to make human beings irrelevant. Applying Metcalfe's Law to the realm of Internet users disembodied the individual. People became abstractions, recognized not as full-fledged persons but as $n$ points on a network or as the "hits," "clicks," and "eyeballs" that interacted with websites and ensured their preposterous market values. Misconceptions about the irrelevance of the human element led VCs to assume that the sheer power of technology networks implied that supplicant e-business entrepreneurs would have to do little to satisfy customers' real wants. In a similar vein, entrepreneurs were no longer expected to have any more personal interest in their proposed e-businesses than they had in the customers their businesses were designed to process. This marked a departure from the traditional venture capital principles of Silicon Valley. Granted, professional VCs and aggressive entrepreneurs have hardly ever been altruistic in their purposes for getting behind new ventures. In the original mold of VC investing in the cluster, however, a modicum of passion—from the VCs and *especially* from the entrepreneurs—was considered a prerequisite for a new company to have any real hope of success.

Randy Komisar, one of the more iconoclastic figures in Silicon Valley's venture capital community, summed up the myopia and impersonal nature of dotcom funding with a fictionalized composite description of the sorts of web business he saw attracting money:

> I sat in on a deal pitch at one of the VC firms where some good friends wanted my opinion. The plan was to sell pet supplies on the Net. The would-be entrepreneurs called their venture PetUniverse.com.
>
> . . . [their presentation] positively gleamed. Here were three guys fresh out of top-of-the-line business schools, and they *had* managed to shrink the world, or at least all pet owners, into a four-cell matrix. Their projections found the perfect balance between the aggressive and the impossible. They clearly recognized this as a "Better-Faster-Cheaper" play and understood the implications, which all boiled down to one simple dictum: execute at light speed. A herd of other aspiring Petsomethings.com startups had been making the rounds during the last month, too. Sand Hill Road was in a pet feeding frenzy, at least for the moment.

> The disconcerting thing about these pet shop boys, all sharp go-getters, was that none of them, they confessed when asked, owned a pet, had ever owned a pet or—so far as I could tell—had ever wanted to own a pet. I wouldn't have been surprised to discover that they were deadly allergic to fur, feathers, and scales.
>
> So why were they doing this? Why was it worth their time? I am always amazed that venture capitalists don't ask that question.[119]

Deterioration in the quality of Valley venture capital signifies a major change, one that had been warned about earlier (and noted to be a disturbing trend not limited to Silicon Valley). In their 1992 book, *Venture Capital at the Crossroads*, William Bygrave and Jeffry Timmons, two leading academics in the field of entrepreneurship studies, had lamented a "merchant capital" mindset in American VC funding that was taking hold. Bygrave and Timmons regard merchant capital as that characterized by "financial engineering know-how, which emphasizes deal making, transaction crafting and closing, and fee generation and is obsessed with short-term gains." This contrasts with the "classic" form of venture capital which arose around the middle of the 20th century, one which entails VCs injecting more than just cash into an enterprise but also "skills that add value in company forming, building, and harvesting."[120]

If the thoughts and actions of Arthur Rock, the Valley's most famous "classic" venture capitalist, are any guide, truly venturesome venture capital involves picking good people over good technology and working closely with investees, even if that means putting in long hours to see a company through difficult times. This proactive, hands-on approach actually typified the present generation of top-tier VC firms during their early years in the 1970s. Robert Swanson, a partner at Silicon Valley's most prestigious venture capital firm, Kleiner Perkins Caufield & Byers, was so enthusiastic about the prospects for a new type of a company that in 1976 he left behind the life of a venture capitalist altogether to co-found Genentech, the Bay Area's (and the world's) first modern biotechnology firm. HP-executive-turned-venture-capitalist

Tom Perkins himself was a noted hands-on investor, frequently seen putting his green Ferrari to use on the Valley's freeway system as he zipped between the board meetings of the small companies in which he would personally manage his firm's investments. [121]

One of the unexpected consequences of success in Silicon Valley's venture capital sector is that the tremendous returns of VCs ended up attracting more funding than the investment firms proved themselves able to manage adequately. By the early 1990s, leading Valley VCs were not just well endowed, they were creating "megafunds." VC coffers had grown to enormous size without venture capital firms concomitantly adding the human resources necessary to keep pace with the increased demands of fund management. The time VC executives had to devote to start-ups subsequently plummeted. With huge amounts to invest and a proportionately reduced capacity to mentor investees, the VCs stopped focusing on needy, truly high-risk ventures and gave attention to safer bets: previously financed companies seeking later-round funding or start-ups that indicated they required cash but not managerial support. This new dynamic in VC funding escalated throughout the decade. In 1995, a well-invested "megafund" might amount to something on the order of $250m. By the start of the 21st century, billion-dollar and multi-billion-dollar megafunds were setting new watermarks. The megafunds feasted on the Net; it had matured into a hyper-valued, low-involvement technology tailor-made for their purposes. Megafund managers came to exemplify a new dominant breed of "merchant" VC in the Valley: savvy investors who operate as skilled moneybrokers but are essentially decoupled from the process of starting up and running firms. These VCs—and the smaller funds that mimic their investment behavior—have abandoned the traditional notion of venture capital, retreating to the role of straightforward financiers. The VCs still exact a high portion of a firm's shares in return for their funding, however. The situation is one of the reasons many start-up founders complain that "VC" today more aptly stands for "vulture capitalist" than "venture capitalist."

This approach to investing, combined with the recent euphoria for Internet plays, also explains how slick start-up teams like Komisar's "pet shop boys" (the kind of entrepreneurs who would be laughed out of the office by an old-style venture capitalist like Arthur Rock) were lavished with cash. The supplicant management team's formulaic approach to establishing and operating a business meant that the new company's leadership required little assistance in managing the enterprise they envisioned. A frenzied IPO market, moreover, allowed a VC to sit back and watch an investment in an Internet play rack up a high-multiple return over a very short period of time.

Another version of this kind of low-maintenance entrepreneur that gained prominence in the Valley during the dotcom funding mania included well-known local figures like Marc Andreessen, the co-founder of Netscape, who practice serial entrepreneurship. Having entrepreneurs who take a second or higher number of tries at starting a firm is, of course, immensely positive for the economic vitality of the region. Serial entrepreneurs are an important and integral part of the overall dynamics of Silicon Valley and other clusters. A qualitative problem in terms of the dynamism of the investment climate, however, is that high-profile serial entrepreneurs once again represent safe bets to venture capitalists. When VCs backed Marc Andreessen in his second venture (which happened to be the Internet infrastructure services company, Loudcloud), the "risk capital" investment went not so much to a person, but a name. For merchant-minded VCs such an investment is a clear winner. The already successful entrepreneur carries enormous brand value in the Valley. Thus, in funding a high-profile serial entrepreneur like Andreessen, VCs get to back a recognized figure in the community who needs no handholding and who confers to their portfolio of investments much added cachet. The focus on prestige paradoxically diminishes the quality of the overall investment climate—more deserving and person-ally committed first-time company founders are ignored as VCs look for sure bets. The risk gets taken out of risk capital.

A further, almost poetically just, irony to this situation is that despite the seeming surety of the merchant capital approach, the detached nature of the merchant capitalist decision-making process usually means that not enough thinking goes into evaluating investment opportunities.

This produces a different set of risks in the investment climate, the kinds of risks that, over the long run, easily trump unwary merchant-style VCs and their investees. A closer look at the VC investment decisions that supported the Silicon Valley enterprises that Andreessen, the poster boy of dotcom mania, was associated with well illustrate this aspect of the cluster's altered investment dynamics.

Andreessen became a major name in Silicon Valley for his role as the whiz-kid who created the Netscape web browser. In August 1995, Netscape made Silicon Valley finance history by pulling off a spectacular Initial Public Offering. Prior to the Netscape IPO, as a rule of thumb a venture would not "go public" without at least four consecutive quarters of profits. Netscape was a young, loss-making company, but with the new calculus of network power that was gaining currency—plus the selling point of Netscape being started by Andreessen's boss, the well-known serial entrepreneur Jim Clark—that hardly mattered. With shares that were initially targeted to be priced at $12, unexpected demand pushed the underwriters to up Netscape's stock price to $28. That increase still underestimated demand. On the first day of trading, Netscape's share price soared as high as $75. The profitless enterprise emerged with a capitalization of more than $2b, turning Clark into a billionaire and giving 24-year-old Andreessen a net worth of $80m. Andreessen became the first fresh young face of Silicon Valley's dotcom mania. John Doerr, the Kleiner Perkins partner who had backed the company, earned a 30-fold return for his firm and was reconfirmed as the reigning VC of Sand Hill Road. An important lesson, or so it seemed, was the perverse logic that an Internet start-up could lose money (in terms of revenues) and still make an outrageous sum (in terms of capitalization). Loss-making Internet-related companies with exponential growth projections, no matter how fantastic, would become the most sought-after investment opportunity throughout Silicon Valley and later the world. The "new rules" for the New Economy had been written. The Valley's latest home-grown gold rush was on.

Four years later, after Netscape had been acquired by America Online and Andreessen was looking for something different to do, the young millionaire announced that he wanted to take another crack at starting an Internet company. True to form, the megafunds of Sand Hill Road began falling over themselves to back what seemed to be a sure-fire business before even knowing the details of what it was about. The partners of the recently formed Redpoint, which had a $600m Internet investment fund, scrambled to lure Andreessen to accept their money. With so many VCs hungry for him to accept their cash, Andreessen had his pick of funding sources. He ultimately accepted an offer made by the fraternity of "e-boys" running Benchmark Capital (a VC which counts among its attributes the statistic that the height of its six partners averages six feet, five inches). Out of a recently formed billion-dollar fund, Benchmark promptly put down $15m in a first round of private financing.

Like Netscape, Loudcloud turned out to be a loss-maker. Nothing to worry about in the summer of 1995. But by the summer of 2000, investors decided that the gravy train was over. Andreessen and his backers nevertheless still hoped to take Loudcloud public before the end of the year with a huge valuation. They sought a $1.25b capitalization but ended up repeatedly delaying their offering and repricing company shares downward, moving from a $12-per-share price to a mere $6. Eventually settling on a valuation of the company at only $440m (nearly a third of the valuation they had originally hoped for), Loudcloud finally went public in March 2001. Its share price quickly tumbled beneath the offer level. Within another two months the newly listed firm announced that it would lay off 122 employees, almost 20% of its workforce, in an effort to stem losses. Loudcloud's operations never fully recovered. By mid-2002, valued at $150m, Loudcloud sold the bulk of its business to Texas-based EDS. Deciding to retain only a third of Loudcloud's workforce, Andreessen and his senior managers reinvented the firm as the software company Opsware.[122]

Just as Netscape's spectacular IPO marked the beginnings of a new financial mania in Silicon Valley, Loudcloud's dismal market performance coincided with the turn toward a far more sober investment mood. Venture capitalists in the cluster now have less capital to work with and act accordingly more conservatively than they did during the dotcom boom. The rediscovered conservatism could mean that a risk-averse, merchant capital mindset will even more than previously set the tone for financing Valley start-ups. But there are also signs of positive responses, examples of where the conservatism does not involve greater risk-aversion but rather a movement to get back to the basics of risk finance. "Classic" venture capital has been making a comeback with a number of respected venture capital veterans leaving big-name firms to set up investment vehicles dedicated to handling new enterprises that seek both funding *and* mentorship. Ruthann Quindlen, a former partner at top-tier Institutional Venture Partners, is one among a group of rebels who have established VCs dedicated to financing high-risk, first-time entrepreneurs. Significantly, her investment strategy reflects more the wisdom of Rock's Law than the formulaic interpretation of Metcalfe's Law. Quindlen focuses on the quality of supplicant entrepreneurs and is attracted by the opportunity to join them in company-building. As she explains her thinking:

> It's the first-time entrepreneurs that make the most successful companies. AOL was started by a first-time entrepreneur. Cisco. Microsoft. eBay. Excite. They do take more handholding, and it's more risky. But the reason they do better is they take more risk. They don't know how it's supposed to be. Marc Andreessen was a first-time entrepreneur when he did Netscape. We want Marc Andreessen when he's at [university], in jeans and sneakers thinking about doing [web browsers], not later when he's got an Armani suit and pitching Loudcloud at a $200 million pre-money valuation.[123]

In Silicon Valley there is a common refrain concerning the assessment of managerial performance: *failure is OK*. The idea behind this principle is that for the leadership of an enterprise to take risks and be experimental, there has to be a basic acceptance that mistakes will occur; without allowing for mistakes the greater danger is that creativity will be stifled. People also know that in fact failure can be more than just "OK": it can provide valuable information for how to be successful in the future. The benefits of failure only become manifest though *if* past mistakes are understood and analyzed as a source for learning. As managers in

Silicon Valley assess the lessons of the cluster's latest boom-and-bust, there is obviously much that can be learned. As the final chapter about the cluster's future (Chapter 6) will show, the learning opportunities go beyond evaluating the fallacies of business decisions made during the heady atmosphere of the dotcom bubble. There is a wide spectrum of issues that merit addressing. Thorny issues and painful lessons, though hardly ever welcomed, can nevertheless be seen as fortuitous whenever they are responded to constructively and used as stimuli for improving conditions and guarding against a repeat of mistakes.

However people in the cluster choose to address the lessons of the past and issues of the present, the remarkably enduring, deeply rooted dynamism of the cluster means that Silicon Valley, for now at least, remains exceptionally well prepared to support whatever new wave of commercial opportunities its entrepreneurs decide to pursue. For a variety of reasons, the exceptional growth rates of the late 1990s will not be seen again any time soon. But growth and change in the Valley will continue in some form so long as intelligent management practices in the cluster still outweigh the unintelligent ones.

# Valley Innovators                                                5

Schumpeter posits that "the defining characteristic" of the entre-preneur "is simply the doing of new things or the doing of things that are already being done in a new way (innovation)."[124] This is a helpful definition because close examination of people who are, according to more standard interpretations, separately labeled entrepreneurs or innovators shows that the approaches to their respective crafts are inherently similar. The entrepreneur/innovator recognizes an opportu-nity and then acts on it to bring about a novel creation, be it a company, methodology, or invention. It is such entrepreneurial/innovative effort that opens the door for economic advancement and keeps an enterprise (or cluster of enterprises) from stagnating.

Yet while entrepreneurship and innovation are closely linked, they also involve separate objectives. In the practical usage of the terms, we tend to think of *innovators* as those who *think up* "new things" while *entre-preneurs* are those who *further act* (commercially or in terms of otherwise effecting organizational change) on the opportunities that innovations present. This chapter probes further into the work of those in Silicon Valley who personify the innovative capacities of the cluster. Previous chapters have looked more at the role of what is commonly seen as "entre-preneurship" in Silicon Valley—the way opportunities were seized on to attract business to the area, the way businesses have been entre-preneurially managed and facilitated, the ways in which new methods and technologies have been exploited. This chapter profiles people in Silicon Valley whose activities are more easily recognized for their inno-vative qualities, people (even those who are *bona fide* entrepreneurs) who stand out most for the new things that they conceptualize and novel idea-generation techniques that they employ.

Innovation is another of the Valley's enduring characteristics. Some commentators would argue that there is an authentic Silicon Valley "way" of innovating. Although the Valley is home to well-known innovation methodologies and certain principles of innovation are closely adhered to, nothing points to a single means of innovation that drives the cluster. What can be seen quite clearly, however, are the ways in which Silicon Valley has come to appeal to innovators, how they and their organizations select the area for their work, and how these people and groups in turn are influenced by and contribute back to the region's evolving capacities in innovation. Accordingly, this chapter provides a selection of snapshots on the diverse manners in which individuals go about innovating and their respective ways of visualizing and managing the innovation process. Though the profiles are not directly related to one another, thematically they help provide a mosaic view of the Valley's qualities as a cluster of innovation as much as it is of entrepreneurship.

In light of the managerial focus of this book, the chapter begins by looking at three Silicon Valley innovators who are, in different regards, operating at the leading edge of management practice. The first is the chief technologists in the Palo Alto R&D operations of the world's largest management consulting firm; the second, a San Francisco-based management guru who works to help companies foster creative behavior within their organizations; the third, a well-known Valley executive who conceptualized the role of a free-floating "virtual" CEO.

The remainder of the chapter takes an up-close look at the efforts of those dedicated to technological innovation, first profiling Federico Faggin, a former Intel researcher whose invention of the microprocessor set the stage for the PC revolution and later waves of modern information technology. A second profile explores the R&I (Research & Innovation) operations established in San Jose by the Japanese consumer electronics maker, Casio. A third and final profile looks at the work of a research team at Silicon Valley's most famous institution for innovation, PARC.

As with the three showcased innovators whose work directly relates to the field of business management, the technology innovators profiled are shown to perform work that is varied in its methods and purpose, helping illuminate the extent of Silicon Valley's intellectual diversity and drawing power.

The chapter illustrates not just the "new things" brought about by Valley innovators but more importantly the thinking and efforts that go into their innovations. It details people's personal commitment to innovation, their varying backgrounds, behavior, and thought processes to shed light not only on the fruits of innovation but its inner workings as well.

## INNOVATING FOR MANAGEMENT

### *Luke Hughes and ATL*

With $11b in revenue and over 75,000 employees, Accenture (which, until a January 2001 name change, was known as Andersen Consulting) ranks as the largest management consultancy in the world.[125] The company has long stood out in the crowded field of firms dispensing managerial advice, not just for its size but for its services, which strongly emphasize IT-based solutions. The company originally made a name for itself in mainframe computer implementation services and consulting. In the 1990s it earned a reputation as a leader in "change management" by showing companies how more modern forms of IT could be integrated to remake organizational structures and improve performance. A high-tech forte distinguishes the consultancy but it serves a wide spectrum of organizations regardless of the technological intensiveness of their operations. The automotive, consumer goods, forest products, retail, transportation, and government sectors are all serviced by Accenture. In a very real sense, the Chicago-based, globally positioned firm is one of the great vehicles for spreading the technologies generated by Silicon Valley and other Siliconia to the world beyond.

Besides relying on available technology to develop client solutions, Accenture has since 1990 had its own technology R&D group, what is now known as Accenture Technology Labs (ATL). Based in Chicago, ATL operates two other research facilities, one in Palo Alto (on the Stanford Research Park) and the other in Sophia-Antipolis, France. ATL's research aims to bridge "the gap between 'state of the art' technology and 'state of the market' business solutions."[126]

Accenture's choice of locales for satellite ATL facilities is revealing in its own ways. ATL's location on the Stanford Research Park—as opposed to one in clusters like Boston's Route 128, North Carolina's Research Triangle, Austin's Silicon Hills, or the Digital Coast of greater Los Angeles—underscores the continued superior drawing power of Silicon Valley as a whole and the cluster's first dedicated high-tech real estate development in particular. As regards ATL in Europe, though Sophia-Antipolis does not have the strong entrepreneurial base, lengthy technological history, or breadth of intellectual resources offered by a location like Cambridge's Silicon Fen, the administration of France's government-sponsored technology hub aggressively recruits foreign investment in order to develop the region—Cambridge's local government agencies, on the other hand, are better known for their discouraging than encouraging substantial investment and build-up in the area.

The background and outlook of the Director of ATL's Palo Alto center, Lucian "Luke" Hughes, also says something about how Silicon Valley continues to draw in highly talented, highly mobile individuals. Hughes' education encompasses many geographies and influences, including studies at the University of Pennsylvania (B. A., Cognitive Science), Edinburgh, Oxford (B. A., Neurophysiology and Psychology), Yale (Ph. D., Computer Science emphasizing Artificial Intelligence), and Northwestern University in Chicago. Another seminal influence on his learning interests comes from his father, Thomas Hughes, one of America's pre-eminent historians of technology, who taught at the University of Pennsylvania.

Like the other innovators to be profiled, Hughes' career exemplifies that of a "footloose" knowledge worker. The demand for his skills means that he has opportunities to live and work basically any place he chooses. As for his personal and educational roots, they lie outside Silicon Valley. One of his greatest intellectual ties is with the Chicago area, the result of Hughes electing to accompany his Ph. D. supervisor at Yale, Roger Schank (a leading figure in the Artificial Intelligence community), who went to Northwestern in 1989 to establish its Institute for Learning Sciences (ILS). If "cumulative effects" or "networked systems" possessed the determining powers in a cluster some attribute to them, Hughes would no doubt still be in the Chicago area. He had great intellectual, professional, and personal ties to the ILS, an organization that he had helped build up. The ILS offered a uniquely creative interdisciplinary environment, one which attracted Hughes with its intensely "rabbinical" atmosphere, a place where he enjoyed how "you learn by argument; you are expected to have your own ideas and be fiercely independent."[127] Using the ILS network, in fact, Hughes joined ATL's headquarters after completing his doctorate degree.

Yet Hughes is now based in the Valley and not Chicago. Though enjoying his job and the benefits of proximity to the ILS, after a few years Hughes felt that the Chicago area did not offer the opportunity that the US West Coast did to see in action the types of technology that he worked with professionally. (The situation contrasts markedly with how half-a-century before the Chicago area drew in Bay Area high-tech firms and nearly became the employment locale for Bill Hewlett.) Hughes contemplated tempting job offers from organizations in locations ranging from Los Angeles to Seattle but in the end he elected to accept an offer from ATL to transfer internally to its Palo Alto research site. The Valley's unique technological environment, which company management stressed as a major fringe benefit to living and working in the area, played a major part in his decision.

Accenture was thus able to retain a highly qualified employee and Silicon Valley was able to welcome into its midst another highly creative thinker. At ATL Palo Alto, Hughes now leads a team of 13 full-time researchers who stay on the lookout for emerging technologies that might have applications for Accenture's client base. If testing shows a technology to possess large enough potential, ATL researchers will integrate it into a prototype that they then show a client. The work supports various symbiotic relationships. Silicon Valley companies benefit by having ATL researchers promote the applications of locally generated technologies to Accenture's customer base. Accenture benefits from increased customer liaising and experimenting with novel technologies. Accenture customers in turn have the advantage of having people like Hughes help them to recognize the applications of Silicon Valley's latest technical creations.

As for his own project work, Hughes tends to focus on experiments that seek to personalize aspects of information content better. MySite@ Work, for example, is his design for an individually tailored Intranet portal that employees can use to organize the contents of incoming information. Another project, Magic Wall, involves a plasma display mounted in a heavily traveled office area, like a main hallway. Sensors in the display can detect an item of employee identification to determine who passes by. They then instruct the display to project information of specific interest to that person—for instance, scheduled reminders, an upcoming meeting agenda, or traffic conditions on the route home from work. On a similar theme, Hughes has also collaborated with others at ATL to set up an audio-visual hallway link between ATL's Palo Alto and Chicago offices. Mounted cameras and screens allow the two office hallways to function as long-distance visual portals, meaning researchers can "bump into" one another and carry out serendipitous discussions as if they were in the same physical space.

Although technologically focused in their research activities, Hughes and his team at ATL Palo Alto are not dedicated to turning out new products but rather to helping companies appreciate the business implications of new developments in high-tech. Like the audio-visual hallway link that increases causal interaction between ATL's Palo Alto and Chicago offices, the efforts that Hughes manages in their own way serve as a bridge, a channel for integrating the technology of the Valley with the management of organizations throughout the world.

## John Kao's Idea Factory

Former Harvard Business School professor John Kao founded the Idea Factory in San Francisco in 1997. He operates what is commonly referred to as an "alternative consultancy" or "guerrilla business consultancy." Kao prefers though to emphasize that he and the Idea Factory's staff serve not as "consultants" in the traditional sense but as people who add value by working with clients in the capacity of teachers and catalysts for innovation:

> If you go to the etymology of the word, "factory" really is nothing more than a tangible set of methodologies for effecting the transformation of raw materials into finished products. From my point of view, a factory can be as much a factory for intangible assets—intellectual capital and ideas—as it can be for a hard product like a widget coming down the assembly line. . . . what we are interested in doing is creating idea factories for companies. We do this at a number of different levels. At the most basic level [we look at] what's the appropriate kind of physical environment in which innovation can occur. I don't mean necessarily some fancy custom-built building but what kind of specific environment can companies use to put some boundaries around the creative process. If you see innovation as simply being a gushy process primarily centered around Bohemian people who get to think of new ideas you're not going to be able to execute a particularly systematic kind of approach.[128]

Unless your firm is a client, Kao does not tend toward specifics about what proprietary methodologies he imparts to companies eager to establish their own internal "idea factories." He does, however, disclose some of the ways in which he will introduce the value of creative management thinking to clients through the use of innovative experiences. For example, a Global 100 corporation once came to the Idea Factory wanting insight into how it should try to conceptualize the state of its business in 10–20 years time. Kao invited executives from the company to a dinner prior to discussing his research findings. Shortly after the meal was under way, a stream of uninvited people began wandering in, disrupting the pleasant banter of the evening and engaging the executives in heated debate. It took some of the senior managers time to realize that the homeless person, environmental activist, and entrepreneur who had stumbled in to hurl pointed accusations about their company's behavior were actually improvisational actors. They had been briefed with future scenario information on the company and were bringing looming dilemmas to life. This is a classic Idea Factory technique for getting clients to think outside the box about their predicaments, not only to contemplate management challenges but to confront them directly.

Kao's approach is no doubt unorthodox, even compared with the methods employed by other alternative consultancies. But Kao is perhaps best described as taking a fundamentalist approach to innovation. As he explains: "We don't want to be the guys who send 30 MBAs in for three months to affect a state of change. We want to be the guys at the front end who deal with the process of innovation with the depth it deserves. There is a world of difference between frivolous brainstorming and a disciplined inquiry into a company's desired future."[129] The approach, however unusual, appears to be well received within the mainstream business community. Idea Factory clients include such blue-chip firms as Citibank, Intel, Nissan, PricewaterhouseCoopers, Shell, UPS, and Young & Rubicam. Kao explains that the types of company that come to him vary but their desire to find better ways to innovate is universal:

> Companies come to us with different complaints but ones that are all themed around issues of innovation. They say, "Gee, you know our corporate ventures system doesn't work, we don't quite understand why but we feel like we need to kill it and start all over. Can you help us?" Or they say, "We're stuck because we're too busy working on the problems of today and we need to start thinking more strategically about how to develop new opportunities. Can you help us do that?" Or they say, "We spent a lot of money on strategy but we don't see anything in our headlights that makes sense to us. We need strategic foresight instead of analytics and strategic planning."[130]

As his methods for fostering innovation suggests, Kao has a rather untypical background for a management consultant. Before graduating from Yale in 1972 with a degree in philosophy and behavioral science, he worked professionally as a musician, playing keyboards for the rock star Frank Zappa. Kao went on to complete an M.D. at Yale and after finishing a three-year residency in psychiatry took an M.B.A. from Harvard. Staying on at the business school, he taught a popular course on creativity for 13 years. During this time he managed to found a biotech company, Genzyme Tissue Repair, and produce the hit film *Sex, Lies & Videotape*. His later experiences in the performing arts world include producing the major motion picture *Mr. Baseball* and the popular Broadway play *Golden Child*. Apart from Boston, New York, and Hollywood, Kao is also connected with one of Europe's leading metropolitan centers of creativity, London. In 1999, he partnered with London-based Fragile Films to purchase the UK's storied Ealing Studios.

Kao's presence in the Bay Area is thus also revealing in the way that Kao himself represents another footloose, well-traveled, and exceptionally talented knowledge worker. He could have chosen any place in the world to establish the Idea Factory. So why did he set up in the Bay Area to spread the gospel of innovation?

> I wanted to be in an environment where there were a lot of people sympathetic to this new company and had values to add ... there were a bunch of people out here that I wanted to work with in the Internet-related sector. I also had relationships with Global Business Network [in Emeryville, near Berkeley] and Stanford and the Institute for the Future [in Menlo Park] so it was a ready-made environment for me to set up something new. I think one of the distinctive aspects of San Francisco is that people are interested in new ideas and they're interested in enabling them. They're not cynical or judgmental about ideas. Also, I wanted to have a ringside seat on the whole Internet boom. In fact, both personally and in the sense of the Idea Factory, I think that we have benefited enormously from being proximate to that in terms of our business and also in terms of what it is that we have learned.

As reflected by Kao's choice to locate his consultancy to the area, the region's enthusiasm and preparedness for "new things" enables the cluster to draw in novel technologies as well as creative thinkers who are attracted by what its environment offers. The Bay Area/Silicon Valley's ready embrace of innovative thinking—both for technology and management—is a continuing source of strength.

### Randy Komisar, "Virtual CEO"

Randy Komisar has played many professional roles in Silicon Valley but is most recognized for having pioneered the position of "Virtual CEO." Born and raised on the East Coast, Komisar attended Ivy League schools (Brown for his undergraduate studies, Harvard for law) and began working in Silicon Valley from 1983 when he accepted a position at the Palo Alto office of his employer, a Boston-based legal firm. He switched to working in (rather than for) Silicon Valley high-tech businesses when he joined the legal department of Apple in 1985. From there he went on to co-found the Apple software spin-off, Claris, and then served as the CFO of Go Corporation. In his final two full-time positions, he worked as a CEO—first for LucasArt Entertainment and later Crystal Dynamics, which both made game software.

Komisar conceived of the Virtual CEO role when he considered work at a variety of appealing start-up businesses after leaving Crystal. He faced a dilemma of having more opportunities to pursue than he could devote himself to full-time. His subsequent career was the result of turning a problem into an opportunity, as he decided:

> ... to take an experiment and do it in an extremely free-form way: total virtuality. To participate in all the different opportunities I wanted to I had to disengage and to detach to take them and still demonstrate that there was a high level of value and engagement in the process. And it has worked, and it has worked extremely well. There are many different forms of it now that are derivative but I think what I did was the next step in the dynamics that are at the core of the Valley. ...
>
> Nobody does it exactly the way I do it. There are interim CEOs, there are advisors and [business] angels, there are a lot of high-level consultants—all of

whom play different parts of the role I play. I think my particular combination of those things is relatively unique just based upon my personality more than anything else.

What's particularly different about my role is that when I engage with a company I engage at the highest level. I'm a decision-maker. I am there with the team, making decisions—I am not just an advisor. But I will ultimately defer because I don't have a position of power in the organization. I bring to it, as a sort of a junior partner, my experience and my contacts and my knowledge. So I'm totally engaged, shoulder to shoulder with the management team. But I'm not present ever really in the same location. I hardly ever attend meetings with them. If I do it's one meeting a week, maybe one meeting a month. My presence though is constant. Seven-by-twenty-four you can get me by phone or by email. I've had more than one executive tell me that I'm easier to reach than people in his own office. In the course of a day I will likely touch a half-dozen or more companies in some meaningful way.

One of the better-known ventures in Silicon Valley where Komisar has served as Virtual CEO is TiVo, a company that spun out of the Full-Service Network Project in Orlando, Florida (a high-profile but failed effort to create an interactive television network). TiVo's service provides customers with greater control over their television viewing, offering advanced features in the recording and playback of shows and in the manipulation of live TV broadcasts. The company's service focus in its business model contrasts to the original intent of TiVo's founders who, when they first approached Komisar, wanted him to help them create a firm that would develop and market technology hardware. After considering their proposed product, but before committing to work with them, Komisar told TiVo's founders that while they had great technology, their company was likely to be crushed by consumer electronics giants if they tried competing as a product manufacturer. He recommended alternative strategies. Rather than being annoyed by Komisar's frankness, the entrepreneurs still sought to bring him on board. Though not adopting his recommendations wholesale, the founders did heed the thrust of his concerns and reconfigured their business so the company would compete primarily as a service provider.

Seldom present physically at the offices of TiVo or the other companies that he virtually works with, Komisar nevertheless regularly interacts with these firms. The value of his Virtual CEO role is that Komisar is available to contribute his experience and knowledge when companies are most in need of such input:

> I try to focus on inflexion points. My goal was to take the CEO job, take the 80% that I consider to be relatively mundane and discard it. Take the 20% that focused on the things that really could possibly make a difference in any single time period and exercise that to the extreme with a set of companies that are at an imperative [point in their development]—start-ups at survival stage.

Komisar's success with his creation of the role of Virtual CEO role says as much about the innovative qualities of his own thinking as it does about the Valley's capacity to integrate innovative management techniques. The willingness of local firms to accept him in the unusual capacity he has designed is an indication of just how much companies in the Valley are committed to experimenting with new forms of management. His activities, moreover, help fill gaps that have arisen in the capabilities of venture capital firms to shepherd startups toward growth. Venture capitalists squeezed for time to provide managerial guidance to the companies they fund now have someone like Komisar to play a surrogate role. In dealing with some supplicant companies, the VCs with whom Komisar works closely will insist that a potential investee get Komisar's blessing or even participation before investing money. Komisar may operate in the realm of Silicon Valley's "virtual" dimensions but his impact as a management innovator is very real.

## FAGGIN'S ENTREPRENEURIAL INNOVATIONS

The career of technology innovator Federico Faggin symbolizes many aspects of Silicon Valley's verve: its cosmopolitan character, the ability of its companies to garner globally mobile talent, and an environment that simultaneously facilitates technical innovation and business entre-preneurship. Faggin is also an immensely iconic figure because he is the principal individual behind what is widely recognized as the single greatest technological innovation ever to emerge from Silicon Valley: the microprocessor.

Faggin was born and grew up in Veneto, the region surrounding Venice in Italy's economically flourishing north. He attended Veneto's Università degli Studi di Padova—the University of Padua, an institution with one of the longest scientific traditions in Europe. Fascinated by mechanics since he was a boy, Faggin had already built his first computer before embarking on his university studies in physics. At Padua he went on to take a doctorate specializing in the physics of solid-state materials, a typical springboard for entry into the world of semicon-ductor research. After earning his degree in 1965, Faggin joined the Italian representative of General Micro-Electronics, a Valley-based Fairchild-spin-out (number seven) that had formed in 1963. GMe was es-tablished with the express purpose of exploiting a promising new technol-ogy that Fairchild had already substantially developed, the metal oxide semiconductor (MOS). The company had been one of Fairchild's most ambitious offshoots. Although in standard fashion it had avoided costly litigation by reaching an amicable out-of-court settlement with Fairchild, GMe was unable to turn a profit. It was acquired in 1966 and in 1967 Faggin left GMe's Italian operations to work at another company associated with Fairchild, the joint venture, SGS-Fairchild in Milan (what is today part of STMicroelectronics, Europe's largest semi-conductor manufacturer).

While at SGS, Faggin continued working on MOS technology and developed the company's first MOS manufacturing process. Taking part in an engineer exchange program, he went to work in Fairchild Semi-conductor's Palo Alto R&D lab for six months starting in early 1968. During that time Fairchild sold its stake in the SGS venture but, aware of the young researcher's talents, Fairchild Semiconductor's management asked Faggin to stay on as an employee. Faggin accepted the offer and he and his wife went from being visitors in the US to being immigrants. Another critical decision for Faggin to make was to choose what line of work he would specialize in at his new employer.

> ... when I joined the lab, I was given a choice of two things to do. One was a circuit design, a shift register using metal-gate technology. I think it was a hundred or two-hundred bit shift register. And the other alternative that I had was to develop a process technology using polysilicon as the gate electrode of the transistors. And I recognized immediately the advantages of using polysilicon and I decided ... I picked *that* one, even if my heart was leaning more and more, even in those days, toward design.[131]

For someone with Faggin's technical abilities, choosing to pursue work on semiconductor manufacturing process technology over circuit design represented a sacrifice. The young physicist realized, however, that any advances to be made in the more cerebral area of circuit design were not going to have the same impact as those in the crucial field of manufacturing process technology. Developing a means of using poly-crystalline silicon, as opposed to metal, to make semiconductor gates (the groups of transistors that perform the AND OR NOT functions in a chip's logic circuitry) implied tremendous ramifications. With their greater density and lower voltage requirements, functional silicon-gate MOS chips would make possible "intelligent" semiconductors such as memories and microprocessors. Building on promising but incomplete work on polysilicon gates previously accomplished by his Fairchild colleague Thomas Klein and others, Faggin designed entirely new configurations for gate architecture. Before the year was out he had resolved key obstacles in manufacturing to produce a working prototype of a silicon-gate MOS chip. Faggin and Klein patented the breakthrough for Fairchild.

Much to Faggin's chagrin, Fairchild did little to move forward with silicon-gate applications and did even less to protect the patent. Robert Noyce and Gordon Moore, by exceptionally strong coincidence, left Fairchild to start Intel right after Faggin had proved his silicon-gate production process. Faggin warned Fairchild management that the Intel founders would likely build their company on the back of his newly patented MOS manufacturing technology. "Well, if they do that, we're going to sue them," a Fairchild higher-up assured.[132] Intel did indeed "do that" and did much more, poaching "dozens of people from Fairchild, down to the lab technician (in the department) who had been working most closely on the silicon-gate process" along its way to racking up successive breakthroughs in developing memory chips.[133] With his employer demonstrating little interest in furthering the technology he had worked so hard on, Faggin himself finally made the move to Intel in 1970 once his immigration status allowed a change of jobs.

The sort of new firm creation and job-hopping that was taking place had a particularly transnational dimension to it. Faggin transitioned to working at Intel just after becoming a permanent resident in the US. He was joining a firm that was founded by two native-born Americans (Bob Noyce and Gordon Moore) but effectively run by Andrew Grove (born András Gróf in Hungary). Faggin's former boss at Fairchild and new boss at Intel, Les Vadasz, was also a Hungarian immigrant. Faggin's first project at Intel involved working with a Japanese company whose liaison, Masatoshi Shima, would also later come to America to join Intel and then team up again with Faggin at Zilog, a company Faggin co-founded in 1974. Silicon Valley in the 1960s and 1970s was not nearly as multi-cultural as it would become by the start of the 21st century but its ability to draw in and retain talent from all over the globe was already apparent. The development of the cluster's pool of human resources can, in many regards, be seen as a manifestation of the American ideal of nation-building: a melting pot. The cluster first served to bring together technologists from across America but has increasingly broadened its catchment base to become a home for the technologically skilled from across the world. Today, 35% of the Valley's residents are foreign born.[134] Whites, though still the largest racial group, since the late 1990s have made up less than half of Silicon Valley's total population.

In a broader conceptual sense, a "melting pot" also metaphorically characterizes Faggin's own experiences with innovation. In developing silicon-gate technology, for example, Faggin pioneered a critical manufacturing process on the back of previous experiments done by others. When later working at Intel, Faggin took the outlines for a microprocessor as conceived by his new colleagues there and largely with his own effort—and under an exceptionally tight development schedule—created the defining specifics that made microprocessing chip technology a reality. His enthusiasm for the potential of the microprocessor (which Intel ignored at first) encouraged him to take another career leap by leaving Intel to co-found his first company, Zilog. At his new firm he pushed microprocessor technology further, leading Zilog's development of a highly versatile 8-bit chip, the Z80. When the Z80 was released in 1976, its functionality and affordability fired the imagination of countless computer hobbyists and provided the major impetus for launching the personal computer revolution. All these technology breakthroughs demanded originality on the part of Faggin but also demanded that he synthesize the ideas of other innovators. As Faggin is quick to point out:

> That's how inventions are made. They are made starting by the work that XYZ did over here and the work that somebody did over there combined with a personal idea; you put together the different pieces and away you go. In general, you never have something that is *ex nihilo*—something coming out of nothing. It appears that it comes out of nothing only if you look at it from the outside, you don't know about the history. Little bits and pieces would have appeared before, but once you are into it you find that any kind of innovation is a delta over something that already existed. You add a new piece, that's how innovation is done.[135]

Another key aspect to Faggin's record in technological innovation is his sheer tenacity. Efforts like Faggin's (and lack of efforts like Lee de Forest's) clearly show that the mere birth of a major invention by itself will not transform the world, let alone a local region. For anything more to happen requires an appreciation of the technology's significance and a commitment to developing applications for it. Faggin's success has relied on combining ideas as well as identifying high-potential technologies and persevering with the quest to see them realize their potential:

> There are historic things that happen because of a convergence of technologies and ideas. They all come together in a way that sooner or later many people will see. So it's just a question of who is the fastest one grabbing the opportunity and going to the finish line, that's the way it has been for me and with my work. That's not to belittle or minimize what was done but rather to say that when I look at myself, all I feel I have done is probably to have shortened by two years what was inevitable. ... I don't feel like I've done such an extraordinary thing. I'm happy that I did it and I certainly don't want to minimize what I did but I also feel that what I did involved seeing an opportunity early on, grabbing it, believing in it, fighting for it, bringing it to fruition with technical skill and personal endurance, and promoting it.
>
> For 10 years, I was probably the most important person in the revolution of the microprocessor. I was the one getting Intel to really go out and announce this product. I was the one fighting inside to let me do the next improvement to it and the next one after that. And then I went further through Zilog by competing [with Intel]—in a way, raising the temperature of the environment so that everybody was rushing into this. Because I believed in it and did what I did, I certainly accelerated by a couple of years at least the process. But as I said, it would have happened anyway.
>
> My contribution is both technical and also emotional or entrepreneurial because I really pushed for development of the microprocessor—I believed in it. ... Not enough is understood for what it took to get it out there. Not just the "doing" of it concerning its technical aspects. People see the technical aspects which were important but they weren't the whole story. In fact, without that energy and that dedication, development would have been much slower.[136]

Apart from explaining the sort of personal commitment it took to spark the microprocessor revolution, Faggin's words also touch on that delicate mixture of combinatorial and singular forces (i.e., those of the group and those of the individual) that drive innovation and economic output in Silicon Valley. The mix is a profoundly important one and its component parts can be easily blown out of proportion. Distorted portrayals will attribute innovation entirely to, on the one hand, the expression of pure creative willpower by rugged Nietzschean individuals or, as is more fashionable today, to a blurred collective genius that denies the centrality of autonomous thought and action. Individuality is the inviolably principal force of innovation. What a cluster like Silicon Valley does so well, however, is demonstrate how creative individualism will flourish in supportive environments whereby "the group"—in the form of the cluster, a company, a team—stimulates and augments the innovative output of "the individual"—in the form of a company, a team (as a unit within a company), a person. In Faggin's case, the resources available in Silicon Valley helped him visualize and act on the possibilities of moving beyond technical innovation and into the realm of pure commercial entrepreneurship. A man who by nature is more interested in engineering design than the business side of high-tech, Faggin has during his time in the Valley seen his commercial abilities blossom. After co-founding Zilog in 1974 and serving as its CEO, he co-founded Cygnet Technologies in 1982 and also served as chief executive during its start-up phase. In 1986, he went on to co-found with renowned Caltech professor Carver Mead the San Jose-based neural network device firm Synaptics, a company where Faggin for more than 10 years served as CEO and currently serves as Chairman. (The positive performance of Synaptics' IPO in early 2002 was one of the first signs of financial rebound for the cluster following the dotcom implosion.)[137] Reflecting on how his career has developed in the Valley and the more likely progression it would have taken had he worked elsewhere (a very real possibility if Fairchild Semiconductor had not offered, and Faggin not accepted, a job in Silicon Valley after the dissolution of the SGS joint venture), Faggin remarks:

> Here is an environment that facilitates the expression of entrepreneurship naturally. There are areas of the world where you can be an entrepreneur all you want but the environment suppresses that. ... Here it is almost like a paradise for entrepreneurs. If you only have an ounce of entrepreneurship in

yourself this environment will bring it out. That's what has made this area so vital and such an economic entity. I obviously had it in me to be an entrepreneur, but I didn't know that. I certainly did not come to this country with the idea that I was going to start a company, never mind three. My intention was to contribute technically and I did that. That was all I could see in my future. But once here you see friends who start a company, they succeed, and you see the excitement and all that—and you think, "Well, why not me?"

. . . In a sense I've had two careers in Silicon Valley: one, a technical career; the other, a managerial–entrepreneurial career. So I've seen the Valley in both its expressions, the expressions of technical achievement and the expression of how to start a company [involving] how to get money and how to earn it . . .

For me the choice to become an entrepreneur was because I wanted to develop aspects of my personality that were manifested in running a company as opposed to developing products. It's a very different set of skills. For me it was not even that natural; it was more natural to be a technical guy than it was to be an entrepreneur. The way I grew up—my family background and so on—did not prepare me. My father was a professor and my mother was a teacher—I did not grow up in an environment where my parents or friends were in business so I could develop some sense of entrepreneurship. For me I discovered that world here. I got interested because of what I saw.[138]

Faggin's comments speak to the crucial interplay of group and individual forces, the dynamic tension that simultaneously invigorates Silicon Valley's collective environment and the independent creativity of its constituents. His experiences also illustrate that remarkable capacity of the cluster not only to draw in innovative thinkers but to help them develop advanced skills as full-fledged commercial entrepreneurs and organizational leaders. Encouraging individuals like Faggin to think up as well as commercialize their ideas is one of the many ways that people have developed the cluster as a New World of discovery.

## CASIO RESEARCH & INNOVATION

Silicon Valley has grown over the years in large part through the contributions of in-migrants (from other parts of the US) and immigrants (from other parts of the globe). Its high-tech economy is also heavily dependent on foreign trade. Because of new supply relationships and patterns of immigration developed in the 1990s, the cluster's linkages to foreign states such as Taiwan, India, and Israel have received growing interest. With the changing nature of the Valley's foreign relations, often lost sight of is the continued importance of Japan, a country that considers its modern economy to be *denshirikkoku* ("made by electronics") and was until recently commonly perceived in the US to be a managerially and technologically superior economic juggernaut; viewed by many as a menacing threat to Silicon Valley. Though no longer feared as an economic predator or celebrated for its business models as it once was, Japan still occupies a position of major significance for the Valley. Japan is both California's largest foreign direct investor and, in a state whose manufactured exports are dominated by Silicon Valley-led sectors, remains California's largest foreign market for industrial products outside the North American Free Trade Area.[139]

Accompanying diminished anxiety over Japan's economic might is the near absence of serious discussion about Japan's once-fabled methods of innovation. Admiration for Japan's supposedly "proven" organizational structures for consensus-driven, intensely collaborative innovation practices has given ground to increased respect for the individualistic approaches to innovation that are a hallmark of Silicon Valley. Major Japanese electronics firms like Matsushita (manufacturer of Panasonic-brand products) have opened incubators and innovation facilities in an effort to tap into the cluster's remarkable capacity for creativity. The revered master of Japanese technological innovation, Sony, has gone so far as to abandon traditional Japanese innovation methods and modeled its Tokyo Computer Science Laboratory on the liberal organizational structure of PARC.[140]

Casio—a company best known for pocket calculators and watches but also a claimant to such original creations as the world's first desktop calculator and the first inkjet printer—has also come east across the Pacific looking for help in idea generation. The company has been operating an R&D center in San Jose since 1994, a facility that originally functioned as a straightforward programming lab. In 1998, Rick Kinoshita (a veteran Casio *sarariman* executive with a background in strategy) assumed the leadership of the San Jose center and decided to expand its activities by integrating a Research & Innovation component. "R&I" in San Jose became a crucial part of Casio's effort to harness Silicon Valley's powers of technical creativity. Casio R&I has experienced a rocky evolution— in synch with the dotcom bubble, its funding swelled and burst. But the mission of Casio R&I has remained unchanged, and the person still driving its activities is a Stanford scholar and innovator, Brian "B. J." Fogg.

Fogg is another person who exemplifies the Valley's eclectic nature, an individual whose background and career shows how even without training in engineering or science, a passion for technology and its applications can take you far in the Valley. Having a strong interest in the artistry and power of information, Fogg majored in English as an undergraduate at Brigham Young University in Utah and went on to take a Masters in creative writing and rhetoric. His later doctoral work at Stanford explored the social psychology aspects of "charismatic computers." After taking his Ph. D. in 1997, he initiated a study group that he later organized into the Stanford Persuasive Technology Lab. In addition to his ongoing work at the Stanford, his career in Silicon Valley combines lecturing, industrial consulting, and a series of stints at the research labs of HP, Sun, Interval Research, and Casio. When Fogg initiated contact with Rick Kinoshita, his intent was to find out if Casio Research would participate in projects with his Persuasive Technology Lab at Stanford. After a few meetings, however, Kinoshita knew he wanted to do more than informally work with Fogg, he wanted Fogg to take charge of Casio's new R&I initiative. Now with both his activities at Stanford and professional responsibilities at Casio, Fogg focuses his research on an area he dubs "captology"—a somewhat tortured neologism for *c*omputers-*a*s-*p*ersuasive-*t*echnology-*ology* (Figure 5.1).

For Casio, the captological dimensions of its R&I activities in San Jose offer the company access to the sort of fresh, unorthodox thinking that it hopes will result in new product breakthroughs. Like the majority of

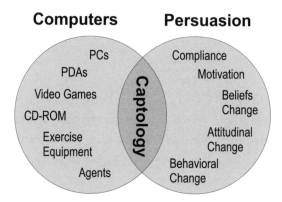

**Figure 5.1** The Captology Space.
(Data from Casio R&I, used with kind permission)

Japanese high-tech firms, Casio has for years successfully competed on the quality, style, and marketing of its hardware. In today's marketplace, while these attributes of manufactured output remain important, as other firms in the world have learned and adopted Japanese manufacturing methods, the playing field has leveled, eroding Japan's previous competitive advantage. For established brand-name firms competing in the consumer electronics space the challenge now is to offer value through the softer side of technology, using the personally enabling qualities of products to appeal to customers. Casio is facing the task of having to distinguish itself on the basis of the presentation, content, and applications of the information its products deliver. The long-term future is one with probable markets for Dick Tracy-style wristwatches that double as PCs and videophones. Applications in the sphere of captology are hoped to move Casio toward development of, as the company sees things, not just watches, calculators, and cameras, but "the next generation of information appliances."[141]

Fogg believes that one of the greatest contributions he makes to Casio concerns not just generating new product concepts but finding ways to leverage the resources of the Silicon Valley cluster:

> In the first year I was here we shifted pretty dramatically from basic engineering and in-house research and innovation to business development as a part of

innovation. Business development concerns looking at what are the opportunities for Casio in areas like the Internet appliance space. Drawing on my network in Silicon Valley—people I knew at Interval or people who are involved in software start-ups and need a hardware partner—I can get people to come in and talk to us about what they're doing. It's really the sorts of alliance and matchmaking that can't be done from Tokyo that's of value to Casio. They don't really need to do engineering here in this office. . . . What they need to do is partner with people who are already doing engineering: start-up companies; then license their technologies and work with them. [142]

Fogg is remarkably human-oriented in his approach to technology innovation, both regarding how he makes use of his personal contacts in the Valley and in the way he employs a user-centric, market-oriented approach to technology research as well. "Our innovation process here is go figure out user needs—what's lacking in the world, what's lacking in people's lives and experiences, and how can we create a product to fulfill that need." [143] This goal is guided by a philosophy, adhered to in the Valley almost canonically, of design-and-test rapid prototyping— a technology development theory strongly promoted by Stanford's interdisciplinary Product Design Program, another Terman era institution begun by creative engineering authority Robert McKim in 1958. McKim's touting of the principle to design and refine products repeatedly according to user wants has spread throughout the research departments of high-tech firms in Silicon Valley. Thanks to the work of the Research & Innovation initiative, it has now made its way to Casio as well. [144]

In introducing the power of rapid prototyping methods, one of the first things Fogg did for Casio was to bring the R&I unit closer to the marketplace by organizing focus groups and consumer surveys. An early project he headed looked at ways to revive the sagging fortunes of Casio's line of cameras—a product whose downturn was particularly hard felt in the company because Casio was an early pioneer in consumer digital camera technology. R&I's research found that the biggest drawback for people in using digital cameras was the need to process photos via a computer, which at the time involved a cumbersome set of procedures. To "take the computer out of the loop," Fogg initiated a partnership with the online photo community Zing. Casio went on to create a co-branded website that allowed Casio camera users one-click uploading of their photos and access to other services in Zing's online photo community.

The work of an enterprise such as Casio R&I offers various shades of meaning regarding Silicon Valley's strengths as a cluster of innovation. In a very basic sense, both Fogg's and Casio's mere presence in the cluster again illustrates how Silicon Valley continues to renew its creative capacity by functioning as a melting pot, attracting talent and investment for innovation from around the nation and the world. In terms of the cluster's evolution, the activities of Casio R&I also signify how Japanese high-technology firms—the companies until recently lauded for possessing superior innovation methods—now find themselves connecting with Silicon Valley not simply to gain access to its industries and hardware, but to access the cluster's "softer" offerings of marketing know-how, personal contacts, and individual ideas.

## PARC'S RED AVANT-GARDE

Excepting perhaps only Stanford University, the most venerated institution for research in Silicon Valley is Xerox PARC. As described in the previous chapter, PARC's origins are closely tied to the area's embrace of new technologies, particularly the Internet. PARC has since become to the current generation of advanced IT, the type of formative crucible that Bell Labs was to an earlier generation of cutting-edge electronics in America. Within the Silicon Valley economy, massively successful products made by companies like 3Com, Sun, Apple, and Adobe can all be traced back to PARC breakthroughs.

Silicon Valley's gain usually has been Xerox's loss. The parent company's failures to capitalize on PARC breakthroughs are legion and long been a sore spot for the American copier giant. An ironic footnote to Xerox's poor record of taking advantage of PARC inventions is that by the start of the new millennium, Xerox was severely suffering in large part because PARC-originated technologies like computer networked printers have, just as PARC researchers had surmised they would, encroached upon Xerox-dominated markets for analog copiers. As of 2001, digital printers used in homes and small offices had emerged as the fastest growing market for document processing.[145] It is a sector that HP, headquartered just down the road from PARC on the Stanford Research Park, has skillfully positioned itself to lead. Xerox finally came to conclude that it would profit more by giving up direct control of its Palo Alto research group and in January 2002 it spun out Xerox PARC to become PARC Inc.

Despite a litany of missed opportunities for its parent company under the former corporate structure, PARC's repeated ability to identify and create massively disruptive technologies testifies to the success of the individuals who led the center's founding and guided its development as a center of leading-edge innovation. In 1996, 25 years after PARC's establishment, the center's then Director, John Seely Brown, brought together employees to assess PARC's accomplishments and chart out new directions. What emerged from this exercise, dubbed PARC 2000, was a new operational framework for the center built around five research themes: Networked Devices, Document Services, Emerging Document Types, Knowledge Ecologies, and Smart Matter. The themes are widely encompassing and rely on interdisciplinary collaboration between an array of PARC laboratories and groups. Working at the forefront of the effort to facilitate new insights and collaborative synergies between PARC's diverse teams has been a highly eclectic laboratory "studio" known as Research in Experimental Documents (RED).

The founder and leader of RED is Rich Gold, a man whose personal background presents a challenge to synopsize. Gold holds a B. A. in English (with a minor in computer science) and a Master of Fine Arts in electronic performance. Among his accomplishments he lists inventing the field of algorithmic symbolism and co-founding The League of Automatic Music Composers. A globetrotting speaker who lectures frequently on the topics of innovation and the social contexts of IT, biographical blurbs on Gold will variously describe him as some combination of composer, cartoonist, writer, and researcher. RED is comprised of six other team members who, as with Gold, have similarly hard-to-classify backgrounds but whose formal training encompasses anthropology, architecture, electrical engineering, engineering design, semiconductors, and sound design. The work RED performs generally falls into two categories. At one level, RED carries out its own experiments with new technologies; at another, it helps other groups develop fresh insights into the ways they conduct their research.

RED's own experimenting seeks to produce functioning prototypes of possible future genres of documents. These projects tend to stretch the boundaries of what common thinking would consider to be "documents" with the standard medium of paper frequently playing an unorthodox, if any, role. One RED experiment, for example, looked at how office work areas could be designed to reduce stress while providing important but noncritical data to staff by sonic messages (a "document" that falls under the category of "audio genres"). The goal was to find ways to keep the sort of incoming data clutter that workers frequently have to deal with subtle enough to avoid being distracting but clear enough to be heeded when necessary. To this end, a mock-up of an office work area was wired to broadcast pleasant-sounding, low-volume sonic effects such as the noises one would associate with an uninhabited tropical beach. The information content or "intelligence" of these sounds—the cawing of seagulls, the crashing of waves, and so on—was conveyed through their relative frequency and intensity. The experiment tried using signals like the number of seagull cries to measure the number of incoming email messages and the relative volume of the roaring waves to indicate the number of colleagues who were at hand near the office area.

Creativity is an activity to which RED's leader has devoted much of his career. Gold sees the abundant material artifacts of our world as the harvest of myriad innovations. Yet he also sees the creative spirit as fractured by divergent schools of thought. Accordingly, a large part of

RED's efforts attempt to harmonize the conflicting values that influence the principles and goals of innovation. Gold's assessment of the schisms that fracture creative output is summarized in a selection from an online treatise he has posted:

> We live in a world of stuff. There are probably close to 10,000 individually invented and sold items in the average room. And this is true for every room. What is interesting is that 95% or more of these millions and millions of items were created by four professional classes: artists, scientists, designers and engineers. Each profession is different: each has their own philosophy, methodology, history, tools, techniques, conferences, dress styles. Some get along OK, others have respectful distrust of the other. Some have active disdain. In RED, we believe that only by bridging all four professional creative classes can we construct a new world that we want to live in.
>
> To give an example, many people outside the creative classes make little distinction between artists and designers, yet if you go to an art college you will find that these two groups do not sit at the same lunch table. Artists feel designers have sold out. Designers feel that artists are too elitist. What is the difference between art and design? An artist paints a painting, looks at it and says: "this expresses my soul, this is me, these are my inner thoughts revealed." A designer paints a painting, and then, turns it around to his/her customer and says "do you like it? No, I'll change it." We would be amazed if Pablo Picasso did user testing on his paintings; we are pissed off when a designer doesn't.[146]

This conceptualization of innovation sees the divide separating outwardly focused design and inwardly focused art to parallel that separating outwardly focused engineering and inwardly focused science. In response, RED attempts to enhance the innovation process by helping people identify the commonality of creativity's four basic manifestations: art, science, design, and engineering.

A graphic rendering of the interrelationships of these four disciplines (Figure 5.2) shows how the fields of art and science, often practised as diametric opposites, can be recognized as related in the sense that they are abstract or "inwardly focused." By the same token, the activities of design and engineering can be appreciated as inherently similar because

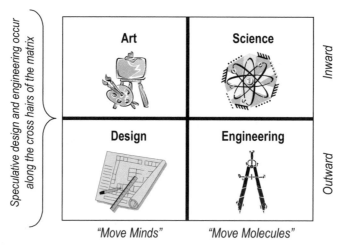

**Figure 5.2** RED's Concept of Speculative Innovation.
(Data from Rich Gold, used with kind permission)

of their practical "outward" orientations. Looked at another way, art and design, often at odds concerning the relative importance of their separate visages of beauty, can be recognized for their unified objective to "move minds." Science and engineering, likewise at odds concerning their separate orientations toward theory or application, can be seen for their common purpose to "move molecules." RED works to impart these perspectives about the subtle interconnections between divergent disciplines in order to assist individuals gain new insights about their work, to break out of the fragmented boxes of the various creative camps. The goal is to have technologists branch out to explore the "speculative" realms of innovation that lie along the frontiers of these separate creative disciplines.

RED's approach to speculative innovation is exemplified by the PARC Artist-In-Residence Program (PAIR), an initiative Gold undertook as a systemic means for helping PARC researchers synthesize insights offered by the Bay Area art community.[147] Each year, several artists from around the region are brought into PARC and matched with a scientist or research team according to mutual interests. The goal with the PAIR program is not to create exciting new breakthroughs *per se* as that already is the job responsibility of PARC staff. Instead, PAIR constitutes an attempt to enhance creativity by stimulating the perceptiveness of the participants, to open up new ways of looking on the significance and nature of their work. PAIR is a vehicle for deep-rooted, human resource development or, as a charter article of the PAIR program states: "PAIR is a project not for creating wonderful art or exciting science . . . but for creating better artists and better scientists."[148]

At the time of PARC's reorganization, Gold and most of the RED team decided to split from the research center and form their own enterprise. Now calling themselves the RED Shift, they still carry out the sort of work that put them at the forefront of PARC's research agenda. The crucial difference is they now serve a much wider community of interests. Although it is still too early to assess the impact the RED group will have with their new organizational structure, what is significant is that they remain part of Silicon Valley. Xerox's loss is again the cluster's gain. The origins and principles of RED illustrate the depth of innovation occurring in Silicon Valley. The recent transformation of RED underscores how the Valley's capacity for innovation not only endures, but continues expanding.

This final principal chapter on Silicon Valley has highlighted the ways that the cluster attracts and retains a diverse body of innovative individuals and the ways these people in turn are impacted by and in their separate ways influence the cluster. One of the more interesting features of this aspect of the Valley's vitality is that, although the collaborative spirit of the cluster undeniably aids the process of innovation, collaborative forces never overshadow the power of individual ingenuity. Far from diluting the power of original, independent thinking, the innovative climate in Silicon Valley helps bring individualism to the fore. It is only in times of complacency or manic euphoria, when groupthink comes to dominate, that this core aspect of the cluster atrophies. The diversity of innovators, variety of innovation methods they employ, and the ways in which they choose to locate to and operate in the cluster further speaks to the way that the Valley does not simply progress according to the momentum of the past but actively pursues opportunities for reinvention. Like their kindred entrepreneurs, successful innovators in Silicon Valley do not follow history, they make it.

# Post-silicon Silicon Valley      6

Leaders in Silicon Valley repeatedly distinguish themselves when rising to adverse challenges or when capitalizing on insightfully envisioned opportunities. Averaging out the booms and the busts—and, in particular, considering the remarkable ways it rebounds from economic decline—the cluster shows itself to be extraordinarily enduring. As for precise estimates about the future, because the cluster has never developed in a linear fashion, trying to predict exactly where Silicon Valley is headed based on its past accomplishments and trends is not so rewarding. The cluster must be observed in real time to see which individuals are leading it in new directions. The Valley's innovators and entrepreneurs will always have much to show us.

What can at present, however, tell us something more about the likely contours of Silicon Valley's future are the sorts of challenges that until recently have been overlooked and still require further thought and action about their root causes if they are to be overcome. For, indeed, the cluster has been so successful at fostering a climate conducive to innovation and new enterprise creation that in numerous ways people have become complacent, lulled into a false sense of immunity from issues looming just beneath the surface of their high-tech paradise.

California's flawed energy deregulation and its consequences for the Valley exemplify the sort of happy myopia that has taken hold. As a collection of businesses whose products and operations are directly dependent on the flow of electrons, Silicon Valley naturally had much at stake in California's electricity deregulation, a process that was in fact initiated along its periphery in neighboring San Francisco in 1995. Yet, incongruously, major Valley corporations and industry groups demonstrated little concern for the regulatory changes afoot. Instead, Old Economy businesses took the opportunity to influence the details of what became atrociously designed energy policy. As one member of the Public Utilities Commission rued in hindsight: "We put in place an answer to the problems of the steel mills and cement plants when Cisco and Qualcomm were becoming the growth sectors in the California economy."[149]

Beyond the cluster's fundamental dependency on a stable supply of electrical power there were other more specific reasons for paying attention to the changing situation. Silicon Valley is unusually vulnerable to supply disruptions because it imports more than 80% of its electricity from outside.[150] General economic development accompanying the 1990s high-tech boom further stressed the Valley's power grid. Making things worse, the technological engines of the Valley's latest "new thing"—Internet services—brought with it new burdens on the region's electricity infrastructure. From 1994 to the start of the new millennium, peak demand for electricity in Silicon Valley grew at an average annual rate of more than 6%, well above the negligible growth rate experienced over the same time in major Californian cities like San Francisco and Los Angeles.[151]

Silicon Valley's vanguard role in the commercialization of the Internet attracted the world's largest concentration of server farms—the electron-guzzling, heavily air conditioned banks of digital routing equipment that process Internet data communications. By the end of the decade, about 40 farms were operating in the Valley. A typical server farm will consume 85–100 watts per square foot, as much as triple the electricity required to power the Valley's previous industrial icon, the semiconductor factory. The largest among the Valley's server farms consumes enough energy to keep four steel mills in operation.[152] Yet, as Valley e-businesses enjoyed phenomenal growth and the whole of the cluster went increasingly online, local commercial and civic leadership not only ignored the chance to help shape deregulation policies but failed to take seriously the statewide crisis that began to unfold.

Well after electricity supply shocks had already hit the Bay Area, in

November 2000, the San Jose City Council unanimously rejected an application for constructing a new power-generation facility in the city. This blatantly ran contrary to the interests of the cluster's economic welfare that the city of San Jose claims to serve so well. Although the political decision to vote down the plant was influenced in part by the cause of a Not-In-My-Backyard campaign carried out by local residents, far more surprising than this populist NIMBYism was that of the corporate variety. Cisco, apparently still convinced of its imperviousness to a variety of changing realities, fought construction because the company planned to build its own 20,000-employee campus adjacent to the proposed generation site. Cisco's stance was doubly ironic considering that the company's networking products lie at the heart of the electron-draining server farms that have inordinately depleted the availability of electricity in the Valley.

This type of aloof detachment from the changing needs of the cluster has not only exacerbated problems with ensuring a stable flow of electricity. Silicon Valley's electricity supply power crisis has its equivalent in a labor supply "power crisis" involving lower income workers.

In 1999, investigative reporting by the San Jose *Mercury News* uncovered evidence that, long after the practice was assumed to have died out, illegal sweatshop labor was still going on in the homes of immigrant, predominantly Vietnamese, families. Investigators discovered that illicitly contracted home production had been providing circuit board assembly for the products of such pillars in the business community as HP, Cisco, and Sun. On another front, in mid-2000 (coincidently just around the time the Bay Area's electricity crisis reached historic proportions), some 5,500 janitors who serve Valley firms and another 1,700 Stanford hospital nurses threatened industrial action. Their demands for increased compensation to provide a "living wage" reflected the extraordinarily high costs that accompany working and residing in the Valley today. One picket sign read "3Com: 1 Minute in Sales"—a calculation of the time it would take the networking company to earn back the rise in pay the janitors servicing its facilities were seeking. The "1 Minute in Sales" placard is also a reminder that Silicon

Valley's once-inclusive concept of familial organizations has, with the decline of such ideals as the HP Way, in many instances come to be replaced by a more utilitarian concept of labor. When asked to reply to the janitors' demands, a spokesperson for another Valley icon, AMD, retorted that, as outsourced workers, the dispute was merely with "the janitors and their employers. They're not our employees."[153] Strictly speaking, of course, the spokesperson is right. The janitors are not the firm's employees. But AMD depends on them as much as it depends on the electricity that is brought in to power the company's facilities. This sort of blindness by firms to the interdependencies they have with the wider environment lies at the heart of new crises facing Silicon Valley.

There are tentative signs of progress. After news broke on the existence of illegal home assembly, transgressing operations were shut down. Federal authorities ordered employers found to have violated minimum wage laws to pay out back wages. The Stanford nurses' strike was settled; janitors were able to get the pay increases they had been rallying for without resorting to a walkout. In late May 2001, under intense pressure to reverse his earlier position, the mayor of San Jose finally backed construction for the 600-megawatt Metcalf Energy Center. Important business associations like the Silicon Valley Manufacturing Group have gone from playing catch-up to taking proactive steps in trying to address energy issues. In early 2001, the CEO of the Silicon Valley Manufacturing Group gained appointment to a reshuffled governing board of the California Independent System Operator, the state agency formed in 1998 to oversee California's electricity supply.

Though encouraging, such measures represent only a beginning. They address the symptoms and not the root causes of basic quality-of-life and resource issues that are affecting people in the Valley at large. Fundamental strategies that ensure that workers within the cluster's supply chains are equitably treated and that the region's infrastructure— be it for roads, housing, public education, or electricity—is sufficiently upgraded has yet to emerge. None of this is to imply that the Valley is somehow doomed to further deterioration and decline. If anything, the cluster has thrived on overcoming adversity. The great, unanswered question, however, is how ingenious will the solutions to its current set of socio-economic dilemmas be.

In 1992, when Silicon Valley was in the depths of what was then its latest market downturn, a report prepared by the consultancy SRI warned that the cluster was "at risk" because of a "growing imbalance between Valley enterprises and its economic infrastructure."[154] If anything, since that earlier time of crisis the Valley, in ways totally unpredicted, actually expanded as a cluster while social and physical infrastructure imbalances likewise grew apace. The future since 1992 has become one of paradoxes. Imbalances now involve issues of livelihood affecting the vast majority of residents, not only the menially employed. Data gathered by the San Jose *Mercury News* toward the peak of the Valley's Internet boom showed that as many as 65,000 households in Santa Clara County (11% of the total) were worth over $1m. Among the Valley's residents were at least 13 billionaires and hundreds of people whose net financial worth exceeded $25m. Yet 71% of Santa Clara County residents were unable to afford the $365,000 median price of a home. Although county residents had the third highest level of median household income in the nation, median household wealth (assets minus debts) placed it 26th—a rating that made the Valley about average with the rest of America.[155] The figure underscores that, while the Mother of All Siliconia offers a veritable cornucopia of wealth and opportunity for certain people, in terms of economic livelihood most people living in Silicon Valley fare no better nor worse than people elsewhere in the US. On the positive side, residents have not indicated they feel overly burdened by the price of membership to the cluster. Surveying 1,040 adults, the paper found that 71% of respondents agreed that "the growth of the high-tech industry has created more opportunities than problems." Thinking ahead 10 years, however, almost the same number (72%) felt that the Valley would stay about the same or deteriorate in terms of quality of life. Those predicting deterioration actually outnumbered those feeling the area will be able to maintain what quality of life it has offered so far.[156]

Public opinion reflects an underlying shift in the mix of entrepreneurial forces at play. Since the early days of Silicon Valley's high-tech build-up, the facilitation of commercial entrepreneurship has increased tremendously: universities are more involved with assisting start-ups, there are more entrepreneurs, more skilled workers, more career possibilities, more money, and a more robust industrial base within which to operate. Conversely, more broad-based forms of entrepreneurship have become a dying art. There is no latter-day version of a Fred Terman—some person or organization with an all-encompassing vision for education, one backed by concrete steps, for enacting measures like putting the Valley's poorly performing public schools on par with its phenomenally well-endowed local universities; or a Dutch Hamann—some can-do public servant or government body willing to roll up their sleeves and take strong action to convert sprawl into density, free up transportation gridlock, and address infrastructure deficiencies; or a Tom Ford—a developer who helps bring forth not only buildings but interactive communities. That is not to say that the Valley is without its social entrepreneurs, its crucial "visionary bureaucrats"; only that these people are not at work in the Valley to the extent the cluster requires if it is to continue to enjoy the type of explosive growth it has thus far. The cluster faces the sort of messily complex issues that are ripe for the innovating of new solutions, perhaps by a new breed of ambitious entrepreneurs and entrepreneurial organizations.

# Introduction 7

Driving north up the M11 motorway from London, to recognize when you have entered the perimeter of Europe's leading cluster for high-tech entrepreneurship is not easy. The squat, undecorated sign proclaiming "Cambridgeshire" is almost made invisible by a sweeping vista of gently swelling hills and farmland. In addition to marking the southern edge of Cambridge's county boundary, the sign approximately demarcates a region historically known as "the fens," a low-lying terrain of once-marshy wetlands that stretches from around the town of Cambridge towards the North Sea. As the car travels on, perhaps passing a line of trucks by using the one additional lane of the motorway, to the left a large aircraft hanger comes into view: the former RAF airfield at Duxford, now a part of the Imperial War Museum. In the 1930s the airfield had been a base for Frank Whittle, inventor of the jet turbine engine, who flew out of Duxford as a member of the Cambridge University Air Squadron. Despite Whittle's groundbreaking creation, which he attempted to commercialize with a company he founded while still a Cambridge student, nothing indicates that his technology has had a lasting impact on the surrounding area. The scene contrasts starkly with the geodesic radar domes, aerospace facilities, and other signs of technology-based activity that have sprung up around Moffet Field, the former US Navy dirigible base, visible off Highway 101 in Silicon Valley. Passing Duxford, one can only glimpse a grassy airstrip and nondescript hanger. The most tangible legacy left by Whittle's invention is a collection of jet aircraft housed inside the Duxford facilities as museum pieces.

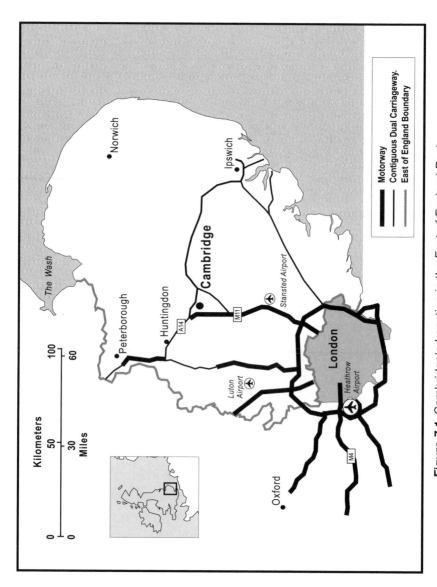

**Figure 7.1** Cambridge's Location in the East of England Region.

(Data from Crown Copyright material, used with kind permission of the Controller of HMSO)

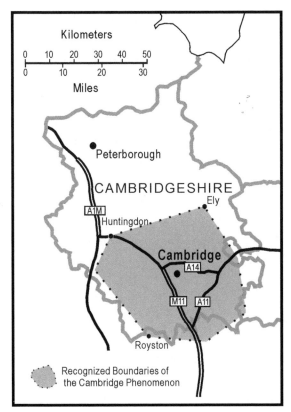

**Figure 7.2** Geography of the Cambridge Phenomenon.
(Data from SQW Ltd, used with kind permission)

Further along the motorway you pass the town of Cambridge itself, center of what the press has taken to calling "Silicon Fen" but from its early days was locally referred to as the "Cambridge Phenomenon." Those familiar with the area can recognize to the right in the distance the Addenbrooke's Hospital site, home to Cambridge's storied Laboratory of Molecular Biology, and later on, closer to the motorway, the quixotically shaped giant tent structure that houses the Cambridge research center of the European energy technology conglomerate, Schlumberger. Other than these few landmarks, the view is thoroughly rural. Little indicates that you are passing through a thriving high-tech cluster. Signs of substantial industrial activity do not even appear until after you have left the town of Cambridge behind and the motorway merges north-westerly with the A14 dual carriageway ("split highway" in the American parlance) that leads to the more economically developed market towns of Huntingdon and, further up, Peterborough.

Though hardly a cruise down the 101, a trip up the M11—the widest, fastest moving roadway connecting greater London to the Cambridge region—has just taken you into a territory that the *Financial Times* proclaims as "The Heart of New Britain."[157] Prime Minister Tony Blair goes further, intoning with a Churchillian spirit (though not quite the eloquence) that "there's no reason Europe can't rival America, no reason why Silicon Fen can't beat Silicon Valley." Rest assured, we are told, those in his government "are committed to the development of the Cambridge Phenomenon which will rival Silicon Valley."[158]

A short ride on the last section of the M11 is enough to demonstrate that Cambridge's economic geography has a long way to go before remotely approaching the scale and denseness of activity that characterizes America's crown jewel of technology clusters. Even a comparison closer to home with development around the "M4 Corridor" (the multilane motorway that runs west from London through Britain's largest collection of high-tech multinational offices) and Scotland's "Silicon Glen" (the UK's largest collection of high-tech multinational manufacturing operations) shows Cambridge only having the third largest concentration of high-tech employment.[159]

Yet the reason politicians, the press, and local boosters get excited about the Cambridge Phenomenon is that it represents Europe's most vibrant region for entrepreneurially driven high-tech. Eighty-six percent of Cambridge's technology firms are home-grown.[160] The cluster thrives on small-to-medium-sized enterprise: less than 3% of its 1,400 high-tech businesses employ 200 or more; most of the fen's 40,000-strong high-tech labor force works in companies that did not even exist 20 years ago.[161] This kind of vibrant, endogenous growth makes Cambridge the location *par excellence* for entrepreneurial high-technology job creation in the UK and Europe.

The preponderance of those small firms sprouting up and populating

Silicon Fen, and lack of small firms that grow into giant corporations, also begs questions: *why does the Cambridge cluster not breed any large companies; where are the equivalents of a Hewlett-Packard, Intel, or a Cisco?* It is also natural to wonder about the more fundamental question of *why has the cluster simply not attained greater economic mass?* A region with 1,400 high-tech firms employing 40,000 workers are impressive statistics for Europe—the Sophia Antipolis cluster in France, for example, even with strong government support has managed to attract only 1,200 firms that employ 22,000 (these figures are, moreover, largely the result of foreign direct investment as opposed to indigenous firm formation).[162] But Cambridge's statistics pale in comparison to the Silicon Valley totals of some 8,000 technology-related firms and employment in the cluster's geographic core that amounts to more than 500,000.[163] The cluster's relative smallness also defies the supposed advantages of being a "first-mover" as Cambridge has enjoyed an unrivalled lead in the fields of science and technology since the time of Newton. University-affiliated technology firms began spinning out of Cambridge's science departments as far back as the 19th century. Another major plus, the presence of a leading scientific university (which is typically assumed to be the key to fostering a substantial high-tech cluster), has in the case of Cambridge actually more often provided a hindrance than help to the large-scale economic development of the area.

The answer to the seeming "mystery" as to why Silicon Fen lacks the mass of Silicon Valley can be found in the way the cluster has been managed, from both the outside and in. Public policy, for example, has influenced the cluster in ways diametrically unlike the laws and government initiatives that helped shape Silicon Valley. Britain's current Prime Minister may sing the praises of Cambridge entrepreneurs but when Frank Whittle attempted to commercialize his jet engine technology shortly after World War Two, Whitehall forbade it. Government at the time sought to protect politically favored big-name defense contractors like Rolls-Royce who wanted Whittle's technology for themselves—a condition that contrasts sharply with the type of Cold War funding Fred Terman managed to funnel toward Stanford's plucky technopreneurs who he hoped would one day create firms to rival GE.[164] National government has since changed its tune but at the same time, apart from stirring rhetoric, offers little by way of directly catalyzing new-growth enterprise and makes almost no attempt to counteract the lingering perpetuation of past policies. At the level of local government, the attitude toward entrepreneurially driven large-scale growth has evolved even less with Cambridge's political structure remaining essentially hostile to substantial economic growth. This is a large part of the reason why the environs around Cambridge stay so verdantly agrarian. Quite unlike the sprawl unleashed in San Jose by Dutch's Panzer Division, Cambridge's government leadership has adopted a vision that stridently opposes significant alteration of the landscape—a position that local public opinion, today at least, seems largely to support.

In addition to the nature of government policy, the management practices guiding Cambridge's commercial enterprises also radically differ from business management styles in the Valley. Innovation and entrepreneurship find altogether different forms of expression in the fens. The cluster's dynamism reflects goals and motivations that are quite unlike the personal drives that propel Silicon Valley forward. Despite what media commentary and political rhetoric might contend, Cambridge does not want to become Silicon Valley. The cluster is content with simply being the Cambridge Phenomenon, eschewing the appearance of Silicon Valley while sharing its fundamental staying power as a cluster driven by the creativity of its innovators and entrepreneurs.

Thus, those hoping for any superficial resemblance between Silicon Fen and the Silicon Valley will be disappointed. No such resemblance exists and the pages of the second half of this book do not bemoan the lack of a Silicon Valley mirror image abroad. At the same time, readers should be encouraged by the way this absence of surface-level similarity makes the story of the Cambridge cluster's origins, dynamics, and innovators that much more compelling. In a far less conducive environment the forces of entrepreneurship and innovation have brought about a different kind of commercial resilience and robustness. With its enterprises operating under different objectives, Silicon Fen offers up a usefully contrasting set of perspectives for appreciating the universalism of how management forces distinguish a successful industrial cluster.

Before delving into an exploration of the Phenomenon of Cambridge, it is worth returning once again to Schumpeter, who argued in one of his most famous postulations that the "essential fact about capitalism" is the drive to alter, to "mutate"—as he borrowed the term from biological science—the constructs of enterprise and industry. This process of mutation:

> ... incessantly revolutionizes the economic structure *from within*, incessantly destroying the old one, incessantly creating a new one. This process of Creative Destruction is the essential fact about capitalism. It is what capitalism consists in and what every capitalist concern has got to live in.[165]

Creative destruction, the best known phrase to come from Schumpeterian thought, gets frequently bandied about in business discourse. It is an especially apt term for the juxtaposed nature of global economic activity today where firms and industries can be found to rise from the ashes of past failures; where the birth of something "new" frequently spurs on the death of the "old." Silicon Valley, which emerged out of a high-tech semi-desert, provides a long litany of noteworthy instances of creative destruction. So it is as well with the Cambridge Phenomenon, a cluster that, while having a much lower profile than its American counterpart, in many regards offers up examples of creative destruction that are clearer, and in certain contexts more profound, than those found in Silicon Valley.

# The Phenomenon of Cambridge        8

The Cambridge Phenomenon's relatively late appearance as a cluster of modern high-tech—active management of Silicon Valley began as far back as in the 1930s; concerted efforts at promoting the growth of what became the Cambridge Phenomenon did not begin until the late 1960s—is historically ironic, mainly in two ways. The first is that the natural environment of the region has long been a stimulant for technical inventiveness. The idyllic pastoral lands that local political powers today so jealously guard constituted a harsh wilderness in earlier times. The development of the fens has entailed people devoting their ingenuity to some form of technological mastery over the territory. And yet it has not been until very recently that the region as a whole has supported a substantial population of technology-based enterprises. This irony is heightened by another: Cambridge's leading role in the sciences. The fundamentals of advanced technology in the world today—from Newton's laws of physics to Thompson's discovery of the electron to Watson and Crick's mapping of DNA—came out of Cambridge. The worldwide (and long-running) prominence of Cambridge science belies the relative global obscurity of the region's commercial technology enterprises.

From Federal Telegraph to Hewlett-Packard, the university-affiliated technology firms that emerged in Palo Alto were initially assisted by Stanford faculty and administrators but also developed as self-reliant, strategically resourceful enterprises. The Cambridge university high-tech spin-outs that began appearing in the late 19th century likewise received a degree of faculty support—some of it quite extraordinary under the circumstances—but the businesses formed were far less independent and commercially ambitious. Before Stanford had seen its first high-tech spin-out Cambridge had already developed a local agglomeration of scientific instrument manufacturers. These organizations were limited in that their purpose of operations was essentially to meet the needs of university science labs and other research organizations, not to open up brave, new markets with their technologies. Out of its scientific instruments base Cambridge did produce two firms that escaped the shadow of their roots as appendages to academia but, owing to management shortcomings, they ultimately failed as competitive enterprises. When government later intervened and nationalized one of these firms—providing the sort of public assistance that was more to the detriment than benefit of the cluster—managerial failures were merely exacerbated. Cambridge's earliest foray into large-scale high-tech industry ended dismally.

It has been out of this morass that a new generation of Phenomenon companies arose. Because the disasters of the past were so pronounced, the ability of high-tech enterprise to emerge again, in new forms and with an increasingly refined understanding of how to manage effectively, is similarly that much more remarkable. Although major recent failures have still occurred among the Phenomenon's collection of high-tech enterprises, there has never again been an overall decline of its industrial base. Instead, firms have become increasingly well adjusted to the parameters in which they operate. The cluster has grown at an impressive rate and out of some of the biggest corporate disasters have come the most capably managed, forward-moving enterprises in Britain. The trial-and-error of creative destruction brought about by Cambridge managers continues to shape the dynamism of the cluster while laying ruin to the erroneous practises of the past.

## FENLANDERS, UNDERTAKERS, AND ADVENTURERS

The word "fen" can be traced back to the Sanskrit *panka* meaning, simply, "mud."[166] The term "swamp" more closely describes the state of the fens before enterprise was organized to drain them. Until the 19th century, lands immediately north of the town of Cambridge were *regiones inundatæ*—much of the territory submerged by shallow estuary waters or soaked as marsh. Frequently calm to the point of being stagnant, the waters when whipped by storms could generate waves high enough to sink ships. The terrain surface and water bottom were spongy, composed of decayed vegetation known as peat, usually the color of pitch and treacherously unstable. The quicksand-like pockets of the fens are believed to have once swallowed an entire Roman column and later the royal treasure of the itinerant King John. The king's death in 1216 is in fact attributed to the shock he suffered at the fen's sudden absorption of his wealth. The area was also known for other life-threatening hazards, notably a form of malaria called fen ague.

From early times the conditions of the wetlands challenged the technical abilities of those seeking mastery over the region. The Romans sought to overcome the poor navigability of the waters by constructing a canal, the first in Britain, which sliced through the fens and connected Cambridge to Lincolnshire in the north-west. At the beginning of the 2nd millennium AD, Canute the Great failed in his attempt to empty fenland waters through the construction of a dyke. During the medieval era, Christian monks, drawn by the seclusion and protection the fens afforded, started a process of incremental land reclamation by using methods of ditch drainage to extend the pastures of their island monasteries. Innovations also were contributed by the local population. Native Fenlanders devised a low-bottomed skiff that could be maneuvered by a pole that dually serves to propel the craft and helps determine the firmness of a mooring site. Today these boats, known as punts, are used in the warmer months for the most famous form of recreation particular to Cambridge: "punting" on the River Cam where its waters meander along the picturesque banks of Cambridge's college campuses.

The greatest of the region's technology projects began during the reign of Elizabeth I when the crown aspired to nothing less than complete drainage of the fens. The kind of official enthusiasm for this undertaking conveys itself in the language of a patent issued in 1580 that certified a would-be technopreneur "to draine certaine fennes and lowe grounds surrounded with waters by certain engines and devices never knowen or used before, which being put in practice are like to prove verie commodious and beneficiall unto the Realme."[167] The local population, however, did not share the government's eagerness for the arrival of such "engines and devices never knowen or used before." The 16th century Fenlander enjoyed an unencumbered frontier lifestyle. The livelihood of the local populace depended on free access to the marshes for hunting and fishing (eels were in particular abundance) along with gathering sedge (for thatch) and dried peat (for fuel). The cluster of colleges that made up the University of Cambridge at the time also stood against drainage because it threatened to eliminate the town's position as a major port and venue for market fairs, activities by which the land-owning colleges profited handsomely.

Disregarding such opposition, the government persevered with its plans and adopted a novel means for their realization. Rather than commit its own resources to the challenge of drainage, the government turned to private investors and management. The investors, offering an early form of merchant-style venture capitalism, were dubbed "adventurers" because of their willingness to "adventure" their capital. These adventurers funded entrepreneurial "undertakers," so called because they undertook the risks of implementing the drainage projects.[168] The context of organizing capital and management in this way was historically unique, as Ross Clark highlights in a book on the history of Cambridgeshire:

> The reign of Elizabeth I was an expansive age, a golden age, even. It was also an age of great individualism. Though the Crown might tax or borrow to fight a foreign nation over some patch of overseas territory, the idea of a government taxing its people to finance what would now be known as "infrastructure investment" was unheard of. The draining of the fens was going to have to be funded by individuals: the world's first industrial-scale joint stock venture.[169]

Of course, the individualism of the era was that for a privileged few. The adventurers and undertakers were politically well connected and their gain in the endeavor was the Fenlanders' loss: compensation from the government for financing and managing drainage projects was title to land freely utilized by the local population.

In the end, the efforts of the state and its commercial pioneers proved insufficient for accomplishing total land reclamation. The equipment employed was limited and unable to withstand repeated sabotage by hostile Fenlanders. Despite sporadic success with projects that attained partial drainage much of the region remained a treacherous bog. Less than two centuries after a rush for the technology-driven development of the fens, the epoch-making invention of the condenser (patented in 1769 by University of Glasgow technician James Watt) offered an applicable technical solution to the problems of fenland drainage. For other parts of Britain, the technology helped spark the Industrial Revolution. As regards the development of the fenlands, however, the managerial will to see through complete draining had subsided greatly. It would be another 50 years after Watt's invention before modern drainage pumps arrived in the area. Not until the middle of the 19th century—with work on isolated areas continuing well into the 20th century—was a network of reliably functioning engines in place, transforming the fenlands into the great agricultural expanse that they are today. Far from Cambridge's modern landscape being the symbol of rustic purity that its appearance suggests, the green lushness of the area is only possible because of an artificially created environment to which the area's earlier inhabitants quite begrudgingly acquiesced.

## THE EVOLUTION OF ACADEMIA AND SCIENCE

The dates and circumstances of ecclesiastic scholars' first gatherings in Cambridge remain unclear. Monks from fenland monasteries may have been lecturing at the market town of Cambridge from as early as the 1100s. By 1209 scholars from Oxford had arrived but the reasons for this are not well understood. Some form of scandal (an exodus in protest over the hanging of an Oxford student for murdering his mistress is one of the more lurid versions of events) typically infuses popular speculation about the migration. Whatever the cause, the coming together of the learned and learning continued, laying the foundation for today's alliance of 31 colleges that lie at the heart of Cambridge's federated university system. Records show that from at least 1225 a chancellor and *universitas* of scholars was officially recognized and shortly thereafter granted special privileges by both Pope and King. The timing proved advantageous. In the 13th century another gathering of scholars was trying to establish a university in Northampton, not far beyond the western expanse of today's Cambridge Phenomenon, but the King forbade it. Another six centuries would pass before royal dictate permitted a third university in England to be formed.

Academic inquiry at Cambridge evolved unevenly with the conditions of the colleges and the quality of their scholarship experiencing bouts of feast and famine. Patronage from church and state, key factors in the university's establishment and growth, could further as much as stifle intellectual development. Special privileges granted to Cambridge's academic community served as buffers against an often-antagonistic local populace. Such protections, however, also demanded excommunication or execution for those who disputed church doctrine or fell out of favor with the monarchy. The first major revolt against this established order occurred some four centuries after the founding of the university when various colleges became hotbeds of Puritan radicalism in a region that itself became swept up in puritanical fervor. Cambridge's revolutionary minds of this era included the dissident John Harvard who emigrated to the Massachusetts Bay Colony where in posterity his library and estate established America's first university. A less academically accomplished Puritan, a college dropout named Oliver Cromwell (a fenland native son), later returned to his *alma mater* leading an army that, after a brief period of occupation, went on to defeat the Royalists and give England a brief taste of republican rule. The Puritan zeal of a young Isaac Newton drove him during his time at Cambridge to uncover what he interpreted to be the divine laws of the physical universe. His search led him to establish the bedrock of physics and computation (the calculus) that provide the basic theoretic constructs for high technology in the world today.

Newton's ground-breaking discoveries and exceptional talent warrant particular reflection because his prolific years in Cambridge occurred around the time when national government (which Newton later joined), financiers, and early industrialists were attempting to develop the fens. Newton, and later generations of Cambridge scientists who followed in his wake, stayed aloof from the pressing technological needs of their eras not to mention those of the local Cambridge area. The intellectual predilections of Cambridge scientists tended toward theory, not application. It was left to those who grasped the practical dimensions of Newtonian physics to transform Britain and eventually the world. Newton biographer Michael White provides a sense for the tremendous economic importance of the Cambridge academic's work in his assessment of the repercussions from the 1687 publication of Newton's seminal work, the *Principia Mathematica*:

> With the *Principia*, Newton not only unified the disparate theories of Galileo and Kepler into a single, coherent, mathematically and experimentally supported whole: he also opened the door to the Industrial Revolution. ... The *Principia* laid the cornerstone for the understanding of dynamics and mechanics which would, within a space of a century, generate a real lasting change in human civilization. Without being understood, the forces of Nature cannot be harnessed; but this, in essence, is what the Industrial Revolution achieved—it dragged humanity from the darkness, from the whim of Nature, to the beginnings of technology and the yoking of universal forces.[170]

Over the two centuries following publication of the *Principia*, Britain emerged as the world's leading industrialized nation. In the birthplace of the science that made this all possible, however, the Industrial Revolution and its multifarious social and technological implications were frequently ignored and typically disdained. Cambridge continued to attract men of talent and ability but the university's goal was to graduate gentlemen of civility and refinement. The ethos of the colleges celebrated amateurism, not the skills that the meritocratic values the age of industry and capital demanded. Students came to Cambridge to, as William Petty famously articulated the ideal, revel in the "Delight and Ornament" of learning.[171] Industriousness and practical knowledge were deemed the province of the vulgar classes. In his study on the role of Cambridge in Victorian England, Sheldon Rothblatt notes the economic implications of the mindset that infused Cambridge University:

> On both sides of the Atlantic it is frequently said that in America business values, incentives and methods were impressed on the university, but in one of England's fairest educational institutions anti-philistinism survived. The result, critics have said is the failure of Cambridge, as well as Oxford, to play a vigorous role in building up the economy and facilitating technological change. The disdain for *homo oeconomicus* in Cambridge was altogether too complete.[172]

Martin Weiner, in *English Culture and the Decline of the Industrial Spirit*, elaborates on these points by arguing that the ethos of England's closely linked prestige universities, Oxford and Cambridge ("Oxbridge"), not only worked against technology-driven change but acted as a vehicle for indoctrinating a spirit of reactionaryism:

> The ethos of later-Victorian Oxbridge, a fusion of aristocratic and professional values, stood self-consciously in opposition to Victorian business and industry: It exalted a dual ideal of cultivation and service against philistine profit seeking. Businessmen were objects of scorn and moral reproval, and industry was noted chiefly as a despoiler of country beauty. . . .
>
> Oxbridge institutionalized Victorian resistance to the new industrial world. . . . If Oxbridge insulated the sons of the older elites against contact with industry, it also gradually drew sons of industrial and commercial families away from the occupation of their fathers, contributing to a "hemorrhage" of business talent.
>
> The educated young men who did go into business took their antibusiness values with them. As businessmen sought to act like educated gentlemen, and as educated gentlemen (or would-be gentlemen) entered business, economic behavior altered. The dedication to work, the drive for profit, and the readiness to strike out on new paths in its pursuit waned.[173]

In addition to the anti-business values of the university there was a strong tendency among Cambridge's academic mainstream to disregard the advances in scientific research being made during the Industrial Revolution. An esteemed Cambridge expert on science, William Whewell (Master of Cambridge's influential Trinity College and a future Vice-Chancellor of the university), was arguing in the mid-19th century that recent scientific discoveries should be banished from the curriculum until they had been irrefutably proven—he considered 100 years a sufficient waiting period. Isaac Todhunter, a leading Cambridge mathematician, was even blunter, contending that scientific experimentation was simply "unnecessary for the student."[174]

Despite such overt resistance to modernizing Cambridge's science curriculum, key faculty and administrators intent on developing Cambridge's scientific capabilities managed to overcome the obstacles in their way. In this case, government was also on the side of the reformers. Parliament, mindful of how other nations were furthering their research-based university systems, wanted to bring the medieval institutions of Oxford and Cambridge into the modern era and pressed them to update their ordinances, pedagogy, and facilities. In 1873, with funding from William Cavendish, the seventh Duke of Devonshire and Chancellor of the university, Cambridge established its first intercollegiate scientific research center, the Cavendish Laboratory. The results of this initiative were tremendous. Over the years a string of paradigmatic discoveries made the Cavendish Laboratory the world's principal incubator for what some consider to be a Second or Third Scientific Revolution. Before the century was out, the Cavendish's first director, James Clerk-Maxwell, had advanced a revolutionary theory on electromagnetism while its third, J. J. Thompson, unlocked the mysteries of the electron—two monumental breakthroughs that paved the way for the era of electronics and information technology in which we presently live. Scholar of science Hugh Kearney equates the historical significance of the Cavendish with that of Padua during the Rennaisance and of Clerk-Maxwell with Galileo.[175] Einstein considered the theory of electromagnetism propounded by Clerk-Maxwell to be the "greatest alteration in the axiomatic basis of physics—in our conception of the structure of reality—since the foundation of theoretical physics by Newton."[176]

Going into the 20th century, as the vigor of England's Industrial Revolution and the health of Northern California's mining industries waned, the proto-phase in industrial development of what later became Silicon Valley and Silicon Fen was already under way. At this historic juncture, Cambridge's emerging high-tech economy had the greatest number of advantages by far. England had already been transformed by industrialization in a way that California never experienced. Progressive Cambridge academics had made the university the epicenter of new scientific knowledge whereas Bay Area universities were still decades away from reaching a similar level of scientific excellence. Before Stanford had even been established, the Cavendish Laboratory was spinning out new technology businesses. To the great benefit of Cambridge's industrial base, these enterprises would not, as happened in Northern California, abandon or be moved out of the region in any significant degree. But leading companies among this early generation of firms would nevertheless eventually decline and vanish as major actors in the cluster. Their demise was not, as in centuries past, owing to physical sabotage committed by disgruntled fenlanders but rather a kind of managerial sabotage perpetrated by leaders in the private and public sectors.

## THE RISE AND FALL OF EARLY HIGH-TECH

To meet the experimenting needs of the Cavendish Laboratory and the university's newly formed medical and engineering departments, the first high-tech company organized in Cambridge was a manufacturer of scientific instruments. Founded in 1878 under special arrangements made by the iconoclastic holder of the chair of Applied Mechanics, James Stuart, the company was housed within the university engineering department's workshop and allowed to operate as a private concern. Three years later, the majority partners of the firm decided to locate off campus and reorganized operations as Cambridge Scientific Instruments

(CSI). Horace Darwin, a Cambridge-trained engineer and ninth son of the famous Cambridge-educated evolutionary theorist, Charles, became CSI's chairman. Another key member of the CSI organization was William T. Pye, a London-based instrument craftsman who Darwin and his partner recruited to serve as shop foreman. CSI first made precision microtomes for tissue sampling but extended its product range over time to include gas and chemical analyzers and electrocardiographs. Throughout the 1950s, in close collaboration with the university, the company pioneered a highly advanced range of electron microscopes.

Under Darwin's stewardship, CSI's corporate culture admirably reflected the university's moral values. Darwin committed the company to undertaking technically challenging projects with little heed to the bottom line. In business dealings he was known to be "over-generous to his customers in his costing methods" and "rarely charged realistic prices."[177] Following an initial equity investment of £1,050 in CSI in 1881, Darwin was a decade later the firm's major creditor, loaning more than £2,000 of his own money to keep it solvent. Devoutly ethical, he championed social causes inside the workplace and out. CSI employees enjoyed a company-sponsored welfare system, benefit fund, and an educational program. Darwin's civic activities included co-founding a local anti-prostitution campaign and establishing a school for mentally disabled boys. He also served as Mayor of Cambridge, Justice of the Peace, and Chairman of Britain's Air Inventions Committee during World War One. His public service earned him a knighthood in 1918.

As regards the welfare of the company itself, Darwin's policies fared less positively for the cause of CSI. One of his less celebrated legacies carried on by successive generations of CSI managers was to embrace technologically elegant but financially unrewarding projects. In the immediate post-World War Two era, at a time when Hewlett-Packard ramped up for large-scale manufacturing, Cambridge's flagship technology company exhibited little interest in the mass market. It preferred instead to pursue intellectually attractive niche projects or to milk revenue from established product lines. By the late 1950s CSI had become a takeover target after a string of technically successful but economically debilitating forays in scanning electron microscopy. One project, the Geoscan, was undertaken at the behest of Cambridge University's Department of Mineralogy and Petrology with little, if any, consideration for actual market needs. The final version of the product was so advanced and feature-rich that its pricing meant only a few Geoscans could be afforded by interested customers. CSI's original purpose as a company dedicated to serving the needs of the university and science, at the expense of pursuing new avenues for revenue growth, had been maintained throughout the years. It prevented the company from acting on a wider range of opportunities.

Despite its ongoing financial difficulties, CSI was at least a success in establishing itself as Cambridge's first prominent technology company. Drawing in technology business talent and readying the ground for the Silicon Fen of today, CSI elevated Cambridge's stature as a location for modern high-tech enterprise. It also produced a series of spin-off companies, the most important of which was CSI's first: WG Pye & Co.

Pye served as the second business pillar during the proto-phase of modern technology-based industry in Cambridge. William G. Pye, son of CSI Foreman William T. Pye, set up his own instrument company in 1896 after having served an apprenticeship at CSI and working as a craftsman in the Cavendish Laboratory. Business did so well that within two years the senior Pye left CSI to join his son. During the recession that followed World War One, WG Pye diversified into the production of radios—a decision that greatly paid off when the government established the British Broadcasting Corporation in 1922, stimulating an explosion in demand for wireless sets. In keeping up with new demand, the electronics section of Pye grew so rapidly that the Pye family felt disconcertingly overwhelmed. Where a typical Santa Clara Valley entrepreneur would have seized the chance to grow the enterprise and move it further into this promising new field, the Pye family shunned the opportunity, attempting to dispose of their radio business by selling off the division to the Dutch electronics group, Philips. Uncomfortable in handling such a transaction themselves, the family asked that WG Pye's advertizing agent, C. O. Stanley, negotiate the sale to Philips on their behalf. Stanley instead countered with an offer that he himself purchase Pye's radio group and establish it as an independent firm.

Once in charge, Stanley built Pye Radio into the largest technology firm Cambridge has *ever* seen. The company's distinctive "rising sun" art deco motif became a recognizable feature on radio and, further out, television sets and other electronics products throughout Great Britain and the Commonwealth. By 1947 Pye's radio technology spin-out had done so well that it even acquired its progenitor, WG Pye & Co. The combined Pye Group went on to become the biggest employer in the Cambridge area, at its peak providing jobs to 15,000 employees locally and another 10,000 abroad.

Stanley's advertizing background meant that unlike CSI and other research- or engineering-focused firms springing up around Cambridge, Pye was distinctively growth-oriented and aggressive in its market strategies. The company unhesitatingly expanded into new areas and Stanley (who also chaired the national trade association, British Electronic Industries) was an active figure in Britain's electronics industry. Mindful of the potentially adverse consequences of government policy, Stanley acted as a powerful and unflinching critic of government regulations he saw as detrimental to Britain's broadcasting sector and Pye's self-interests. He failed, though, to develop within the Pye Group effective financial controls to balance out his marketing and public leadership skills. A poorly orchestrated drive into the rental radio and TV markets in the mid-1960s caused Pye to rack up £9m losses and precipitated a boardroom putsch. The auditors were brought in and Stanley and his son, who served as deputy managing director, were ousted. The Philips conglomerate was finally able to act on its interest of 40 years earlier and purchased Pye's core electronics business plus the much-broadened corporate portfolio of the Pye Group.

Under new management Pye initially conducted operations as before. Within a decade, however, it was whittled down by an inability to marshal an effective response to the forces of foreign competition and Philips' efforts at cost-cutting. By the late 1980s, dwindling in corporate size and market presence, Pye was finally removed as the trade name of all operations previously affiliated with the Pye Group. Manufacturing and other headquarter activities at the group's former multi-divisional complex—Cambridge's first and so far only large-scale corporate campus—were vacated in a long, drawn-out process that continued into the start of the 21st century.

Among the handful of Cambridge's big-name technology company failures, by comparison Pye fared well: though it was crippled by financial difficulty it never went bust; after being taken over it was competently managed as a going concern; its downsizing and reorganization in Cambridge was well handled and done for defensible, if controversial, reasons. Actions surrounding the demise of Cambridge's original technology firm, Cambridge Scientific Instruments, entailed a far more sordid affair.

## THE CSI SAGA

After its string of big and unprofitable product development projects in the 1950s, by the mid-1960s CSI at last had a new management team that was serious about growing the company. The reformers were headed by a chief executive, Jack Race, who made it his personal goal to revamp a company that he saw as having "slumbered" through its first 80 years.[178] The company designed and priced its newest mainline product, the Stereoscan electron microscope, for wide-scale industrial and research applications, marketing it in conjunction with a worldwide corporate identity campaign. Commitment to growing its international sales base was also underscored by the company offering product delivery via express air shipment rather than ocean transport, as was standard for its industry.

Unfortunately, efforts to remake CSI came about too late. Soon after CSI launched its new initiatives Britain's instrumentation sector began to consolidate—the result of evolutionary changes in the industry and government fiat. CSI was pressured to merge. Two larger groups, the Rank Organisation (of Rank/Xerox fame) and George Kent Ltd (an engineering combine based in nearby Luton), made offers. Of the two bids Rank's was the strongest across many measures. Rank bid earliest and it bid aggressively, expressing the determination and boasting the resources to outbid any competing offer from the market. Rank already had a subsidiary successfully competing in the scientific instruments space. This subsidiary was enjoying robust growth and had good prospects for more: in only three-quarters of the time it had taken Kent to build its market position in the instruments sector, Rank's operation was earning twice the sales revenue of Kent's. Paralleling CSI's new strategy, Rank was already pushing wide-scale industrial applications for its scientific instrument products. Rank's strength in optics and lenses furthermore complemented CSI's core strengths in microscope technology. Most of all, Rank's intense bidding strongly suggested its likely long-term commitment to developing CSI's competitiveness. Rank's deputy chairman noted that the greatest advantage of a Rank acquisition for CSI was his company's plan to inject into the Cambridge firm "more skills in marketing and more finance for research."[179]

Kent's offer, on the other hand, proposed to have CSI grafted on as a new division within Kent's existing corporate structure. Kent's instrument product lines—industrial process controls, domestic water meters, precision equipment—offered comparatively little synergy with CSI's lines of scientific and medical instruments. The export customer base of the two companies was also dissimilar. Where CSI and Kent were alike was in terms of history and corporate size. Both also operated as businesses still heavily influenced by the family descendants of their founders. Kent's bid held political appeal to the reigning powers on CSI's board because, with differences in business activities between the two companies, there would be no need for organizational streamlining after operations were combined. Acquisition by Kent meant that further structural changes at CSI—uncomfortable but necessary if the firm was to succeed in a globalizing marketplace—could be forgone.

CSI's board repeatedly and emphatically rejected Rank's offers while embracing Kent's. For reasons not made clear (or easy to understand) the UK government concurred with these sentiments and decided that combining CSI with Kent was in the best interests of the British taxpayer. In 1968, the government's Industrial Reorganization Corporation made an unprecedented move and violated its own policy of non-interference. It spent more than £4m of public money (purchasing shares at a 37.7 price-earnings ratio) to ensure that Kent won control of CSI. The government's extreme measures opened what would become a veritable black hole for public funds.

An immediate effect of government interference was to alienate the Young Turks who had been pushing for change in the company. Within a few months of the takeover, CSI's reformist CEO, Jack Race, resigned. His departure was followed shortly thereafter by that of the company's sales director. By 1973 CSI's entire pre-merger board had been replaced; several of the senior management replacements in turn left after only short tenures. Throughout this period performance deteriorated severely. Between 1972 and 1973, the division hemorrhaged losses at the rate of about £100,000 per month. When another Cambridge-area technology firm and university spin-out, Metals Research, raised the prospect of relieving Kent of the CSI division, Kent was willing to dispose of its Cambridge acquisition for as little as £3m—far less than what the government and Kent had paid out to acquire CSI only five years earlier. After assessing the likelihood of the Cambridge division's continued heavy losses, however, Metals walked away from the deal.

When Kent's own financial difficulties resulted in its acquisition by the Swiss conglomerate Brown Boveri, the foreign acquirer was careful to exempt Kent's CSI operations from the merger. CSI thus spun out to emerge once again as an independent but (in comparison to its former self) severely weakened company. The firm continued floundering in spite of additional government spending in the form of £2m in loan guarantees. As a promised final solution to resolving the firm's ongoing difficulties, the Department of Trade approached Metals Research with enticements of £4.5m in equity capital and interest-free loans to support its takeover of the suffering instruments company. Although Metals accepted the offer, after the merger losses continued mounting (eventually totaling £3m per year) and the government found itself delivering an unrelenting stream of subsidies. In the five years following the firm's acquisition by Metals Research, support from public coffers totaled more than £15m for the combined firm. Since intervening in the market in 1968, the government ended up owning 87% of the equity in the former CSI. Deciding to cut its losses, in 1979 the UK's National Enterprise Board reorganized the government's position and sold 75% of the voting shares in CSI for a mere £500,000.

The company's purchaser was an American: the Welsh-born, San Diego, California-based physicist, Terry Gooding—an entrepreneur who had a track record of building up and turning around instrumentation companies. Gooding's new management team reformulated CSI's hopelessly misleading cost accounting system, sold off the medical instruments side of the business, and had the remaining operations carry the name Cambridge Instruments.

CI's major accomplishment was to transition from its long-standing concentration on scanning electron microscopes to developing a world-wide market for its line of electron beam lithography equipment—the latter a technology that had been pioneered at Cambridge University with collaboration from CSI in the 1960s. In the 1980s, as the circuitry of semiconductors approached the level of one micron (one-millionth of a meter, or about one-hundredth the width of a human hair), CI's range of electron beam lithography and related equipment offered promising emergent applications in semiconductor manufacturing. Cambridge Instruments expanded throughout most of the decade. By 1987 it had earned a record £7.7m in annual profit and was listed on the stock market.

The fatal flaw of the new strategy was its overestimation of the demand that could be relied on in the electronics sector. When the global IT industry nosedived in the second half of the 1980s, CI found itself without an alternate revenue base and was unable to adjust to its new predicament. The firm founded by Darwin's son finally succumbed to the harsh realities of survival in a free market. Unable to revive itself, in 1989 CI's shares were acquired by the privately held Swiss optical group, Wild Leitz, the manufacturer of Leica cameras. A form of Cambridge-based operations has since been retained under a series of new management structures. Yet with a Cambridge workforce numbering 800 in 1988 (on the eve of CI's takeover by Wild Leitz) and only 150 ten years later, what is now the Cambridge division of Leica Microsystems exists as a faint, hardly recognizable shadow of the former pre-eminence of Cambridge's first major high-technology company.


## PHENOMENALLY CAMBRIDGE

As of 1979, the health of Cambridge's established high-tech firms gave little indication that the area had a thriving technology cluster. At the time not only CSI but also Sinclair Radionics, a quirky but sometimes wildly successful local maker of calculators, personal computers, and assorted electronic gizmos, was being sustained by emergency financing and management from the British government. Philips-Pye was entering a final phase of decline. Another highly regarded high-tech enterprise, Cambridge Consultants Limited, had overexpanded and been close to total dissolution in the early 1970s. It only escaped corporate oblivion through a bargain-priced buyout by the American consultancy, Arthur D. Little, which turned CCL into its European technology research headquarters.

Despite these scenes of corporate carnage and decay, 1979 also saw new forms of Cambridge high-tech enterprise arise to break fresh ground and occupy spaces vacated by the previous high-tech base. Two trend lines were crossing. The old way of managing technology business—and government's bureaucratic attempts to manage markets—was in decline. Conversely, small, entrepreneurially minded firms operating in an increasingly free and dynamic market climate were on the rise. A university once remarkable for its complete "disdain for *homo oeconomicus*" was also on its way to producing a new class of technology elite: Cambridge's "millionaire dons." Most importantly, a new generation of management was, through an uneven process of trial and error, gaining expertise and pursuing nontraditional business models that would take Cambridge-based technology companies to new levels of global competitiveness.

## Hatching Biotech

Although often overlooked as a symbol of the early "Phenomenon" era, a company that well illustrates the fullness and the types of change taking place is Celltech, the firm that essentially created Britain's modern biotech industry. The events that led to Celltech's birth were part of a broad-based awakening to opportunities missed through mismanagement of British, especially Cambridge, technological innovations.

Work by scientists at the university and its affiliated laboratories throughout the 20th century had firmly established Cambridge as a world-leading center for the life sciences. Most famously, in 1953 Cavendish researchers James Watson and Francis Crick made the paradigmatic discovery of how to model the double-helix structure of Deoxyribose Nucleic Acid (DNA). Two decades later, César Milstein and Georges Köhler, working at Cambridge's Laboratory of Molecular Biology (LMB, a government-funded Cavendish spin-out), discovered a technique for producing monoclonal antibodies—proteins hailed as the "magic bullets" capable of eradicating all variety of disease.

Although Cambridge minds had solved some of the greatest mysteries of biological existence, they had failed to secure patents or help build companies around their intellectual assets. This differed with the situation in California where Sand Hill Road's star VC firm, Kleiner Perkins—founded by Traitorous Eight member Eugene Kleiner and ex-HP executive Tom Perkins—was aggressively funding life science spin-outs from University of California campuses in San Francisco and San Diego. The spectacular rise of Genentech, the Valley start-up established in 1976 around recombinant DNA technologies, caused the world to wake up to the potential of discoveries in a field that was being called biotechnology. In Cambridge, Genentech's success served not only as a wake-up call but was also a cause for questioning why home to the discovery of DNA had yet to capitalize on its biotech capabilities. The soul-searching intensified after the 1978 launch of San Diego's Hybritech, a company formed around the very monoclonal antibody technology Milstein and Köhler had pioneered at Cambridge's LMB.

The event created a national furore in Britain for assigning blame in the failure to protect and commercialize some of the UK's most valuable, and publicly owned, pieces of intellectual property.[180]

Amid the uproar and finger-pointing, an entrepreneurial Director of the Science Division in the National Enterprise Board (NEB) decided to do something. This "visionary bureaucrat" was Cambridge-trained bio-chemist, Gerard Fairtlough. He proposed that the best response to the UK's past failure to exploit its life science assets was to establish a biotech firm in the style of Genentech. Having also led the government's disposal of its stake in CSI, he had intimate familiarity with how techno-logically "smart" firms can be unintelligently managed. Fairtlough became Celltech's chief executive. He and his management team decided that while Celltech would at first base its core technologies around the intellectual property of the Cambridge LMB, they would not limit the company's technology supply sources. All leading academic life science centers in the UK would be approached as potential partners for the new company.

Fairtlough and his team studied aspects of Silicon Valley for insights that they felt could be applied to Celltech. Mindful of the approximate geographic dimensions and logistics of the Californian cluster, Celltech's management chose to headquarter the company in Slough, about 60 miles directly south-west of Cambridge. This location offered the same basic proximity that exists between San Jose and San Francisco and gave the company a position along the M4 Corridor, making it far more accessible to the outside world than any location available in Cambridge. (More fundamentally it was the only location in the region that offered a lab of the necessary size.) The team also felt that this geographic positioning would allow the company to take advantage of a "Golden Triangle" of knowledge, finance, and management resources available between Cambridge, London, and Oxford[181] (Figure 8.1). After analyzing Genentech's business model Fairtlough modified its constructs into a framework for encouraging innovation at Celltech through an organizational structure he dubbed "creative compartments."[182]

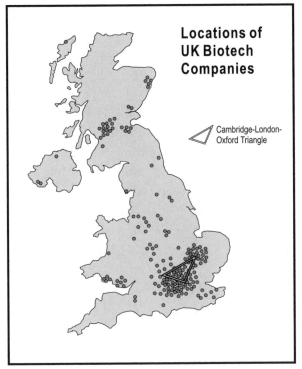

Locations of
UK Biotech
Companies

Cambridge-London-
Oxford Triangle

**Source**: Department of Trade and Industry, Ernst & Young, 1999

**Figure 8.1** Clustering Around the "Golden Triangle".
(Data from Crown Copyright material, used with kind permission of the Controller of HMSO)

For Celltech's finance, a government committee considered the catalytic role played by venture capital in the US and flatly conceded: "There seems little prospect of similar companies being set up in the United Kingdom at the present time by wholly private finance."[183] Celltech accordingly sought investment via a combined public–private partnership. At the company's founding in 1980 the NEB took a 44% equity stake, something it wound down to complete divestment in 1985. Compared with the bungling of the Industrial Reorganization Corporation in 1968, the NEB's action represented a major step forward. It also in its own way showed how government support of enterprise can, if tempered, well managed, and done for the right reasons, be a positive force in the creation of vital new industries.

Since Celltech was established, Britain has developed the second largest number of biotechnology firms in Europe, bested only slightly by Germany. The UK's largest concentration of biotech companies now cluster around the very Golden Triangle of points that Fairtlough and his team had earlier identified. Toward the emergence of Cambridge's own locally concentrated cluster of biotech firms, Celltech served as a model for the first Cambridge-headquartered biotech start-up, Cantab Pharmaceuticals. Founded by Cambridge University professor Alan Munro in 1989, Cantab was formed after Munro had spent a sabbatical at Celltech to learn how a successful modern biotechnology firm operates. Fairtlough also served as an advisor to and investor in Cantab. Cantab in turn then became a model for much of the Cambridge biotech sector, helping to incite an interest in establishing firms throughout the immediate area.

Celltech's formation and development represents the type of fundamental transformation that had taken place with Cambridge's technology community in the span of only a few decades. When Celltech formed in 1980, it signified that Cambridge life scientists were, in a big way, being broken out of their sheltered existence from the Real World. Celltech's birth also represented the breaking of British officialdom's monopoly—and inaction—on patentable technologies generated by government-sponsored laboratories like the LMB. As a private enterprise, Celltech has demonstrated great strength; its stock market performance showing the company to be an unusually solid performer in a notoriously volatile sector. Celltech reinforced its links to Cambridge when in 1999 the company bought out the Cambridge-based biotech firm, Chiroscience, thereby finally establishing a direct corporate presence in the fens. The acquisition of Chiroscience also gave Celltech a new market capitalization of £696m, making the group Europe's most highly valued biotech firm at the time.[184] Most importantly for the Cambridge economy, by seeding the UK's biotech industry with Cambridge-originated technologies and providing special support and investment in the Cambridge cluster, Celltech has returned to the Phenomenon foundational building blocks for its own clustering of biotechnology enterprise.

## Sparking Phenomenal IT

Since its modest beginnings in the early 1990s, Cambridge's biotechnology sector has outpaced growth in all other high-tech sectors to represent now almost one-quarter of Cambridgeshire's total high-tech employment.[185] Yet the majority of the cluster's output still comes from the more traditional, physics-based sectors of high-tech. The activities of these IT- and engineering-related enterprises of the Phenomenon are distinct from those of Cambridge's biotech sector in several ways. For one, Cambridge IT firms evolved without the type of unique government assistance that benefited Celltech and have had to forge ahead largely on their own accord. Another major difference is that, while regional biotech firms tend to hold a broadly encompassing view of their technology community as part of an expansive "Golden Triangle," Cambridge physics-based high-tech firms tend to be much more locally focused—arguably parochial—and view the geographic core of their activities to be based within a small radius of roughly 15 miles from Cambridge University (see Figure 7.2 on page 143).

Cambridge IT start-ups came on the scene in noticeable numbers during the 1970s. There were various factors contributing to the surge in entrepreneurial activity. Silicon Valley had already been receiving worldwide attention for its activities and the accomplishments of its firms attracted widespread interest from scientific communities like Cambridge's. Changing regional demographics and attitudes in the university made the idea of starting a high-tech company more appealing a proposition than it had been in earlier years. Cambridge University also practised an extremely liberal policy toward intellectual property, allowing researchers to exploit their discoveries without the university demanding a percentage of royalties. In 1970, Trinity College founded the UK's first science park on the northern edge of Cambridge—a first, albeit timid, step by Cambridge academia to accommodate the presence of research-based high-tech industry. The Trinity College Science Park was, it should be noted, in no way akin in spirit to its Stanford equivalent. The Trinity development was not part of a grand vision, like that promoted by Fred Terman, to bring academia and industry together through mutually supportive cooperation that would in turn substantially develop the surrounding region. The park was not backed by a proactive recruitment drive and the initial response from the private sector was also far from overwhelming. Occupancy moved along at a slow rate—as late as 1979 the park was still characterized more by empty lots than built facilities. Nevertheless, the park's establishment was a watershed event, representing a departure from earlier policies in the post-war era where Cambridge had diligently turned away science-based businesses.

The first concerted effort at actively facilitating the region's nascent IT cluster came in July 1979 when around a dozen people involved with recently formed companies met in a pub near Cambridge's market square to consider ways to collaborate. One of the chief architects of this initiative was actually not a technology business leader, but a banker: Matthew Bullock, a Cambridge graduate and son of the famous Oxford University historian and Vice-Chancellor, Lord Bullock. Enjoying strong ties to Cambridge's academic and IT circles, Bullock had initiated a special loan program for technology companies at Barclays Bank in Cambridge. Out of the July pub gathering he became the leading organizer of what was dubbed the Cambridge Computer Group. (It was, incidentally, at this pub meeting when Bullock asked what people thought of the growing high-tech activity in the area. "Someone turned and simply said: 'What we have here is a phenomenon.'"[186] The moniker of the "Cambridge Phenomenon" has been in use ever since.)

As with the arrival of Trinity's Science Park, the changes the establishment of the Computer Group heralded were impressive but still nothing close to what had taken place in the Santa Clara Valley. In the area of finance, for example, Barclays' outreach efforts meant that new companies could more easily secure funding through loans and overdrafts. Yet this was a far cry from having nearby access to venture capital. Cambridge's veterans of high-tech businesses were also dwindling in number along with the fortunes of companies like CSI and

Pye. There were no senior members of either the academic or business communities to mentor the enterprises of the Phenomenon—young, relatively inexperienced managers like Bullock and the technopreneurs he worked with were left to figure out things on their own. Cambridge, furthermore, lacked a cadre of local professional firms interested in servicing the needs of the new companies—there was no equivalent of a Wilson Sonsini. Most of all, the university, though awakening to the positive dimensions of high-tech enterprises in the area, still kept a safe distance from the commercial sector. Apart from its hands-off stance on intellectual property and Trinity's creation of a partially occupied science park, there were no programs in place to promote the flow of knowledge between academia and industry. What was happening in Cambridge may have been phenomenal, but it would take some time before the environment could significantly aid the growth and competitiveness of firms in the embryonic cluster.

In these mixed atmospherics of positive stimuli but limited facilitation mechanisms, entrepreneurs persevered nonetheless. A 1984 report commissioned by the Cambridge Computer Group titled *The Cambridge Phenomenon* found that 100 new technology firms had started up in the area throughout the 1970s. By 1984 that number more than doubled, with some 260 firms operating as part of new (post-1960) high-tech growth in the region. These new-growth companies employed nearly 14,000, accounting for 17% of total jobs in the Cambridge travel-to-work area.[187] The data were touted as comparing favorably with the Bay Area, where there had been an estimated 250 high-tech firms established along the San Francisco Peninsula in the 1960s.[188] Cambridge was heralded as having "an 'effervescent' and dynamic business culture" that flourished not only in spite of the decline of companies like CSI and Pye, but in the face of poor national conditions: a "period of almost unabated economic recession in Britain."[189]

In the years since the 1979 pub meet, the cluster has amply demonstrated its "effervescence." Though lacking the support structure and ambitions of their Valley counterparts, Cambridge entrepreneurs keep building businesses. Cambridgeshire County Council figures indicate that the area is home to around 1,400 high-tech firms employing more than 40,000.[190] In 1984, 73% of technology firm start-ups in Cambridge were by local residents (the rest were the result of relocation or expansion of companies based outside the region). By 1998 the ratio of local firm start-ups had reached 86%.[191] Cambridge's entrepreneurial engines have if anything increased their resilience with time.

Recalling the 1984 comparison with Silicon Valley, however, it is striking how much Silicon Fen less and less resembles the world's largest cluster of high-tech. In the early 1980s, 20 years after a few hundred high-tech firms had been established in the Silicon Valley region, that cluster had developed massively sized corporations. It was on its way to pioneering entirely new global industries around technologies such as microprocessors, personal computers, workstations, applications software, and networked computing. At the start of the new millennium, some 20 years after 261 firms had arisen as part of the Phenomenon, Cambridge entrepreneurs can be found to be involved in exciting high-tech developments but no one is building companies of enormous size or pioneering entirely new industries. Instead, Cambridge firms have adapted to changing market conditions by becoming niche players, pursuing the "option numbers two and three" strategies that Andrew Grove and other managers at Intel had considered for their company in the mid-1980s. Cambridge high-tech firms are now characterized by their "avant-garde" and "special purpose" technologies that other companies focused on mass markets will avoid. Cambridge firms have been immensely successful with this strategy, many attaining high profitability and a select few reaching multi-billion pound market capitalizations. But pursuit of this strategy also means that the firms have yet, and are unlikely ever, to attain high sales revenue or employment figures. Cambridge's flagship IT firm, ARM Microprocessors (the closest thing the area has to an Intel) is a darling of the stock market and celebrated as the leader of a resurgence in world-beating, entrepreneurial technology business from the UK. Yet ARM only employs around 500 locally and posts annual sales of around £100m. In all of Cambridgeshire, less than 40 high-tech enterprises employ 200 or more people.[192] For years, it has been rare in Cambridge to find a high-tech firm employing more than 1,000.

None of these statistics point to failure on the part of entrepreneurs involved in the Cambridge Phenomenon to build businesses. They simply point to a different set of choices Cambridge entrepreneurs have made. The figures also underscore why good-versus-bad comparisons with Silicon Valley's cluster are irrelevant. It is revealing to see how and where the two high-tech regions have diverged in their separate evolutions but impossible to say which has done better or worse: the goals set out by the individuals involved in their respective developments are markedly different. Firms in both clusters stand out for their achievements in the markets in which they have chosen to compete.

The limited size of Cambridge's IT firms means that no companies have come to dominantly symbolize the successes of Phenomenon the way mega-corporations such as HP and Intel have for Silicon Valley. A sense of the cluster's economic progress, however, can be illustrated through highlights of the Phenomenon's more outstanding IT business sectors and its areas of technical expertise.

***Computer Companies.*** By far the most spectacular of start-ups from the early stage of the Phenomenon was the computer company Acorn. Founded in 1978 by Chris Curry, a self-taught engineer who had worked at the erratically performing Sinclair Radionics, and Hermann Hauser, a debonair Austrian who had completed a Ph.D. in solid-state physics at the Cavendish, Acorn was the closest the Phenomenon in its early days came to producing a noticeably exciting high-tech firm. Acorn exuded a style and market presence somewhat reminiscent of Apple, its fiercest global competitor. Beginning life with a total of £200 in start-up capital equally contributed by each founder, Acorn first sold assembled computer boards to enthusiasts through mail order. Building on early success, the young managers next took their firm into the mass market with a fully assembled computer, the Atom. Comparing its machine with the Apple II, Acorn boasted significant advantages: a superior operating system, a processing speed that was twice as fast, a clearer monitor resolution (one that was, moreover, in color), easy up-gradability, plus a network connection that was standard with every unit sold. Acorn's management was also aggressive. Putting together an eleventh-hour bid, Acorn won a contract with the British Broadcasting Corporation in 1981 to manufacture the BBC Micro. The contract gave the fledgling Cambridge firm an enormous boost. Acorn was now supplying a machine that was not only officially endorsed but was being featured in a TV series as part of a government campaign to increase computer literacy. The company's sales surged by 800% and Acorn came to dominate the UK's personal computer market. By 1984 the firm had nearly £100m in turnover and was being hailed by people like Industry, Information, and Technology Minister Kenneth Baker as a "sobering and encouraging little story" that should be "replicated and continued one hundred fold."[193]

Although enjoying tremendous success in its first few years, Acorn failed to expand further. Outside the UK, the company never became a big player in the world's PC markets. Its sales push into the US, executed when Acorn was at the height of its popularity in Britain, was strategically ill conceived and ended up depleting the company's financial resources just as the UK's PC market entered a major shake-out. In 1985, with trading in the firm's shares suspended and creditors clamoring for a wind-up, Acorn was acquired by the Italian conglomerate Olivetti. From there on, under various ownership arrangements, Acorn remained a well-regarded brand in the UK for its high-performance computers but its presence became increasingly insignificant. The firm retreated into fewer and less promising markets until finally stopping production of its last major computer product, high-end workstations, in 1998. It disappeared as a company entirely the next year.

Despite its difficulties and ultimate demise, Acorn unquestionably succeeded as a stimulant for the growth of other firms. There are now more than 30 companies in Cambridge that have formed as offshoots or invested enterprises of Acorn. Cambridge's most prominent high-tech firm, ARM Microprocessors, is a direct spin-out of Acorn's RISC processor design group. Acorn co-founder Hermann Hauser remains one of the most active leaders in the Cambridge cluster and is regarded by many to be the "Father of Silicon Fen." Throughout the 1990s he was Cambridge's most prolific venture capitalist; first as an "angel" investor (i.e., an investor of his own money) and since 1997 as a founding partner in Cambridge's best known formal venture capital firm, Amadeus. Hauser was also a driving force in the birth of the Cambridge Network, an umbrella networking and public outreach organization formed in 1998 that in many ways acts as a more evolved surrogate for the long-since defunct Cambridge Computer Group.

**Technology Consultancies.** The technology consultancy Cambridge Consultants Limited is another firm that despite earlier disaster has remained a central force in the ongoing generation of high-tech enterprise in Cambridge. With its founding in 1960, CCL pioneered what for Britain was then a radical concept: providing outsourced R&D to the nation's poorly performing manufacturing sectors. After a slow start, CCL expanded rapidly but failed to manage its growth adequately. Over-extension followed by poor earnings brought the company to its knees and it was purchased by the Cambridge, Massachusetts-based management and technology consultancy Arthur D. Little in 1972. CCL still acts as a major player in the cluster. As a source of new enterprise, it can be traced back as the origin of at least two mini-clusters of the Phenomenon: one formed around companies like itself (technology consultancies, sometimes referred to as R&D or science-based consultancies) and another formed around industrial ink-jet printing manufacturers.

Cambridge's concentration of major technology consultancies began when CCL's Director of Electronics, Gordon Edge, left CCL in 1970 to establish a technology center for the London-based management consulting firm, PA. The PA Technology Centre later begat Scientific Generics (also founded by Edge) and then The Technology Partnership—all have prospered and deepened the region's base of enterprises dedicated to innovation services. These consultancies have further served, at first inadvertently but now by strategic design, as incubators of numerous spin-offs. The CCL spin-out Domino Printing gave rise to an "Ink-Jet Alley" north of Cambridge along the A14 highway that currently produces a large portion of the world's industrial ink-jet systems. Because of defense contract work begun in the 1980s, CCL also developed an expertise in wireless communication chips. Some of CCL's wireless communication chip experts later created, with the company's blessing and investment, a 1998 spin-out, Cambridge Silicon Radio. CSR has already grown into a large (200-plus employees) company for Cambridge and shows potential to become a major player in its global niche markets.

**Communications.** An early seeder of communications and telecommunications technology capabilities in Cambridge was Pye. Various communications technology research groups in the university have also contributed spin-outs. Even scientists engaged in the rarified field of radio astronomy have started several firms, the best known being Cambridge Positioning Systems, a company formed in the 1990s to offer location-fixing technology for mobile phones. All of Cambridge's major technology consultancies have also produced spin-outs involved in telecommunications. In 1985 network communications guru David Cleevely augmented Cambridge's base of scientific consultancies by founding a high-profile telecom strategy consultancy, Analysys. From out of The Generics Group consultancy, telecommunications engineer Nigel Playford ventured out on his own to establish the fixed wireless telephone network firm Ionica in 1991—for a brief time Cambridge's best performing venture of the decade with 1,000 employees and a spectacular IPO that made it the first Cambridge firm to acquire a one-billion-dollar capitalization. Ionica ended up pursuing a business strategy that was poorly thought out and had the company engaging in a turf war with the British Telecom monopoly over the local phone services market. Not surprisingly, Ionica lost this battle, going bankrupt barely a year after its headline-grabbing IPO. Of ongoing benefit to the cluster, however, Playford and other managers from Ionica stayed involved in the area and went on to start or join other local ventures.

Other technology consultancies such as The Technology Partnership and PA Technology have also spun out successful mobile communications technology firms such as TTP Com and Ubinetics.


**Computer Science and Computer Networking**. In the areas of computer science and computer–computer communications, Cambridge has long enjoyed outstanding technical capabilities. Only recently, however, has any commercial success in these fields attracted much attention.

Even before Cambridge had a railway station, the town was the workplace of the world's first computer scientist, Charles Babbage. Babbage was a great eclectic who, as holder of the Lucasian Chair of Mathematics (the same post once occupied by Isaac Newton and today held by Stephen Hawking), assembled a digital mechanical calculator in 1832. Babbage went on to envision an "analytical engine"—a device whose punched-card data inputs, memory storage, and sequential control mechanisms essentially described the functions of the first generation of modern computers that emerged in the mid-20th century. Subsequent computer pioneers in Cambridge include Alan Turing, the famous World War Two code-breaker and artificial intelligence theorist, and Maurice Wilkes who in 1949 invented the world's first programmable electronic digital computer.

Despite Cambridge's historical leadership in computer science, no computer-related businesses of even remotely proportional stature to this scientific capability ever emerged until the 1970s when firms like Acorn appeared on the scene. Cambridge's ruling powers also rejected the sort of investment from computer technology giants that San Jose courted so assiduously. In the 1950s IBM selected Cambridge as the location for its European research facilities. It turned out that, though IBM may have chosen Cambridge, Cambridge did not choose IBM. Big Blue's planning application was summarily rejected by local officials and the company located its European R&D operations to Switzerland instead.

In the 1990s Cambridge entrepreneurs built successful companies on the back of Internet-related technologies. Cambridge became home to Britain's first commercial Internet service provider, PIPEX, with that company's establishment in 1992. PIPEX's founder, Peter Dawe, had previously worked as the head of engineering for a Phenomenon firm that he felt was ignoring too many promising market opportunities. Wanting to do more than the pace of work that his employer allowed, Dawe took notice of a US-made Internet protocol software package that was gathering dust on the company's shelves. Purchasing its UK sales rights, he started up his own software marketing firm and later took the additional step to found PIPEX. Dawe has since left PIPEX (which he sold to MCI/Worldcom) but has stayed active in the cluster as a serial entrepreneur, angel investor, and outspoken voice in the debate about how best to develop the Cambridge region while retaining the area's cherished environmental qualities.

With the UK Web-based enterprises that have arisen in the wake of PIPEX's founding, Cambridge did not become a hotbed for dotcoms (which tended to take root in London) but it did become a breeding ground for Web technology firms such as Muscat (a producer of Web search engines), Zeus (Web server software), and, of particular repute, Autonomy (which makes neural network-based information management software). Zeus, founded in 1995 by two Cambridge undergraduates operating in a college dormitory room, grew to the point that in 2000 it took over the landmark facilities vacated by the failed Ionica. *Fortune* magazine introduced Autonomy, which has its principal offices located in both San Francisco and Cambridge, to the world at large by officially anointing it a "cool company" in 1998.[194] The coolness factor is underscored by the personal style of Autonomy's CEO, Dr. Mike Lynch—a man who, along with his arcane knowledge of Baysean algorithms, exhibits a mod taste for clothes and a sardonic sense of humor that violates the stereotypical image of a Cambridge University computer scientist. In response to Tony Blair's call to arms—the rallying cry for Silicon Fen to beat Silicon Valley—it is widely understood that Lynch dryly remarked: "Having Cambridge take on Silicon Valley is like having a seagull fly into the engine of a 747." Lynch claims this is a misquote, stating that what he really said was that if one thinks of Silicon Valley as a jet, Cambridge is a "seagull" that should fly alongside, rather than *into*, Silicon Valley's powerful engines.[195] Faithfully quoted or not, the oft-repeated utterance has obtained mythic proportions to become something of a cult refrain within the local high-tech community. The deeper truth of the remark is its accurate characterization of the cluster's ironic sense of itself.

The seagull quote also captures something of the Cambridge cluster's psyche and capacity that national politicians, outside observers, and wistful-minded insiders typically overlook: Cambridge's entrepreneurs are basically content with building small-scale niche enterprises. A politician wants a Cisco. A Cambridge entrepreneur wants at most an ARM and many will happily settle for much less.

That is not to say that Cambridge could not become a cluster that includes mega-corporations. It *is* to say that lingering attitudes and prevailing conditions in the business environment make that possibility exceedingly unlikely. Until entrepreneurs from the commercial and other sectors seek to marshal the range of resources necessary to change key elements of the cluster's operating parameters, large-scale firm growth will remain more vision than reality.

As with the previous section on Silicon Valley, the next two chapters of this section on Silicon Fen will examine the present-day dimensions of the cluster's dynamics and the experiences and methods of leading innovators. These explorations will get further at the root causes of why the Cambridge cluster operates the way it does while considering the managerial insights the Phenomenon offers.

# Cambridge Dynamics 9

The 19th century clergyman and novelist Charles Kingsley observed in a fittingly evocative yet enigmatic line that "Cambridge lies in an attitude of magnificent repose, and shaking lazy ears stares at her elder sister, asks what it is all about."[196] What the area, now in the guise of its technological Phenomenon, is "all about" has hardly become any less mystifying with the passage of time. If Silicon Valley is best conceived of as a state of mind, Silicon Fen is best pondered as a riddle; whereas the Valley is a series of "wow!" events the Phenomenon is more often a series of "why's?"

Taking a closer look at the how's and why's of Cambridge's present-day dynamics, this chapter begins by examining the major features of Cambridge's built environment. Physical infrastructure loomed large in the plans of Silicon Valley's strategists who worked to ensure that the area could attract and accommodate substantial economic growth. Cambridge has had nothing like this. Commercial and residential developments are of limited scale; key high-tech enterprises are frequently prohibited from expanding. The area's meager road system became congested almost as soon as the Phenomenon took off. In the fenland biome, the built environment is dwarfed by the natural; the trappings of the infrastructure expected for a global technopolis are hard to find.

These physical constraints are but the proverbial tip of the iceberg, the more obvious manifestations of impediments to firm growth whose roots stretch down to matters of popular will, political economy, social structure, and personal identity. With an understanding of these constraints to business growth, it becomes clear that, unlike the sort of mismanagement that characterized Cambridge's earlier technology firms, the management styles that typify the Phenomenon's exclusively small-firm economic base are not the result of entrepreneurs failing to appreciate the requirements for running competitive capitalist enterprise. Rather, Cambridge management techniques reflect how local entrepreneurs have accommodated their personal goals for developing companies and the region. Management of Cambridge firms also must contend with a NIMBYist antagonism to economic development from today's local residents and a living tradition in local government for suppressing technology business growth.

The creative dynamics of the cluster are shaped by the innovative ways in which individual entrepreneurs respond to these forces and the means by which leaders of the Phenomenon are working to make the business climate more conducive to firm formation, collaboration, and growth.

## THE LOGISTICS OF LOCATION

Modern forms of transportation have never been a Cambridge strongpoint. The perils of navigating the fens were finally eradicated in the 19th century, but in the sectors where Phenomenon companies compete today it is important to have ready access to places like San Francisco or Tokyo. Yet getting to any transcontinental destination from Cambridge can be a chore. Stansted and Luton—Cambridge's closest major international airports—have existed for decades as part of a greater London air transport system but, apart from occasional flirtation with ex-EU routes, generally only provide service to domestic and intra-European destinations. Cambridge's own small airport provides a shuttle to Amsterdam but is otherwise cut off from direct access to destinations in countries important to the Cambridge cluster. For direct flights to anywhere beyond Europe, one is faced with the prospect of about two hours of travel in moderate traffic to fly out of London's notoriously crowded Heathrow Airport. The situation is not dire but, for a center of advanced technology that relies on global mobility, compared with other major Siliconia, the airport infrastructure connecting Silicon Fen to the world outside provides more drag than stimulus for the cluster.

Airport proximity and other transport advantages are among the major reasons foreign high-tech multinational corporations locate their headquarters and sales and service operations along the M4 Corridor and, apart from R&D functions, essentially shun Cambridge.

Cambridge's road system presents another set of problems. The M11 motorway, which emanates out from London and passes through the cluster, flows well enough but is not Silicon Fen's principal transport link. That role is occupied by the A14 dual carriageway, a limited-capacity highway whose traffic volume has trebled since 1981.[197] The section of the A14 running between Cambridge and Huntingdon, the cluster's transportation artery, ranks among the most congested portions of Britain's trunk-road system.[198] The gridlock is bad enough to have earned the carriageway the nickname "the road from Hell." The worsening conditions are compounded by a patchwork of local surface roads of only one or two lanes per direction. The usual clogging that occurs during peak hours turns into near paralysis in the event of accidents or road construction work. Traffic congestion has already been cited or suspected as a reason for firms moving out of Cambridge's landmark Science Park complex.

The most efficient means of ground transport available is the train although coverage is limited. In the first half of the 20th century local industry benefited by Cambridge serving as a regional railway hub. Britain's post-war government dismantled the regional rail system, however, and today the main advantage of train transport for the cluster is a one-hour express service to London. Such enhancements have not been supporting the cluster for long, though: trains to Cambridge were not even electrified until 1987. The location of Cambridge's train station, which unusually for a city is located a full mile away from the city center, is also a lasting reminder of the university's 19th century reactionaryism. When rail links to Cambridge were first proposed, university authorities strenuously fought against their introduction until finally yielding to an 1844 Act of Parliament. One of the university's hard-fought concessions was to banish the station to a location as far from town as possible. The dons moreover won special privileges like the right for university authorities to board trains at will in search of under-graduates trying to escape their sequestered existence.

Location also says something about the intended role of the Cambridge Science Park. Developed in the 1970s on derelict land owned by Trinity College, the park provided the first site in the vicinity of the university to welcome high-tech business. In the wake of local policies that had actively discouraged industrial build-up, the park's land-scaped plots offered a kind of sanctuary for entrepreneurs or corporations wanting to set up in the emergent cluster. Still, the park's location on the city's northern fringe (at least three miles from any university science facility), defeats the possibility of regular, casual interaction between the academic community of the town center and the business community of the park. Considering the political context out of which it emerged, the park in effect functions to keep high-tech near to Cambridge but, like the railway station, at the same time distant enough to be comfortably out of the way. Cambridge's leading technology incubation facility, the St. John's Innovation Centre (built in the 1980s on another parcel of fallow college land directly opposite Trinity's Science Park) and other developments nearby have enhanced the benefits of the park's overall location. But this newer complex of facilities still remains remote in terms of the spatial dynamics of the university and cluster, a remoteness only intensified by the worsening traffic congestion.

People have at least recently been taking positive steps to improve aspects of the Science Park complex and expand on the facilities and programs related to university–industry interactivity. In 2000, a young restaurant entrepreneur struck a joint venture with Trinity College to create the Science Park's first multi-purpose building for conferences and informal socializing: the Q.ton Forum. Cluster leaders like Hermann Hauser also have lobbied successfully for the establishment of a Cambridge University Entrepreneurship Centre that was founded in that same year. University–industry interaction has been bolstered further by the efforts of university Vice-Chancellor Alec Broers. An Australian-born former IBM executive, Broers has distinguished himself by being not only tolerant but personally supportive of technology build-up in the region. One of the biggest projects he has championed is development of the West Cambridge Site, a large research complex built around the Cavendish Laboratory, which since Broers' tenure has attracted new funding from such American high-tech luminaries as Bill Gates and Gordon Moore.

The university's swelling enthusiasm for synergistic relations with the commercial world has yet, however, to be shared by local planning authorities and residents. The political climate in the county district of South Cambridgeshire, which has jurisdiction over development of land abutting the university, has been particularly hostile toward the expansion of technology enterprise. Famous cases of recent years include rejecting the Generics Group's request to double their modestly sized facilities and blocking a £100m extension of the Wellcome Trust's Genome Campus. Wellcome became so frustrated that in 1999, after three years of pressing its case, it began looking for more supportive locations in Germany and the US. Tellingly, the Stanford Research Park was among the sites it considered for relocation.[199]

Rather than looking to Silicon Valley as a benchmark for Cambridge, residents and planning authorities are more likely to invoke Silicon Valley as representing exactly the type of location they *do not want* Silicon Fen to become. Arguing against plans to increase the supply of local housing, a resident in a South Cambridgeshire village that neighbors the Science Park declared: "We don't want a huge metropolis ... just go to Silicon Valley in California to see just how oppressive urban sprawl on this scale is."[200] However much sincerity (or intentional irony) is voiced in the debate over the cluster's growth, the virulence is hard to ignore, as evidenced by the comments of one concerned citizen:

> Many a farmer is now under siege from all directions because land is wanted by developers. They want land owned by both the aristocracy and the monarchy and they will destroy them both to satisfy their greed. Now is the time to stand up for Queen and countryside, take arms against a sea of International Business Men, and, by opposing, end them.[201]

## ORIGINS OF THE COUNTERREVOLUTION

References to "Silicon Valley" and "International Business Men" can give the misleading impression that anti-growth sentiments are a simple reflex against the modern form of aggregated high-tech enterprise in Cambridge. But, as the previous chapter showed, antagonism to technology-driven development has long been a recurring theme in the evolution of knowledge-intensive enterprise in Cambridge. A closer look at ways in which the local power structure has been responding to the forces of industrial progress since the 19th century sheds light on how and why Cambridge's political economy still works to reign in development of the high-tech cluster today.

The changes conservative factions at the university feared would follow the arrival of the railroad did indeed occur. By 1860, 15 years after Cambridge's out-of-the-way railway station began operating, the population of Cambridge had swelled from 20,000 residents to 45,000.[202] A migrated working class and the factories in which they labored coalesced around the railway station and urbanized the outlying parts of the town. University reforms—abandonment of mandatory religious tests, the creation of experimental science faculties, the general expansion of university facilities—stimulated growth of the academic population and fueled local economic development. Led by CSI and Pye, Cambridge became home to such technology-oriented industries as scientific instruments, electrical and wireless products, chemical manufacturing, and engineering services. Jobs in Cambridge were plentiful. Unlike the high-tech "semi-desert" that appeared in the Bay Area during the Depression years, high-tech businesses remained in Cambridge. In 1931 local unemployment was only an estimated 2%. Between that year and 1948 employment in the sectors of scientific instruments and electrical/wireless products grew 163% and 130%, respectively.[203]

Despite what would by most standards of today be considered positive change—solid but not runaway growth accompanied by the creation of an advanced industrial base—the Cambridge establishment still did not welcome the transformations taking place. Shortly after the conclusion of World War Two, local government authorities and the university formed a committee chaired by a respected expert on town planning, Professor William Holford of University College, London. Holford's committee was charged to focus singularly on the "problems" brought by growth and recommend a course of action. The committee's findings were distilled in a document, commonly referred to as the *Holford Report*, issued in 1950. This report articulated a vision, the Holford Principles, that has served as a guidepost for local planning policy ever since.

The inductive logic of *Holford* emanated from two central assumptions. The first was that the people of Cambridge simply did not want any further economic development. "One has the impression," a key observation of this type runs, "that in each decade since 1900 many people in the town have been dismayed at this continuous growth and have hoped that they would soon see an end of it." The second article of faith asserted that it was incumbent upon local authorities to protect the citizenry from the onslaught of development, arguing that "unless preventive measures can be agreed and carried out Cambridge will grow rapidly ... if this happens the average citizen of Cambridge will gain nothing and lose a great deal."[204]

Consequently, *Holford* called for limiting all variety of growth: population, buildings, businesses. It took specific aim at high-tech sectors—what the study refers to with alarm as those "go-ahead scientific industries"—and considered them to be the most likely culprits for greater Cambridge to "grow quickly unless active measures stop this happening."[205] The document goes to lengths to emphasize that halting growth was all for the benefit of the general public, repeatedly claiming to speak for the "average" or "ordinary citizen." The report does, almost as an aside, concede that it also had the interests of the university at heart, noting that it is "the body most likely to suffer from a rapid growth in the town's population."[206] It is rather short on tangibly describing why growth would harm the university, however. In one instance, *Holford* speculates that collegiate athletics might be adversely

impacted—an assertion that rests on the assumption that, to accommodate a larger population, college sports grounds would by necessity
have to be converted into housing sites. *Holford* was not so opposed to development as to completely ignore the benefits of at least some change.
It admitted that one aspect of modern life, "a public indoor swimming
pool," had the potential to improve local living conditions.[207] But it
was perfectly clear that Cambridge did not need additional economic development if all the town really lacked were the blessings of indoor
swimming.

The sometimes dubious logic that pervades *Holford* naturally invites
speculation about ulterior motives. The notion that college sports
grounds were under threat, for example, was completely false. As
college property, developers would be unable to force the colleges to
forfeit their lands. At the same time, continued growth could easily be
seen to threaten the ancient economic structures of the colleges. The university and the colleges have traditionally been, and are today, the single
largest employer in the Cambridge area. Providing the local population
with increased job opportunities and higher wages would work against
keeping the costs of living and employment at the low levels the
colleges had enjoyed for centuries. Whatever the real reasons for the
university's antagonism, the report is notable for the uncompromising
nature of its viewpoints—the total disregard for any positive changes
that thoughtfully managed economic growth might bring. *Holford*
utterly ignores the opportunities to strive for a balance: that development
could somehow be accommodated while still preserving designated
areas of historic and ecological value. Instead, the committee resorted to
dogmatic assertions: "It is impossible to make a good expanding plan
for Cambridge. ... no advantage in further growth."[208] The Holford
committee was of course entrepreneurial, exhibiting great creativity in
their lines of reasoning. They were also, like any innovator or entrepreneur, seizing an opportunity. Yet the opportunity seized was to lead
the area backward, not forward. The team, in fact, expressed great pride
in the novelty of its proposal: "We make this recommendation with full
appreciation of the difficulty of carrying it out. No ancient town

comparable with Cambridge has ever tried to limit its population. Until very recently nearly every town has tried to attract population."[209]

The reasoning of the Holford Principles interestingly compares with that of Fred Terman's Steeples of Excellence. Both Holford and Terman were united in the goal of bolstering a university's scientific research capabilities. Where the two leaders differed was on how to realize this objective. Terman believed that industrial upgrading was key, that developing a "strong and independent industry" would be good for Stanford and good for the region. Holford and his committee, on the other hand, asserted: "the Government desires to expand University education, especially on the science side; and we have tried to show that the work of the University would be hampered, and probably gravely obstructed, if Cambridge grows rapidly."[210] Terman had been inspired by the windfall of benefits he saw in the technology-based industrialization that had occurred around Stanford's East Coast academic rival, MIT. Holford and his team were likewise inspired by the industrial build-up that had taken place around Cambridge's academic rival, Oxford—*negatively* inspired. The Holford Committee saw automotive industry growth around Oxford as evidence of a "lopsided expansion" and feared that industrialization "of this kind might repeat at Cambridge the story of Oxford."[211] The two divergent lines of interpretation meant that at the middle of the 20th century, a crucially formative period for laying the groundwork to accommodate the next generation of IT industries, the Santa Clara Valley and Cambridge's fenlands were prepared to respond to future opportunities according to sharply opposed ideals.

In the years since the recommendations of the *Holford Report* were instigated, the combination of attempts by local authorities to adhere to artificial growth caps while progressive forces have pushed Cambridge's high-tech economy forward has brought about predictable results: skyrocketing prices for residential and business real estate, higher costs for goods and services, neighboring villages and towns caught unprepared for spillover population growth, and traffic that grinds to an infuriating standstill.[212] The costs in terms of lost opportunities for industrial upgrading have been even higher. *Holford* made basic concessions to pure research enterprises, those that had existing "connections with the scientific work of the University."[213] Yet the report sought to banish all high-tech manufacturing, including light-manufacturing activities like product prototyping, from the immediate vicinity of the university and town. Such production-related operations, the very seeds of an industrial cluster, were designated to locate no closer than 14–18 miles from town. The outer limits of this "exclusion zone" in fact exceed the boundaries of what would later become the Cambridge Phenomenon (see Figure 7.2 on page 143). In effect, the intent of implementing the Holford Principles was to prevent anything on the order of the Cambridge Phenomenon from ever occurring.

As little as a decade after the Holford Principles were adopted as official policy, university science faculty began reaping the negative consequences of their anti-growth regime. Even acceptable, nonmanufacturing scientific research organizations that established themselves in Cambridgeshire but outside the town of Cambridge proved to be located too far away to achieve the close collaboration with the university. University scientists discovered that after having helped with the establishment of these enterprises, cooperative activity quickly dropped off. The companies became simply co-locational—sharing general proximity to the university but not working with faculty and students in any meaningful way.

The first concerted attempt at halting this trend was organized in 1967 by Professor Nevill Mott, Director of the Cavendish Laboratory and a future Nobel laureate for his work on noncrystalline semiconductors. Mott qualifies as a revolutionary in the Schumpeterian sense, but the struggle he led was not one that intended a storming of the Bastille. The university committee Mott headed accepted the basic integrity of the Holford Principles, adding—in what seems to be a rationalization for the planning authority's earlier rejection of IBM's proposed R&D operations—that "research laboratories employing a thousand or more scientists and technicians ... would, in the Sub-Committee's view, be undesirable for this area."[214] The committee also echoed *Holford* in opposing "research based units from developing into large-scale manu-facturing processes."[215] In completely rejecting manufacturing and any sizable commercial research activity, Mott's team may have been expressing their own elitist biases or simply offering a realistic appraisal of the situation, recognizing that a full-fledged attack on the Holford Principles would have been suppressed outright.

Whatever their reasons, Mott's committee did at least advocate a change in policy to allow "desirable" small-scale commercial research activity, the kind that in total would bring in no more than an additional 1,500–2,000 high-tech workers.[216] The figure warrants repeating. The *total* increase Mott proposed for the high-tech working population of Cambridge was a maximum of 2,000 people. To consolidate this small-scale activity and exempt it from the entrenched no-growth policies of local authorities, Mott and his team advocated establishing a science park, a proposal which the leadership of Trinity College acted on in 1970. The design and intent of Trinity's Science Park clearly shows how not all such developments are created equal, nor are they somehow responsible for unleashing a snowballing set of processes that then create a thriving cluster. What saved Cambridge from becoming little more than a curious footnote in the history of Siliconia was not the establishment of the science park but the entrepreneurs who never limited themselves to the compromised growth targets set out by the *Mott Report* and the park that was developed based on its recommendations. *Mott* had marginally overturned the restrictions of *Holford*, but local entrepreneurs have totally overthrown the modified restrictions of *Mott*. They and their enterprises are the ones responsible for the cluster's "phenomenally" effervescent vibrancy, growth, and job creation.

## BROADER CONTEXTS

The rationale and actions of the Holford and Mott committees, like those taken by Fred Terman and "Dutch's Panzer Division," reflect aspects of differing national attitudes and policy frameworks. Hamann and Terman utilized opportunities that arose during an expansionary post-war America: from copious US government funding made available for military-related research to important aid packages like the 1956 Federal Highway Act, which helped state and local authorities to shape what became the Valley's freeway system. Similarly, the Holford and Mott Committees found inspiration and justification for their basic stances to restrict growth in the tenets of British national policies like the Town and Country Planning Act of 1947. Divergent national conditions helped people like Hamann and Holford promote their respective visions to the communities they served. By the same token, it cannot be said that national conditions ultimately determined the development of these regions. Valley entrepreneurs and community leaders did far more than rely on federal assistance to develop their cluster of high-tech; Cambridge's visceral antagonism toward modern economic development stood out even among the heavy-handed bureaucratic controls put on business activity by post-war British governments. Initiatives taken at the local level, both in businesses and in policy-making bodies, have provided the final defining characteristics of the ways in which these divergent clusters have evolved and now function.

Bearing in mind the primacy of actions taken at the local level, it is still informative to see how matters of not only local but also national dimensions influence the Cambridge cluster's verve. In particular, two aspects of the larger milieu stand out: Britain's financial regime and its social norms. Both the UK's financial regulations and various social characteristics particular to Britain undeniably positively influence the Phenomenon. But to understand why this indigenously entrepreneurial, effervescently vibrant cluster remains of such limited economic mass requires an appreciation of the hindrances posed by these factors as well.

## Financial Regimes

**Taxation.** When Peter Mandelson visited Silicon Valley in 1998 as the UK Secretary of Trade and Industry, he was eager to promote Britain as having the Right Stuff to generate the investment enthusiasm he saw in the Bay Area. "We are intensely relaxed," he said in a peculiar turn of phrase, "about people getting filthy rich," quickly rushing to add: "as long as they pay their taxes."[217] Therein lies the rub; taxation poses many difficulties for operating a high-tech enterprise in the UK. Cambridge business leaders like ARM Chairman Robin Saxby, for example, have stridently criticized UK policies on taxing employee share options. As for investors in high-tech businesses, they have for years faced a maximum capital gains tax rate of 40%, twice as high as that in the US. After persistent complaints from the business community, the rate was finally lowered in 2001 so that for assets held for at least two years, the capital gains rate drops to 10%, one-half that in the US. This is a positive step toward improving the tax environment, one of several the Blair government deserves credit for advancing, but other developments in the area of taxation have been found to add burdens as well. For example, incremental improvements to share option taxation are seen by many high-tech businesses as confusing and incomplete. Another deeply unpopular statute introduced in 2000 known as IR 35 in effect increased taxes on independent contractors—a sizable component of Britain's free-floating pool of high-tech, especially software, professionals. After decades of organized labor in strident conflict with British industry, the way IR 35 reduces flexibility in Britain's IT sector seems particularly inappropriate at this stage of the country's industrial modernization.

***British Venture Capital.*** Venture capital in the UK simultaneously points to strong and weak points in the nation's financial infrastructure. Britain's £7.8b worth of annual VC investments makes it home to the largest and most developed market for VC finance in all Europe (and worldwide is second only to the US).[218] This prominence, however, belies a quality of British VC that makes most of it more properly labeled merchant venture capital. A Bank of England study found that the proportion of what constitutes truly high-risk VC investments in the UK comprised only 1% of all venture capital funding. Investments in early-stage technology firms fared even worse, accounting "for only a part of this already small total."[219] Danny Chapchal, while serving as CEO of Cambridge Display Technology, lamented that diehard conservatism among British financiers means that: "We have capitalists but there's no venture involved."[220] British venture capital remains primarily a funding mechanism for management buyouts and buy-ins. As a percentage of GDP, the UK puts in three times less venture capital into high-tech companies than does the US.[221]

***Capital Markets.*** In 1980 the London Stock Exchange introduced a second-tier market to allow the trading of shares in young companies with a limited corporate track record. In the 1990s that market was replaced by a newly structured one, the Alternative Investment Market—an attempt to simplify further and ease the process of securing a public listing for small firms. Despite such progress in the restructuring of markets, liquidity has been drying up for smaller quoted company shares. Consolidation among Britain's financial firms has meant that institutional investors and fund managers, the dominant players in the UK's equity markets, are increasing the size of the minimum amounts they invest. This effectively eliminates the prospects for them putting money into small capitalized firms. The Department of Trade and Industry has reported that small-cap companies have been finding "their businesses poorly valued and researched. . . . Their cost of capital has increased and the ability to attract high caliber staff has diminished."[222]

Europe's first pan-European exchange, Easdaq (which along with crossing fragmented national capital market boundaries has the advantage of being small firm-friendly), only came into existence in 1996—a full 25 years after its model, America's Nasdaq. Easdaq, moreover, may imitate Nasdaq with its name and market model, but it is a long way from attaining the crucial bottom-line characteristics of its US counterpart. Even in the pre-crash heyday of technology stocks in 2000, Easdaq was listing slightly more than 60 companies with a combined market capitalization of €30b ($28b); Nasdaq was listing over 5,000 companies with a capitalization of $4t. Poor liquidity in the new pan-European exchange is worsened by the policies of some fund managers who refuse to purchase Easdaq-quoted shares. Recently created exchanges like Germany's Neuer Markt (owned by the Deutsche Bourse) and the UK's TechMark (owned by the London Stock Exchange) offer better volumes, capitalizations, and liquidity but boast nothing close to Nasdaq's statistics and, equally importantly, are part of the problem of having nationally based exchanges—a situation which merely contributes to the continued fragmentation of Europe's region-wide capital market structure. Overall, any small, growing firm in the UK (or elsewhere in Europe) faces the kind of obstacles in going to domestic and pan-European capital markets for funding that are unheard of in the US.

**Investment Advertizement.** Section 57 of the 1986 Financial Services Act criminalizes the pitching of a new business plan to potential angel investors whom an entrepreneur has never met. The law was designed with good intent—to protect unsuspecting individuals from being misled into illegitimate investments—but its application has produced unique absurdities. For example, at business angel network meetings, management teams are prohibited from presenting to their assembled audience estimations for a start-up's financial growth. There are ways of finessing the law but the net result is to make the process of securing angel financing that much less direct and unnecessarily cumbersome. Nigel Brown, who runs the largest association of angel investors in Cambridge, has creatively solved the problem by arranging for breakout sessions when investors gather to hear formal business plan pitches. In these post-presentation gatherings, supplicant management teams and potential investors introduce themselves to one another. Since after personal introductions and "shaking hands" the two sides are considered legally "familiar" to one another, the management team can then safely present their financial projections. "If you don't find a mechanism for getting around this," Brown explains, "in order to raise just a little seed money a company is going to have to issue a prospectus. And the prospectus is going to cost—I don't know—100–150 grand. If the law was actually applied, nobody would start a business, in effect. The government has removed *caveat emptor* from the marketplace."[223]

## Social Norms

For the development of a high-tech region like Cambridge, aspects of national and local social norms play a multifaceted role. In economic terms, Britain (specifically England) is the birthplace of an individualistic, equity-based "Anglo-Saxon" style of capitalism: the very expression of capitalist existence that seems to serve the US so well. As limitations with the UK's financial infrastructure illustrate, however, the benefits of Britain's "equity culture" can be offset by more fundamental issues. Within the context of Europe at least, Britain's socio-economic environment offers its own sets of opportunities. As Hermann Hauser, replying in 1981 to an incredulous British reporter who asked why he chose the UK of all places to start Acorn Computers, the future "Father of Silicon Fen" observed: "Where else can you set up your own business for a mere £100? In Germany, it costs far more to start a company and on top of that there are expensive social benefits. This country is packed with people with clever individualistic ideas, whereas in Germany there is a feeling that if it is a good idea why don't Siemens develop it."[224]

The social parameters in which a regional economy functions can, depending on the outlook of innovators or entrepreneurs, be perceived as either an inducement or impediment to their efforts. Regardless of how important the social norms or "culture" of a cluster may seem, these elements by themselves serve as a poor basis for understanding a cluster's performance, let alone its relevance to the world at large. Culturally influenced behavior inevitably differs between societies. The challenge for those pushing forward the development of a cluster is to work within the context of an endogenous value system, to find ways to stimulate commercial creativity without destroying a local area's sense of identity. In the case of a cluster like Cambridge's, it can at least be said that however its constituents perceive the significance of the social norms with which they must contend, the Phenomenon's social dynamics present their own unique obstacles to any quest for building up economic mass.

**Getting on with Things.** In England, or perhaps more precisely, in Cambridge, the general expectation is for individuals to simply "get on with things" when it comes to developing new ideas; not busy themselves with selling a concept. Cliquish networking among one's social set is practised as a fine art, but schmoozing with strangers in order to talk up a business plan is considered gauche (not to mention illegal in some cases according to the Financial Services Act). No less a personage than Nigel Brown, Cambridge's master networker, expresses mystification at the way people go about building up their businesses:

> It never ceases to amaze me, considering how diligent we are, how many companies emerge through the pages of the local newspapers that we never heard of. And we're trying really hard. We have a very big network and we get into most nooks and crannies. But still we miss things. ... I think it's a reflection of the entrepreneurial spirit in a perverse way. It's just people "getting on with things" before they start joining in and talking to others. I know that's different from America where people go and talk around a lot and then they get on with it. But here I think people just start something in the garage and go from there. Cambridge has always been a very difficult place to figure out actually.[225]

James Watson, the American who with Englishman Francis Crick identified DNA's molecular structure at the Cavendish Laboratory in 1953, went so far as to attribute English notions of propriety as having held back early genetic research at Cambridge. Before Crick and Watson began their research in earnest, another scientist, Professor Maurice Wilkins at King's College in London, had already begun similar investigations. Thus:

> ... molecular work on DNA in England was, for all practical purposes, the personal property of Maurice Wilkins ... It would have looked very bad if

Francis had jumped in on a problem that Maurice had worked over for several years.

The problem was even made worse because the two, almost equal in age, knew each other and, before Francis remarried, had frequently met for lunch or dinner to talk about science. It would have been much easier if they had been living in different countries. The combination of England's cosiness— all the important people, if not related by marriage, seemed to know one another—plus the English sense of fair play would not allow Francis to move in on Maurice's problem. In France, where fair play obviously did not exist, these problems would not have arisen. The States also would not have permitted such a situation to develop. One would not expect someone at Berkeley to ignore a first-rate problem merely because someone at Cal Tech had started first. In England, however, it simply would not look right.[226]

The sense of probity that held back Crick's research efforts noticeably differs from the productive competition waged between the nearby rivals of Stanford and UC Berkeley—a rivalry that helped establish and spur forward Silicon Valley's scientific research base. With England's "cozy" social relationships the problem is not that there is a lack of personal networks but that the expected behavior for members of such networks can serve to stifle as much as aid the transmission of ideas.

English society may have moved on from the norms of the mid-20th century but research shows that the practice of collaboration in Cambridge has progressed only slightly in the very industry that the discovery of DNA made possible. A 1999 study by the economic consultancy SQW surveyed biotechnology companies in the East of England (the wider territory that encompasses Cambridgeshire) to find out how much value they placed on local business linkages. Results showed that more than a third of firms considered linkages with local customers to be "critical/very important" and 20–25% of firms similarly rated as "critical/very important" ties to local suppliers, venture capital sources, university faculties, and other research organizations.[227] The report concluded that biotech industry in the region thus represents "much more than a co-presence of organizations: in supply-chain terms, it really is *functioning* as a cluster and the organizations within it are enjoying the commercial benefits of co-location."[228]

The findings do of course indicate that a significant proportion of firms highly value local relationships, but there is also significance to the converse of these statistics: namely, that a clear majority (65–80%) of firms *do not* consider such linkages "critical/very important." In fact, more firms are not just indifferent to such connections but in all categories (excluding linkages with local customers) a greater percentage of firms viewed local connections actually to be "unimportant/of very little significance." Particularly surprising is how links with sources that one would expect to lie at the heart of the workings of a high-tech cluster—venture capital, university resources, specialist suppliers—are rated in a way that can hardly, on the basis of the survey, be seen as strong points of interaction (Figure 9.1).

The data may not be as incriminating as they seem. A higher percentage of firms rated linkages *outside* the region to be of greater importance than linkages inside, a reflection in part of the transregional and global orientation of many local biotech firms and the industry they serve. Nevertheless, excluding ties with customers, linkages to any geography (local or international) were rated to be important by at most only 40% of firms surveyed. The statistics again speak to how managers in Cambridge's high-tech sectors generally do not view local networking as a vital component of a firm's strategy or one's personal career ambitions. Prevalent thinking in Silicon Valley in recent years has assumed too much about the value of networks and led to instances of extremely poor decision-making. Prevalent thinking in Silicon Fen appears to suffer from the opposite extreme, undervaluing the way networks could be leveraged for greater individual and organizational gain.

**Working to Live.** British entrepreneurs are routinely criticized for a perceived tendency to create "lifestyle companies": firms that meet the limited aspirations of their founders but are never managed for substantial growth. Cambridge firms in particular are viewed as emblematic of this

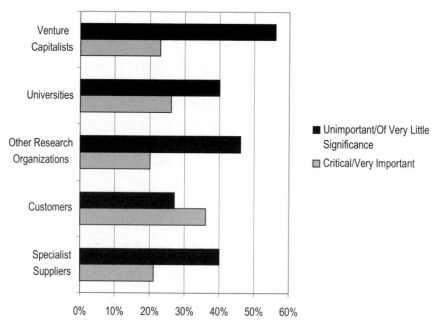

**Figure 9.1** Valuing Regional Enterprise Linkages.
(Data from ERBI Ltd, used with kind permission)

condition. A report on the Cambridge telecommunications sector summarizes common perceptions of the issue:

> Although Cambridge has continued to spawn companies specializing in innovative use of technology, they have been dismissed as "lifestyle companies" and Cambridge has been regarded as a place in which bright but self-satisfied people indulge their interest in technology by setting up companies which they have no intention of ever developing beyond their control.[229]

Although the cluster's leadership generally takes umbrage at such dismissive characterizations of the entrepreneurial spirit infusing the Phenomenon, these assessments are largely accurate. There is an instinctive reaction to deny charges of self-satisfaction and limited ambitions. Yet accepting the label of "lifestyle entrepreneurship" as a fair reflection of the cluster's economic dynamism does not imply the cluster is somehow flawed. Entrepreneurial ambitions are, after all, a matter of personal choice. Moreover, such lifestyle choices entail their own rewards, especially compared with the frenetic pace of work life in the Valley. By not building large companies that provide greater economic mass and employment opportunities for the area, of course, the local community loses out in many ways. Yet this too is a situation to which many parties contribute. Cambridge's residents and political leadership go to nothing less than extraordinary lengths to restrict the growth of the cluster. Cambridge's "lifestyle" entrepreneurs, albeit a symbol of the cluster's unrealized economic potential, cannot be viewed as doing anything other than behaving rationally in light of personal goals and the prevailing socio-economic climate.

The American journalist Jonathan Rauch perceptively observed that what is often described as the "British Disease" underpinning the UK's comparatively anemic economic performance may simply be the result of "sane" behavior by Britons who forgo the economic passions that drive Americans. You "can be a good and decent country if you are sane," Rauch comments, "but not a great and exuberant one."[230] By the same measure, the Phenomenon's driving spirit can be seen as producing a cluster that forgoes the manic highs and lows of greatness for pursuit of a more sedate and steady dynamic.

**Perceived Status**. The particular way in which British society confers status is another, much discussed but often underappreciated, ingredient in the country's overall social milieu. The political scientist, Stephen Haseler, sees the royal honors system in particular as dampening Britons' creative spirit:

> The honours game of the royal-state is more than a simple public recognition awards system. Rather, as well as reinforcing the country's peculiar sense of importance, it legitimises ancient class sensibilities—and in the process sanctifies the idea that achievement is not enough, that even in the twentieth century

achievement cannot speak for itself. While captains of industry fall over themselves to be called 'sir', and trade unionists and academics manoeuvre for peerages, the money made, the business created, the invention produced or the book written assumes little value in itself. The ultimate prize is something much more precious: the medieval title, a position in an eternal social hierarchy, the opportunity to parade a kind of social apartness based on an illusion of nobility, or at least gentrification.[231]

Haseler writes polemically but nevertheless persuasively encapsulates how the British tradition of conferring and observing social status, however modernized and refined, can detract from a *laissez-faire* means of rewarding accomplishment. If nothing else, the honors system underscores a sense of capricious social stratification—anathema to the horizontal structures, fluidity, and meritocratic values that high-growth businesses espouse and use to motivate their employees. In the same vein, technology enterprises in Cambridge, with their elitism purportedly based solely on individual competence, can perhaps be seen as somewhat insulated from the effects of the nation's wider social hierarchy. Yet, even if adhering to egalitarian scientific values, Cambridge (and, considering the university's traditional role in grooming the upper classes, perhaps *especially* Cambridge) cannot entirely divorce itself from a larger social fabric where the issue today, as another commentator has observed, is not the functioning of a class system *per se* but the workings of a "class psychology: the preoccupation with class, and [its] symbols."[232]

## STIRRING THE FIRE

Against the backdrop of societal constraints and personally imposed restraints, the work by members of Cambridge's high-tech community to facilitate more synergistic, growth-oriented dynamics is all the more impressive. The first concerted attempt at building business cooperation, the Cambridge Computer Group, folded with the downturn of large technology companies like Acorn in the mid-1980s. But many of the core activities of the Group have been revived and expanded upon by Walter Herriot, Director of Cambridge's "Innovation Centre" administered by St. John's College. Herriot is especially qualified for carrying on the original services provided by the Computer Group because, as another Barclays Bank technology accounts manager, he was involved in its establishment and managed the enterprise during its final years. What he sees to have been particular valuable in the Group's services was the way it allowed him and his colleagues to:

> ... get to know the people and help them translate their business plans into a language financiers could understand. We talked to people to encourage them to start up businesses, to show them how to reduce risk, and gave practical advice like pointing out when they were not charging enough or helping them write cash flow forecasts and business plans. We also identified a number of people who we thought were potentially important and we should really follow almost through thick and thin because the individuals had the personality to succeed.[233]

Now, as Director of the Innovation Centre, Herriot remains a central figure in the Phenomenon. His vast connections and familiarity with local goings-on make him a must-speak-to person for anyone who considers starting a new firm in the cluster. The Innovation Centre also manages projects for the government's Small Business Service and an equity advisory program that assists some 250 businesses a year. "We'd make more money," Herriot admits, "if we just stopped running those programs and charged for consultancy services. It means that we remain substantially a *pro bono* organization and haven't developed as a purely commercial business in our own right. Although we could do other things which would generate more income that probably would not be so positively helpful to businesses in the Cambridge area."[234]

In regards to dedicated professional service organizations—lawyers, accountants, financiers, human resource specialists—these groups have been streaming into Cambridge in noticeable numbers since the late 1980s. Even with reasonable proximity to London, all the major international accounting firms now have a sizable presence in the cluster. Local attorneys are a long way from fostering a legal community like that found in the Valley, but the Phenomenon has become home to nationally recognized attorney "rainmakers" and technology legal specialists. The UK's *Legal 500* rates Cambridge's locally based law firm of Mills & Reeve as "steadily transforming itself from a regional to a national heavyweight."[235] The firm is the first in Cambridge's legal community to design packaged offerings that combine legal and business advisory services specially tailored for local technology start-ups.

Additional examples of ongoing improvements in professional services are related by the experiences of Rob Arnold, Partner at PricewaterhouseCoopers. Arnold heads PwC's pan-European biotechnology corporate finance operations out of offices on Cambridge's Castle Hill (Silicon Fen's minicluster of professional service organizations). Arnold first came to Cambridge from London in the late 1980s. The changes he has observed since then give a feel for how much the business environment has advanced. At the time he arrived, the Cambridge practice (then operating as Coopers & Lybrand) had only 20 staff; now it has 250. Arnold recalls how Cambridge's outlook was promising but uncertain when he arrived, with big-name local firms like Sinclair and Acorn "falling apart. ... We knew that some companies weren't going to survive." There were also issues with local business ways:

> I and others who had come to this newly established practice began to realize that people in Cambridge didn't walk through the door for advice, you actually had to go and find them. It makes me think of how different the situation was from those amazing stories about the VCs in Silicon Valley, the notion that you basically "stand beneath a tree and wait for somebody to come along and you throw money at them." That wasn't the case here so we started knocking on doors, which for accountants was a bit risqué.[236]

By the start of the 1990s things began looking better as Arnold worked with new-growth biotech firms that began to emerge. Exciting technologies were being spun out of Cambridge labs and Chris Evans, who

would go on to be recognized as the UK's most prolific biotech entrepreneur and venture capitalist, was active around Cambridge following
his buyout of the enzyme research group at British Sugar's nearby facilities. Although Arnold did not handle the acquisition, he got to know
Evans through it. Later the two worked together when Evans founded
the diagnostics company Celsis in 1992. By then Cantab Pharmaceuticals
had also spun out of Cambridge University's Department of Immunol-
ogy. To Arnold, both firms were instrumental in seeding the biotech
sector in the area and helped Cambridge recognize the potential of
biotechnology as an industry. Evans and Arnold also took a highly
entrepreneurial approach to handling constricting financial regulations:

> At the founding of Celsis, the idea was "despite the rules of the stock exchange
> in London, we're going to float this company, boyo, and we're going to do it
> in six months." The rules of the LSE at the time were such that you just
> couldn't do it. But Chris with his gift for the gab and we and other advisors
> were able to establish that really the business had actually existed for quite a
> long time and we found a way around the rules. It was that which subsequently
> led the stock exchange to change its own rules. Just for the historical record,
> British Biotech had by then also emerged and it listed in London just margin-
> ally before Celsis. But what was remarkable about Chris' company is that it
> had gone from nothing to the market in under a year. The flotations of
> British Biotech based in Oxford and Celsis and Cantab Pharmaceuticals over
> here was what really woke us up to what was going on. I think that was also
> in all reality when Cambridge woke up to it as well.[237]

Another major figure within the current generation of Phenomenon
business facilitators is Nigel Brown. Brown moved to the area in 1972,
intending simply to live in Cambridge as a commuter while managing
an insurance brokerage that he had founded in London. By the end of
the 1970s, he realized that the growing prosperity of the region meant
he could skip his daily journey and serve a large enough base of high-
net-worth individuals in greater Cambridge instead. He thus repositioned
his company, NW Brown, to become a Cambridge-based financial
services firm. On the heels of the Thatcher-era tax reform in the early

1980s, Brown expanded his firm's offerings to include stockbroking. Following London's 1987 stock-market crash, he recruited displaced investment banking talent from London to add investment management and corporate finance to NW Brown's range of services as well. In 2000, with the launch of its Gateway fund, NW Brown became a local provider of formal venture capital.

Arguably, Brown's greatest contribution to the financial vitality of the cluster has come from his organization of the angel investors' group, the Great Eastern Investment Forum. GEIF's roots stretch back to the early 1990s when Brown found that: "having the network that we have, new companies were coming to us and we couldn't fund them" due to NW Brown's charter to invest only in publicly quoted stocks.[238] Rather than turn away interesting start-ups, Brown decided to send letters to potential investors inviting them to business plan presentations. As word about these occasional presentations spread, demand for them grew to the point that Brown decided to organize his matchmaking service more formally. Starting out with only 40 members in 1995, within five years GEIF membership numbered 450. Of 600 companies that approached the Forum during this time, 90 were accepted to present and subsequently raised £20m from GEIF members. Although a Cambridge-based organization, GEIF draws supplicant entrepreneurs from throughout the UK and other parts of the world (even entrepreneurs from France's Sophia-Antipolis can be found making presentations). In the light of the Forum's drawing power, Brown jokingly describes the greater Cambridge region he serves: "as stretching from Edinburgh down to Southampton across to Manchester."[239] The situation exemplifies how the cluster may still lack mass but is at least gaining magnetism.

Brown also banded together with other Cambridge business leaders in 1998 to found an umbrella organization for the cluster, the Cambridge Network. The Network has since become Cambridge's major vehicle for information sharing, PR, lobbying, and outreach efforts. Many regard it as having brought an unprecedented degree of interactivity and cohesiveness to the Phenomenon. Not insignificantly, the make-up of the six organizations that created the Network (three financial firms, a strategy consultancy, a professional services provider, and Cambridge University) are all part of the peripheral enterprise base that support the cluster's core of high-tech firms. The sort of initiative and involvement that the Cambridge Network represents is an indication of the Phenomenon's growing support structure and also the ways in which the need for more collaborative interaction is being addressed.

Of all the leading enterprise facilitators in the Phenomenon today, Hermann Hauser, the co-founder of Acorn and now Cambridge's biggest name venture capitalist, is by far the most prominent. Hauser represents something of an ideal form of Cambridge innovator and entrepreneur. A Cavendish-trained Ph.D., as a young physicist he transitioned to the business world in 1977. His varied experiences as an academic, inventor, business entrepreneur, senior executive at two large technology firms (Acorn and then Olivetti), and role as a high-profile technology funder make him a unique and influential Cambridge personality.

After earning his first £10m from the IPO of Acorn, Hauser started a sideline career as an angel investor in the early 1980s. An easily identifiable role model for others, Hauser enthusiastically promotes the cluster and, running against the grain of Cambridge's traditional norms, is a prolific networker. His business partnership with Acorn co-founder Chris Curry traces back to a conversation the two, as strangers to one another, struck up at a local pub. Through an ongoing association with former labmate Richard Friend, today holder of Cambridge's Cavendish Chair of Physics, Hauser has stayed intimately familiar with cutting-edge developments at the Cavendish Laboratory, giving him the opportunity to act as the chief deal coordinator on companies built around some of Cambridge's more exciting IT-related breakthroughs: light-emitting polymers (a discovery out of which Cambridge Display Technologies was established) and plastic transistors (the technological seed of the company, Plastic Logic).

Hauser is especially excited about the broad-based wealth that the cluster's firms are bringing back to the region. Speaking in the summer of 2000 about Cambridge's three highest capitalized IT companies at the time—ARM, Virata, and Autonomy—Hauser observed that the Phenomenon no longer just produces millionaire dons but millionaire employees as well:

> The options in ARM, Virata, and Autonomy are worth almost $2b, which is the amount of money that will flow into this region over the next couple of years or so. This option thing will have two very exciting consequences. The first consequence we've already seen and that is the attitude that people have to options. It's changed from an attitude where they thought that options were a ruse to get the base salary down to "hey, these options are really worth having because look at ARM, Virata, Autonomy." We made 200 millionaires in ARM, 100 millionaires in Virata, and another 50 millionaires in Autonomy. Some of these millionaires have tens of millions. Robin Saxby is worth 200 million and Mike Lynch a billion. This kind of wealth generation can be done in Cambridge as well as in Silicon Valley.[240]

Hauser was speaking at around the height of a global technology stock bubble. Estimates would suggest that only one year after Hauser's comments, the actual number of employee millionaires had dropped to a level closer to 100. Regardless of how such numbers may fluctuate, Hauser makes an important point about the way wealth is being recycled back to the cluster. This trend shows no sign of abating over the long term. For example, two Phenomenon companies featured in the next chapter, The Generics Group and TTP Com, conducted successful IPOs in the bleak market dark days of late 2000–early 2001. They and other leading new-growth companies continue to generate their own numbers of newly wealthy. As Hauser sees the future, such emerging *nouveau riche* offer the real hope of providing the cluster with the sort of properly guided, high-risk capital infusions that can finally allow the Phenomenon to achieve sizable mass:

> Until two years ago I was 50% of the business angel money in Cambridge—not a very realistic situation. Whereas over the next two years, with [the money] coming into the Cambridge area from options that people will cash in on, this will change things radically. This will be a bigger change than anything that has occurred in the past. There will be more money from these business angels going into the Cambridge region than any venture capital fund, than

any government initiative, than any corporate funding. . . . I'm delighted to say that Cambridge is really the first such region in Europe where this is happening quite to that extent. You need rich people to make these crazy investments and prepare the undergrowth of exciting new companies that the venture capital community then can grow into very large companies.[241]

Of course, growing "very large companies" will require more than just monetary injections. Cambridge managers will have to rise to the tasks required to build fledgling enterprises into major global corporations. Company management must also be successful at doing this within a framework of policies and popular attitudes that work to hold firm growth in check. The current phase of the Cambridge Phenomenon owes its existence to small, niche-focused firms that arose out of the debris of fallen giants. For Cambridge firms, and the cluster as a whole, to achieve greater economic weight will demand applications of different management skills than are currently the cluster's forte. Perhaps, along the lines of what Hauser anticipates, with time, the recycling of capital and experience into the cluster will provide enough resources and kindle the necessary ambitions to create more radical change. Even with a heightening of the cluster's economic means and expectations, however, tremendous challenges await those who seek to go further in overturning remnants of the Old Order that still influence what Cambridge is and what it truly aspires to be.

This chapter has looked into how and why particular dynamics sustain and shape the Phenomenon. The ways in which the cluster is "creatively destructive" have been highlighted with the emphasis tending more toward the entrepreneurial aspects of organizations than their purely innovative dimensions. The next chapter shifts focus to hone in on the capacity for innovation in the cluster, considering in greater detail the novel aspects of leading management strategies, the ways in which innovators are attracted to Silicon Fen, and how they contribute back to the creative environment of the cluster and its firms. As has been the case with this chapter, no attempt is made to demonstrate Silicon Fen as somehow superior or inferior to Silicon Valley. The lessons offered by the innovators featured are interpreted in order to appreciate the particular characteristics of the cluster as well as to recognize the insights they offer about enterprise creativity in general.

# Phenomenally Innovative 10

The English "innovate/innovation" and identical or similar phrasings in other European languages—*innovation, erneuern, inovación, inovação, innovazione, innove, innovez*—all derive from the Latin *novus* (which itself derives from the Greek *neos*) meaning "new." An indication of the universality of this conceptualization is how in non-Western languages as well the notion of innovation appears with similar connotations. In Chinese, for example, the equivalent term is 革 新 (*gexin*, sounds like "geh-sheen") which literally means "to peel away the old to create the new." The same phrasing also appears (identically written but separately pronounced) in Japanese and Korean as *kakushin* and *hyoksin*, respectively.

What is interesting about so basic and widespread a concept as innovation is that the practice of innovation can vary in significant ways. In the case of the Cambridge Phenomenon, its knowledge workers do not typically seek to transform the world, let alone their firm, with the "insanely great" ideas that are a hallmark of Silicon Valley. Instead, as the expression goes, there is a tendency to "get on with things," retreating to a garage, cubicle, or laboratory to toil independently until the innovator can produce some marvelously crafted solution or invention whose ingenuity, it is hoped, will simply speak for itself. Finding ways beyond this bottleneck to create synergies and build stronger personal interactions within the cluster and its innovation-driven enterprises in particular represents a major challenge for managers. Any growth that is driven by innovation/entrepreneurship in Cambridge also becomes contained by the limits of personal motivation and restrictions imposed by external powers, especially those of local government. Observing how management responds to such challenges reveals much about the nature, purposes, and broader relevancies of innovation in the Phenomenon.

This chapter begins its exploration of Cambridge innovation styles by looking first at the flagship firm of the Phenomenon's present generation of enterprise, ARM Microprocessors. Although technologically innovative, what has done the most for ARM's success in the marketplace is the innovative conceptualization and execution of its business strategy. Having emerged from the wreckage of Acorn, ARM is distinguished by its management's demonstrated ability to learn from the mistakes of the past and pursue novel means for developing a dominant presence in its global markets. ARM's strategy has proven so effective that its products have become standards for microprocessors manufactured throughout the world. (Standards are often dubiously used as "proofs" that industries become "accidentally" dominated by firms. The upcoming examination of ARM's conceptualization and implementation of its strategy will show just how much thought and effort the firm has had to put into gaining its dominant market positions.)

The remainder of the chapter looks at ways in which leading Cambridge innovators have come to be part of the high-tech cluster and how they promote innovation within their organizations. The innovators individually profiled are associated with three of Cambridge's major technology consultancies: Cambridge Consultants Ltd, The Generics Group, and The Technology Partnership. Much of Silicon Fen's stature in the world of Siliconia is lent credence by the presence in Cambridge of R&D operations from major corporations such as Microsoft, AT&T, Hitachi, Marconi, Monsanto, Nokia, Toshiba, Wellcome, and the much storied Xerox. Particularly Cambridge-esque methods of innovation, however, are best found in locally established, though less globally renowned, R&D consultancies like the ones featured here. The innovation management techniques that are showcased provide a sense of the inherent creativity of the Cambridge Phenomenon. The leadership styles and company histories of these multidisciplinary technology consultancies also offer useful views on ways to foster and manage an innovative workforce, be it based in Cambridge or elsewhere.

## ARMED TO THE CORE

Only a few years following Acorn's acquisition by Olivetti in 1987, the dozen members of Acorn's RISC (reduced instruction set computing) processor design team found themselves threatened with job cuts as the new management streamlined operations. The team was talented, demonstrated by their creation of a unique 32-bit RISC chip that offered the "killer application" of drastically reduced chip size and power consumption—attributes ideal for intelligent portable electronics. Unfortunately, the team had developed this technology at a time before hand-held devices like mobile phones and personal digital assistants represented the tremendous global markets that they would in later years. At least one company was pushing the envelope on developing such products, however: Apple. The Silicon Valley firm needed just the type of processor the Acorn team had designed to drive the Newton, Apple's much ballyhooed hand-held computer. An arrangement struck in 1990 transformed Acorn's RISC design team into Advanced RISC Machines Ltd, a joint venture struck between Acorn, Apple (the major shareholder), and the Silicon Valley semiconductor manufacturer, VLSI.

ARM initially intended to license its RISC chip designs exclusively to VLSI, which would then build them into processors for the Newton. The prospects for such a narrow application of ARM's technology worried key figures in Cambridge behind the deal, individuals such as Hermann Hauser and ARM's founding CEO Robin Saxby. People previously involved with Acorn linked that company's failure in the market to its inability to set global standards with its products. ARM's Cambridge-based management therefore wanted to target as broad a customer base as possible. Proceeding along these lines it developed "the partnership model" as a strategy for unrestricted licensing of ARM's intellectual property. Partnering for ARM came to mean that the company would provide standardized processor design "cores" to RISC chip manufacturers (like VLSI) and chip integrators (like Apple). The cores would act as a foundational building block on top of which

ARM's "partner" customers could then customize and produce a processor's complete architecture.

The partnership model first bore fruit in 1993 when ARM secured a license agreement with Texas Instruments (TI)—ARM's first deal with a partner outside Apple's supply chain network. The partnership with TI was tactically important because it signaled to the market that ARM was of enough caliber to collaborate with any top-tier semiconductor firm, not just firms connected with its major shareholder. The deal also represented the first step for ARM to have its cores widely adopted in a market other than that for hand-held computers. As it turned out, TI used the ARM core in a popular chipset for mobile phones, opening for ARM an important inroad to a market that was set for explosive future growth. A "lucky break," perhaps, yet ARM's securing a relationship with TI had nothing to do with luck but rather prescient strategizing and effective follow-through. By the mid-1990s, with the Newton slipping into extinction and Apple in danger of doing the same, ARM found that its strategy for a diversified customer base and wide range of partnered applications for its cores was paying off. It allowed the small Cambridge firm to pursue alliances with a variety of leading semiconductor makers and integrators and led to important partnerships with the likes of Intel, 3Com, Ericsson, IBM, and Toshiba. With a widening array of digital products requiring the chip characteristics for which ARM cores serve as a platform, ARM's presence in the world of electronics has spread enormously, though its market positions are largely unnoticed by the general public. Sales of ARM cores leapt from under 10 million units in 1997 to 175 million by 1999.[242] Internal estimates indicate that ARM cores can be found in microprocessors running 85% of the world's mobile phones.

ARM's strategy for diversifying its customer base has required considerable finesse and perseverance. ARM's major investor, Apple, had previously competed with Acorn; Apple co-founder Steve Jobs himself had earlier journeyed to Cambridge to acquire other Acorn spin-offs outright. If Apple deemed ARM's intellectual property to be a potential competitive threat, the company could have vetoed ARM's efforts at partnering. Instead, ARM management did so well in managing its investor and partner relationships that in 1998 it succeeded in organizing a complex divestiture-cum-market listing that dissolved ARM's joint venture structure, reconfiguring the Cambridge firm as an independent company. Now free from the need to appease the interests of a single large investor, ARM still has to tread carefully. Its unrestricted partnering strategy means that the same ARM cores used by one customer are used in the chips of that company's direct competitors. As ARM increases the range of applications for its cores, it also works even more closely with the chip integrators to which chip manufacturers themselves sell. Because of ARM's increasing partnerships with integrators, managers at some of ARM's semiconductor customers believe that the company is more properly seen as a competitor, not a partner. With ARM's Executive Chairman Robin Saxby declaring: "I want to be the engine inside every digital product" and the company attaining the growth and market positions to make such a statement more than wishful thinking, concerns are not entirely misplaced.[243] So far at least, ARM has managed to show that partnering is a win–win proposition and that its cores represent "solutions," not threats to its principal base of semiconductor firm partners. Its accomplishments in this regard are a result of not only outstanding marketing efforts led by Saxby but also strengths that ARM has developed in its execution of global account management and after-sales service.

Although ARM is very much a product of the Cambridge Phenomenon, the greatest resource ARM management has made use of in the Cambridge cluster has been the opportunity to learn from Acorn's failure—the lessons they gleaned have been more critical to the company's long-term success than the technology ARM inherited. If ARM management had merely relied on the merits of the company's technology and stayed as a dedicated supplier within the Apple supply network, the company would probably no longer exist. Instead, managers took an aggressive market approach and have led ARM to the top of the global semiconductor intellectual property market, edging out Silicon Valley-based rivals (Table 10.1).

**Table 10.1** Top Five Semiconductor Intellectual Property Firms.

(Data from Gartner Dataquest, used with kind permission)

| Company | Location | 2001 Revenue ($m) | Global Market Share (%) |
|---|---|---|---|
| 1. ARM | Cambridge Phenomenon | 179.0 | 20.1 |
| 2. RAMBUS | Silicon Valley | 107.3 | 12.0 |
| 3. MIPS Technologies | Silicon Valley | 70.2 | 7.9 |
| 4. Synopsys | Silicon Valley | 45.0 | 5.0 |
| 5. TTP Com | Cambridge Phenomenon | 34.9 | 3.9 |

ARM's rise is impressive, both for the company and the Cambridge cluster as a whole. In 1999, ARM became the UK's 45th largest company in terms of market capitalization. This showed to Britain the enduring potential of Cambridge high-tech. Perhaps more importantly, it showed to other companies in the Phenomenon that well-managed niche positioning can reap big rewards. In ARM's wake, other promising specialist semiconductor firms have emerged. For example, the semiconductor design firm, Cambridge Silicon Radio, not only follows a niche positioning strategy but also uses ARM cores as the platform for its chips. Another high-potential niche company of the Phenomenon, TTP Com, has itself risen to join ARM in the ranks of the world's top five semiconductor intellectual property (IP) firms. The market positions of ARM and TTP Com mean that Cambridge's combined share of the global semiconductor IP market roughly equals that of Silicon Valley's. Although this does not equate to having companies the approximate size of an HP or an Intel, it does indicate that Cambridge firms can manage and profit from innovation as well as their Valley counterparts do.

## CCL AND SIM

Cambridge Consultants Ltd. (CCL) began life in 1960 when a 24-year-old Cambridge chemical engineering graduate, Tim Eiloart, called together a handful of former classmates and acquaintances to found with him a company intended to "put the Brains of Cambridge University at the disposal of the Problems of British Industry."[244] Beyond Eiloart's circle of young, idealistic friends, the initial response to his call to arms was chilly. At first, neither the mainstream of Cambridge academia nor British industry saw much point to collaboration. Although making few converts in the university, CCL's enthusiastic leaders eventually garnered serious interest from the business world. Having begun as a part-time commitment by the founders, who all had day jobs at local firms or university labs, demand for CCL's technical consulting grew and management became a full-time affair. By the end of the decade the company had expanded beyond the ability of its inexperienced leaders to cope. The company had reached the point where it needed the "brains of industry" to survive.

At the time the Phenomenon was in its early phase and there were little by way of local resources for CCL to turn to for support. Eiloart brought in from the outside an ambitious, but minimally experienced, man from the commercial world (someone even younger than Eiloart himself) to help him turn things around. The grand but poorly conceived directions CCL pursued as a result of its new leadership nearly destroyed the company. On its last legs, CCL was acquired by the Cambridge, Massachusetts-based management consultancy Arthur D. Little in 1972. Despite being under foreign ownership, CCL has remained a central force in the cluster. The company has produced the second largest number of spin-outs after Acorn and was a highly visible early occupier of the Trinity Science Park. With 300 employees it is now one of the park's largest tenants.

CCL has also evolved from a company whose technological preoccupations once blinded it to its own managerial deficiencies. Today it blends original capabilities in technology consulting with management lessons learned from the firm's experiences. In fact, the company has advanced so far in its insights on management processes that it has become a proselytizer to clients throughout the world of an innovation management technique that was originated at CCL in 1987: Structured Idea Management.

SIM was born, like many a useful tool, out of frustration. As a newly hired Cambridge University physics graduate at CCL, Lucy Rowbotham decided—after being subjected to "some brainstorming sessions that were the most painful of experiences"—that there had to be a better way for thrashing out ideas.[245] Rowbotham saw the tendency of brainstorming meetings to wander aimlessly as a fundamental problem. Another was the habit of people who acted as note transcribers to compensate for the chaos of discussions by emphasizing a single point of view, usually their own, in the write-ups and action item lists that followed. Rowbotham took the initiative to search for an improved discussion framework that would guard against both extremes, preventing unfruitful meanderings beyond an intended discussion topic while also democratizing the mechanics of a brainstorming session and its follow-up. She especially wanted to protect the voicing of off-the-wall ideas, to allow creative, unorthodox thought "to percolate upward."[246]

As Rowbotham developed the particulars of SIM her work caught the attention of Jean-Philipe Deschamps, the continental-based founder of Arthur D. Little's international technology and innovation management practice. Deschamps provided guidance on ways to integrate the SIM methodology broadly and introduced Rowbotham to others at ADL Europe with interests similar to hers. Discussions and refinements resulted in a seven-step process that now characterizes the heart of Structured Idea Management (Figure 10.1).

To progress a SIM-based project requires a strong sense of team buy-in. Garnering upper-level involvement begins with the first step in the SIM process: the setting of project goals. Here, the manager in charge of implementing proposals is not allowed to get away with vaguely describing expectations for the project but must sign off on the specific criteria that will guarantee the kind of proposals on which action will actually be taken. This avoids lack of focus during the idea-generation process and prevents demoralization among project participants who might otherwise find their final proposals casually discarded for "not being what management wanted." After criteria have been set, a team of SIM participants is picked with a view toward bringing together person-

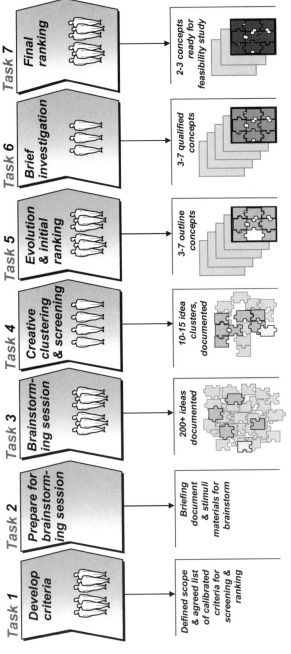

**Figure 10.1** CCL's Structured Idea Management Sequence.

(Reproduced by permission of Cambridge Consultants Ltd)

alities and skills that will achieve diversity and synergy during discussions. At the initial brainstorm meeting, all ideas are given an unencumbered airing—negative commentary or judgmental opinions are strictly banned. At later meetings, the group critically evaluates the mass of proposed ideas, discarding those it deems inappropriate and gathering together those deemed acceptable into thematic clusters. From these clusters the group will then develop several concrete proposals. A typical SIM-based project will see more than 200 unconnected thoughts winnowed and combined into two or three concrete proposals for trial implementation.

SIM's means for boosting the efficiency and purpose of otherwise haphazard brainstorming sessions has become especially popular with CCL clients in the Nordic countries, Germany, and Japan—nations where firms are inclined toward organizational hierarchy but thrive on creative breakthroughs. Despite undertones of formality and linearity, which creativity aficionados might instinctively reject, SIM can be appreciated for achieving a practical, easily implementable means for liberating an organization's creative powers. As anyone who has sat through enough brainstorms can attest, apart from chaotic meanderings, what passes for "brainstorming" at some firms really amounts to "brainwashing" a group to back a manager's preconceived pet project. SIM offers a pathway to avoid entering the Dilbert Zone. The accountability, transparency, and objectivity that infuse the process offer hope to those who have to suffer the immediate and long-term consequences of aimlessly progressed or groupthink-dominated brainstorms. As Rowbotham and an ADL Europe colleague argue in an exposition of SIM, the process guards against bureaucratic foolishness as it precludes the all-too-common practice for concepts "to 'float' around the organization, acquiring currency in proportion to the personal and political power of the champions who promote them."[247]

Another attractive feature of SIM is the way it neatly accommodates the dueling organizational forces of structure and creativity and does so in a way that is widely applicable across sectors. After perfecting the methodology in-house, Rowbotham and others from CCL have gone on to teach SIM to clients in a broad range of industries, including fast-moving consumer goods, industrial equipment and processes, chemical-based products, retail distribution, telecommunications, and electronics. In one instance, the Domestic Appliances and Personal Care division of Philips employed four teams using SIM that individually generated four successful product ideas. One of these SIM-generated products, the electric razor Philishave Cool Skin, earned for Philips revenues of over $100m in its first year on the market and received an IDEA award for innovative design.

The birth and applications of SIM offer further examples of the learning processes that spur Cambridge's innovators to continue to improve upon the technical and organizational creativity of the cluster. That SIM has been adopted as an innovation management tool by major companies outside the Cambridge cluster further testifies to how Cambridge's management capabilities are coming of age. Philips' adoption of the SIM methodology offers a poignant example of how companies outside the cluster now look to Cambridge not only for acquiring technologies or businesses (such as the Pye Group) but for gaining insights on management as well.

## GENERICALLY INNOVATIVE

Gordon Edge, founder of the Generics Group, comes from the old school of high-tech. Someone "just besotted" by his first radio when he was eight years old, Edge has not paused to stop playing with technology ever since.[248] An honors science undergraduate at the Bolton Institute of Technology, Edge was drawn into Cambridge's pre-Phenomenon high-tech community through summer apprenticeships and postgraduate work he undertook at Pye laboratories. From contacts he developed there, Edge was given—and took—the opportunity to help establish Cambridge Consultants Limited with Tim Eiloart. Considering the difficulties Edge and his colleagues at CCL experienced, it is rather impressive that CCL and Edge have remained active in the Cambridge area at all:

> The original idea of Cambridge Consultants was to link together [Cambridge] university and industry. And this proved to be an extremely bad idea because the university really wasn't interested in formalizing the relationship for the transfer of technology (as we would call it today) into what was seen as trade. Social class and role distinctions in Britain were still very, very, very strong in the 60s. British industry wasn't interested in technology transfer from academia either. There was an arrogance about British industry, a perceived self-sufficiency that they were all-powerful, that they didn't need any external support. They were very hierarchical, *extremely* hierarchical—getting a meeting at senior level in a British company was almost impossible.[249]

Edge has nevertheless stayed committed to the nature of his work and to remaining based in the Cambridge area. In 1970, he accepted an offer from PA Consulting in London, then Europe's largest management consultancy, to set up and run the company's new technology center. Edge first chose the town of Cambridge to locate PA's R&D labs but after being served notice by the city council for "creating what they called an industrial environment" he relocated operations 10 miles south to the village of Melbourn.[250] In 1986, Edge and a close group of associates left PA to found in the village of Harston (roughly midway between Melbourn and Cambridge) the technology consultancy Scientific Generics, the principal operation of what is now the Generics Group. In a repeat of Edge's earlier problems with local authorities, Generics was denied planning permission to expand its Harston facilities. After years of fruitless negotiation, the company ultimately appealed to the UK government's Planning Inspector who finally ruled in 1999 that Generics' welfare was "of significant importance to the national interest" and struck down local obstacles to expansion.[251]

The main reason Edge refuses, despite the unwelcoming attitude from the local political establishment, to give up on Cambridge is the benefits he sees in being part of the region's uniquely creative environment.

Edge has in fact designed Generics to function as a distillation of the innovative forces he believes underpin the Cambridge Phenomenon:

> Generics was set up essentially to become a kind of microcosm of the Cambridge area—a place where we would actively create spin-outs. Generics gets its name from investing in those areas of science and technology which are basic, simple, and ubiquitous. It's the old English use of the word "generics." Unfortunately, in the American usage it has a connotation of meaning the lowest common denominator whereas we use it to refer to a fundamental sense of pervasiveness. In fact, looking at the Cambridge Phenomenon as a whole you see it is very much an interdisciplinary phenomenon. . . . It's so diverse. You can see very little symmetry in it.[252]

Based on Edge's conceptualization of the Phenomenon, Generics will support new companies—whether spin-outs from Generics or other enterprises in the region—that it deems to be "generically" innovative. For example, Generics was an early supporter of the Cavendish Laboratory spin-out Cambridge Display Technologies, a firm it assisted with business advice (and, later on, capital) in exchange for equity during the company's initial phases of development. What excited Generics management about Cambridge Display Technology was that its product, illuminescent polymers, blends cutting-edge theories from biology and physics. This kind of interdisciplinary approach is exactly what Generics strives for in encouraging innovation within its own organization.

To be good at "generic" innovation Generics tries to provide a "homogenous" work environment—homogenous in the sense of being *permeable, without internal segmentation or division.* Apart from the inherent merits of encouraging workplace interaction, promoting a climate of homogeneity also addresses the Cambridge habit of "getting on with things." To ensure that knowledge is not confined to lone individuals or within certain corners of the company's facilities, all office areas— even Edge's own executive office—are without partitions. Labs, as much as possible, are housed in heavily trafficked areas and contained within glass walls to produce situations where "electronic engineers can see biologists working, get familiar with their work, and then associate with them at the coffee machine and elsewhere."[253]

Generics backs up its physically homogenous work environment by trying to promote enthusiasm for the nature of work among its rank and file. In a Generics pamphlet on innovation, the company offers a highly philosophical set of arguments for the innovative spirit it seeks to encourage. It begins by taking issue with the trumpeting of Reason heralded by the European Enlightenment. Calculative reason, in Generics view, has overtaken the powers of intuition and passion. Nowhere is this clearer than in the "vocabulary of management," which tries to dictate the nature of thinking in the workplace. Companies are seen to have become obsessed with emotionally sterile notions such as *analysis, planning, assessment, prediction, efficiency,* and *productivity*. To help people think inspirationally, Generics own vocabulary of management emphasizes a sense of purpose in work, relying on concepts such as *enjoyment, enthusiasm, intuition,* and *excitement*. This change in the language of management intends to inculcate a different way of visualizing opportunities and to help break down the mental barriers that inhibit creativity and interaction.

At an even deeper level, Generics promotes a communal form of decision-making known as "action rationality," a concept originally advanced by the Swedish academic Nils Brunsson. Action rationality asserts that managerial authority is by itself an insufficient basis for organizational leadership. The group as a whole must be enthusiastically engaged for creativity to flow; one's feelings must precede thought for a company's goals to be met and sustained. Generics explains the strengths of action rationality in the following terms:

> [Action rationality] suggests that inspiration arises through social interactions, the development of trust and social communities. It implies that inspiration arises from action, not just thought (an example of the role of momentum). It questions whether the rational model of defining goals and objectives, generating alternatives and evaluating them are the best basis for action.

> And it emphasizes that actions require motivation and commitment, not just thought and decisions.[254]

The management philosophy and vocabulary that Generics promotes may verge on the idealistic but the Generics style of innovation is nevertheless credited with delivering bottom-line results. Generics has invested in or otherwise incubated more than 20 Cambridge companies; it credits its technology consulting services as having generated more than $10b worth of innovations for clients.[255] Senior R&D managers from companies such as Siemens, Dow Chemical, and ABB speak at seminars and forums to sing the praises of Generics capabilities. At the same time, among Generics' employees, the open but deeply intellectual, consensus-driven management style can prove too ponderous and conservative for some to bear. Turnover rates for many years were estimated to run as high as 25–30%. Prominent Generics defectors include Nigel Playford, founder of Ionica, and Andrew Dames, a leading Generics inventor who left to establish the Cambridge technology incubator, Sentec.

Since such departures Generics has updated the company's management practices to better align its innovation philosophies with corporate growth. Lobbying for governmental approval of its facilities' expansion, which is intended to accommodate a doubling of Generics 200-plus workforce, has been a first step. The group has also implemented changes within the organization, notably in the way it facilitates spin-outs. In the past, Generics-invested spinoffs would stay rooted within the parent company, legally operated as independent businesses but effectively administered as internal business units of Generics. Beginning with the founding of the spin-out Absolute Sensors in 1998, Generics-sponsored offshoots have been given the freedom to manage themselves. Commitment to the new policy was shown when shortly after launching Absolute Sensors, the new company's management on their own elected to accept an offer to merge with Federico Faggin's Synaptics and become the Silicon Valley firm's European base of operations. Synaptics UK is now completely separate of Generics' management structure but has nevertheless chosen to remain based in Harston at Generics incubation facilities.[256] Another step toward growth came with Generics listing 30% of its shares on the London Stock Exchange. Conducted in late 2000, during the days of severely negative investor sentiment, the offering was five-times oversubscribed. With its more aggressive growth targets, and now the legal permission to pursue them, Generics—a company that serves to replicate the innovative dynamism of the Cambridge Phenomenon—may yet be able to show how much further enterprises like it can expand when possessing the will and given the freedom to do so.


## TTP, INNOVATING FOR GROWTH

The Technology Partnership (TTP) began operations in 1987 when Gerald Avison brought together about two dozen of his colleagues from PA Technology who had grown unhappy with the changes in the organization since the departure of Gordon Edge. Avison had joined Edge at PA in 1972, before PA's R&D operations had been forced out of Cambridge. Prior to that Avison had managed British Aerospace's electron-beam welding facility in Bristol. A former member of his staff who had gone over to PA Technology suggested that Avison also consider taking a position with the firm. At a time when the whole world was awakening to the meaning of a place called Silicon Valley, Avison found himself struggling just to familiarize himself with the basics of getting around Cambridge:

> I had never been to Cambridge before I came for a job interview here. Cambridge is not a place you naturally go through. There are some parts of the country you inevitably come across in your travels, and Cambridge is definitely not one of them. You go to Oxford more than you go to Cambridge. And it was not an easy place to get to. The railway connections were not good at all . . . and the town was a mile's walk from the station.[257]

Fortunately for the cluster, difficulties with the train and lack of other conveniences—he recalls that Cambridge "only had one restaurant"—did not deter Avison from accepting work at PA. He remained with their operations until the late 1980s when he founded TTP in Melbourn, only a few miles from PA's facilities, within the converted estate grounds that once housed Metals Research (the firm the British government had prodded, with disastrous consequences, into acquiring Cambridge Scientific Instruments). Carrying with him a sensitivity to the stimulative effects of the built environment that had been a hallmark of PA Technology under Gordon Edge, Avison has ensured that TTP facilities be designed with purpose and symbolism. TTP's office space is open plan, conference rooms are decorated according to iconographically thought-provoking themes, laboratories are easily accessible, and nonconfidential project work is subject to interdepartmental scrutiny and input.

Where TTP differs from other Cambridge consultancies—and indeed the majority of firms in the Phenomenon—is in its strategy for growth. Typically, when a firm intentionally nurtures a new offshoot, it sets up a separate enterprise that, while enjoying various degrees of support from its progenitor, still lives or dies by its ability to generate revenue. TTP is more actively involved with its company-sponsored spin-offs. When TTP identifies a promising new opportunity, it will form a team, sometimes taking the structure of a department or division, to explore the product's market potential. This project-based, as opposed to firm-based, model for innovating new technologies and incubating enterprises around them avoids overburdening a still untested business concept. "If you do it the other way around," Avison reasons:

> ... then you dissipate a huge amount of effort on company-related things which aren't actually central to what you're trying to do. You have to set up your own recruitment operation, you have to set up your own accounts, you have to set up your own mechanism for dealing with [tax] and personnel issues. .... What we're doing is growing a project just as part of the rest of the business and then gradually shaping it into a corporate entity over time. Only when we've got the technology fully developed are we ready to turn it into a separate company.[258]

The major advantage to this project-based approach is the overall flexibility it provides. If an originally identified market opportunity does not materialize or a more attractive opportunity arises elsewhere, staff and capital allocations can easily be adjusted, minimizing costs. The structure also allows project managers to keep an open mind and avoid overcommitting to a given business plan. Such policies appear to have been sufficient in satisfying the entrepreneurial impulses of the workforce. So far, TTP has only suffered one major spin-off as a result of employee defection. In the meantime, the company has taken an active role in nurturing several projects that have ultimately succeeded in becoming significant independent enterprises in their own right.

TTP's method for innovation and incubation took shape shortly after it had finished a contract to produce customized automation equipment for Celltech in the late 1980s. The contract represented a one-off deal but TTP staff involved were intrigued by the long-term possibilities for the equipment they had designed. TTP surveyed the market and found that not only was there growing demand for such equipment, but that the sophistication and quality required supported healthy profit margins for manufacturers. TTP thus elected to establish an Automation Division that gradually built expertise and a reputation as an advanced equipment supplier to the biotech and pharmaceutical industries. By 1994, TTP's Automation Division had matured from producing customized orders into more streamlined production. Having reached what was judged to be a state of critical mass, the division was transformed into The Automation Partnership (TAP) and made a wholly owned, 45-employee-strong subsidiary of TTP. TAP continued growing, doubling in size and establishing a US branch in 1997. In 1998 managers on both sides agreed that TAP would do best as a fully independent enterprise and TAP demerged from its parent company. By 2000, already employing 125 and expecting 25% annual growth, TAP moved two miles south from its former facilities at TTP to new purpose-built facilities in Royston, Hertfordshire.

TTP has repeated this means of growth and "industrial mutation" with its most recent spin-off, TTP Com. Also originating from a client assignment undertaken by TTP in the late 1980s, the TTP Com project team initially worked on first-generation mobile telephony. It later moved on to design a key part of a GSM (Global System for Mobile Communications) satellite telecommunications system for British Aerospace, which BAe ended up terminating midway through because of financing difficulties. Not wanting to disband what it saw as a high-potential project group, TTP sought out other applications for its newly acquired GSM capabilities. This ultimately led to a 1993 agreement with Analog Devices in Massachusetts for the TTP Com division to design the architecture for a new generation GSM chipset. TTP Com went on to establish other valuable alliances, including one with Hitachi to design integrated radio semiconductors for GSM handsets. The group also initiated collaborations with local companies like Plextek (a mobile communications design house) and Cambridge Positioning Systems. Like ARM, TTP Com has done so well in building alliances and partnering with customers that it now ranks in the top five of semiconductor IP firms.

In 1998 the company decided to structure TTP Com as a subsidiary. Within two years, TTP Com was employing 160 and earning a healthy profit margin of around 26% on £19m in sales—not stellar earnings but enough to validate the subsidiary's business model. Management of both the parent company and subsidiary agreed that TTP Com was ready for complete demerger via public offering. Even in the bleak market days of early October 2000, when high-profile companies from Intel to Yahoo! were being pummeled by severely negative investor sentiment, the TTP Com IPO was nine times oversubscribed, raising nearly £40m and giving the company a valuation of over £540m.

TTP has found a remarkably effective means for accommodating innovation and growth within the firm. Like most business leaders in Cambridge, TTP's CEO Gerald Avison is not interested in running a large company. He estimates TTP's ideal size to be about 300 employees. At the same time, and rather uniquely, Avison does not want to preclude pursuit of high-potential projects because of TTP's self-imposed growth restrictions. He furthermore recognizes the need to provide room for the innovative impulses of entrepreneurial staff or risk losing them. What TTP refers to as its "incubation and separation" strategy of growing projects and then spinning them off as full-fledged companies aims to balance these conflicting objectives. TTP management is able to maintain an optimum size for operating the firm while allowing the company as a whole to benefit from pursuing new directions. In effect, TTP reaps much of the creative turbulence that comes from a high-growth enterprise without the company itself growing beyond a manageable size for its leaders. TTP's long-term viability is further enhanced by the future revenue streams earned from the shares it holds in demerged subsidiaries. TTP is managed to address that "essential fact" of capitalism that revolution inevitably comes from within. It is run as an enterprise that works to harness, rather than be overtaken by, waves of creative destruction.

TTP's ability to work with the forces of innovation also stems from ways the company motivates its workforce to be cohesive and creative at the same time. TTP Group is 75% owned by its staff and former employees—the only major Cambridge consultancy (and perhaps the only major Cambridge firm) where staff, and not only founders, own a clear majority of the company. The organization eschews incentive plans for rewarding individual performance. Instead, TTP rewards group performance in order to motivate all employees and demonstrate in real terms that TTP's management supports an inclusive culture. Share options are made available to every worker at TTP *except* those among the firm's founders. This is done to continue "recycling the ownership of the business into the next generation."[259] Employee ownership can begin from as early as the first day of work. New hires who have to wait for share options to vest can immediately take advantage of an interest-free company loan made available for purchasing stock on TTP's internal market. Avison sees equally sharing in the fruits of TTP's growth as vital to building the firm's innovative potential:

> There's nothing that goes on here that doesn't require a team of people to achieve it. So anything that reinforces the team approach—any subliminal

message—that's what the ethos is about actually, the message that everybody benefits equally. Anything that reinforces the team message is positive, anything that reinforces the individual message is potentially negative. That isn't to say that individuals don't have a role to play ... You need the inspired individual but they have to work within a team. The formula you need is $2 + 2 = 5$.[260]

As a company that is predominantly employee-owned, TTP's policy for returning value to its shareholders offers an added twist to the generally negative impression of a Phenomenon "lifestyle" company. In the TTP model, the lifestyle of the workforce is actually foremost in the company's thinking about wealth creation:

With our model we try to return value to our shareholders, broadly, as much as possible, in a way that will be life *enhancing* but not life *changing*. I'd much rather make 200 people very well off so it enhances their lives than make two people extremely wealthy so they can totally transform their lifestyles. Life changing can work for good or ill actually, it's not always good news. With the life-enhancing bit you can start doing things which you couldn't do before, you can stop worrying about things which you used to worry about. What you're trying to do is improve the quality of your life, not completely transform it.[261]

TTP's comprehensive innovation management model is most striking for the balances it achieves—between work and lifestyle, individual and group, growth and stability. In the context of the Phenomenon, TTP's thoughtful but pragmatic business strategy, corporate self-sufficiency, and largely uninterrupted record of success make it stand out from among the cluster's leading consultancies. At the same time, being the last major technology consultancy formed to date, TTP's management techniques are in many ways another indication of how members of the cluster have been "learning by doing"; that the evolution of the Phenomenon has advanced through the intelligent use of hindsight and finding means to improve upon past or existing methods of business management. TTP's successes with its incubation and separation strategy to drive ongoing innovation may yet further inspire other firms in the cluster. TTP's philosophy of employee lifestyle and wealth enhancement, moreover, offers a promising vision: one of genuine corporate steward-ship and truly innovative management practice that, especially in a century that began with business news overshadowed by the demise of greed-driven dotcoms and other purportedly innovative companies like Enron, the leadership of any enterprise would do well to reflect upon.

Since its beginnings as a center of scholarly education and learning, Cambridge has been blessed with an abundance of intellectual resources. In recent centuries and decades, the scientific ingenuity emanating from the university has laid the theoretical groundwork underpinning the Industrial Revolution and the pervasive information and life-science technologies of our world today. What the region has traditionally lacked, however, has been effective means for local enterprise to profit economically from Cambridge's creative genius. This makes the recent success of the innovators and innovation methods of the Cambridge Phenomenon all the more remarkable.

The continuance of a thriving concentration of knowledge-based industry in Cambridge still faces many challenges, from the reluctance of local innovators to interact synergistically (or competitively) with others to a variety of direct limitations placed on the growth of high-tech enterprise. Leaders in the Phenomenon have been identifying ways to address such obstacles and now the cluster demonstrates an impressive capacity for not only producing novel concepts and technologies, but in-novative, effective management techniques to profit by these creations as well. Cambridge innovation methods are contributing to the success of business activities within the Phenomenon and are proving applicable to markets and firms located far beyond the tightly circumscribed borders of the cluster. The innovative capacity of the Phenomenon shows how even if Silicon Fen stops short of producing large firms, the cluster distinguishes itself in creating enterprises and methods that are impacting the world in large enough ways.

# The Future of the Phenomenon     **11**

To a greater degree than the residents of many places, the people of Cambridge carve out their future according to deeply held views of the past. How those who move the cluster forward interpret and respond to current issues *vis-à-vis* the perpetuation of historical legacies will very much define the Cambridge Phenomenon of tomorrow. The issues that are likely to continue challenging Cambridge's leaders can be observed at local and national levels.

## *Local Issues*

More so than in Silicon Valley, Cambridge entrepreneurs confront the growing possibility that their revolution is reaching a plateau—not *dying*, but leveling off. So far, modern fenland technopreneurs have skillfully adjusted to the restrictions put on them by the local environment and provided the cluster with impressive, though not spectacular, growth. As the cluster further develops, limitations imposed by matters of laws and attitudes can be probably creatively addressed. Matters of physical restraint will prove to be more absolute, however. Cambridge's roads are choking with traffic; the amount of land people are willing to give over to development is diminishing. The problem is no longer a matter of having room for individual enterprises to grow, but simply having enough space to accommodate the birth of still more enterprises. As the cluster's physical infrastructure is currently configured, the Cambridge Phenomenon is close to reaching saturation point.

On the positive side, though the Phenomenon is unlikely to maintain the rate of growth it has enjoyed during its first three decades, there is little sign that the cluster will shrink through a hemorrhage of talent or business. The area will, like Silicon Valley, in all probability stay a preferable place to live for those who can afford it and are able to put up with the worsening conditions of daily life. Santa Clara Valley offers a reminder that the disadvantages of frustrating commutes, high living costs, and merely average levels of personal wealth do not easily deter people from the tremendous opportunities still associated with working in a thriving industrial cluster. There is no reason to expect that this will not similarly apply to those who consider the costs and benefits of being part of Cambridge's economic geography. An additional advantage: the cluster's staple of small, nimble firms will probably be unsusceptible to the types of pain and errors of excess that have recently plagued their larger-scale Valley counterparts. Thus the Phenomenon is unlikely to be blindsided by spiraling demands for energy, an increasing alienation of the lower levels of its workforce, or the sort of wrenching readjustment that comes after frenzied overexpansion during the latest technology craze.

Cambridge is not without its blind spots, however. In fact, the unique identity of the Phenomenon—a great source of the cluster's strength and integrity—has misleading, potentially self-defeating elements in it as well. Despite possessing a guarded, ironic sense of self-importance, the high-tech community in Cambridge can also be seen to suffer from an oddly persistent *folie de grandeur*. The misplaced sense of pride expresses itself in the preface to the *Cambridge Phenomenon* report of 1985, through seemingly innocuous sentences that convey some of the original spirit of enthusiasm for new growth in the cluster:

> There is a local excitement of it all. The visiting financier or industrialist, so often now from overseas, soon discovers this when the taxi driver from the railway station is full of information (gossip even) about the University; like the story of Lord Butler's now legendary remark at high table in Trinity to the [French] foreign ambassador who was waxing eloquent about his country's educational system—"You realize, your Excellency, that this small college has borne more Nobel prizewinners than your whole country, don't you?"[262]

Just as in the 1980s, the happy "fact" that Trinity College has produced more Nobel prizewinners than all of France still gets recited in a wide variety of discussions when talk turns to Cambridge's performance in high-tech. Apart from reports like the *Cambridge Phenomenon* and the scuttlebutt of chatty cab drivers, the Trinity versus France statistic makes appearances in speeches, casual conversation, and even some scholarly writing. The persistence of this comparative statement is revealing on several fronts, not the least of which being that the claim is pure mythology. Trinity has not produced more Nobel prizewinners than the nation of France.[263] Yet even if the boast were correct, the more important oversight in its frequent recitation is that a Nobel prize tally has no direct bearing on a region's competitive standing in the world of high-tech. The greater myth being perpetuated is that raw brainpower somehow serves as an adequate gauge of a cluster's positioning. A major lesson that comes from the squandering of Cambridge's early lead in high-tech industries concerns how promising, technologically astute businesses such as CSI and Pye failed by being unable to manage themselves. The resilience and vibrancy of the Cambridge cluster today results from practical management, not cerebral knowledge. Until the collective consciousness of the cluster grasps more of this reality, the Phenomenon will to some degree be limited by the myopia of popular opinion in facing the challenges and opportunities that lie ahead.

Unfortunately, such (admittedly subtle) delusions of grandeur appear in other ways and point to a similar lack of appreciation for Silicon Fen's true standing in the world of commercial technology. Powers falsely credited to the cluster's most celebrated firm, ARM Microprocessors, offer some examples. Managers from ARM can at times be heard to claim that, although the company only employs several hundred workers, it is more accurate to think of ARM's employees to number in the tens of thousands. Why? Because of the knock-on effects of the company's partnerships—ARM's cores make possible twenty or more jobs elsewhere for every single job created in Cambridge. Cambridge boosters will also point with pride to how ARM's yearly "shipments" (i.e., the number of chips using ARM cores) since 1999 have exceeded the number of chips annually manufactured by the semi-conductor industry's reigning power, Intel. This line of reasoning has been broadened. At the Cambridge Technology Conference held in May 2001, when a debate emerged about which sector, biotech or IT, would be more important to the Phenomenon in the future, a member of the audience challenged anyone from the life sciences sector to predict how long it would be before a local biotech company "produced" 400m units, as ARM already had with its cores. The implication of the question seemed to be that biotech companies needed to work harder at being more like ARM before they could claim to be leading the cluster.

There are many legitimate reasons for admiring ARM's accomplishments. To make assertions, however, that the company should be specially credited for the employment of multitudes of workers outside Cambridge or that it should serve as a benchmark for other firms to attempt producing hundreds of millions of "products" profoundly confuses ARM's true accomplishments. In particular, claims that ARM has somehow surpassed Intel eerily echo misleading comparisons between Trinity College and the nation of France. What ARM "manufactures" is semiconductor intellectual property (IP). That ARM cores have come to underpin the architecture of hundreds of millions of chips indicates genuine success. These facts, however, in no way imply that the company itself employs more people than it shows on its payroll or that ARM outperforms a company like Intel, whose sales and employment figures (if such comparisons are to be made) are respectively about 200 and 140 times larger than ARM's. ARM's success likewise does not mean that it can be claimed to perform better than all other Cambridge firms, especially those in the biotech sector where they compete in market-places entirely different from that for semiconductor IP. Exaggerated claims about ARM's accomplishments hint at a sentiment, prevailing in some quarters of the cluster, that apparently seeks to compensate for feelings of inferiority—feelings that are as undeserved as are the exaggerations that they spawn.

The people of the Phenomenon deserve to take pride in what they have accomplished, they should just do so for the right reasons. Cambridge's enduring urban legends are problematic in that they distort and misappropriate the true strengths of the cluster and its enterprises. They also mask the areas that would benefit from further improvement. The success of the Cambridge Phenomenon rests mainly with those individuals who managed to make sense of the mistakes of the past and subsequently directed enterprises toward more fruitful endeavors. Now that the track record of the Phenomenon offers more successes than failures to learn from, fostering an accurate understanding of exactly how and why the cluster has succeeded—and where further improvements could be made—will become increasingly important.

### National Issues

Misconceptions about Cambridge's position in the world of Siliconia also cloud the real issues Britain's leadership faces if it hopes to see the cluster developed substantially further. A Silicon Fen that comes even remotely close to rivaling Silicon Valley will demand that the UK's political establishment depart from the patterns of fundamental negligence shown to the cluster so far.

One of the most basic and least controversial ways that national government could support the cluster's growth would be to provide for better infrastructure. Improvements of this type would in no way ensure the continuation of high growth rates for the cluster or guarantee the creation of large-scale companies. Such improvements would, though, provide the Phenomenon with better odds at achieving either objective. Physical upgrading could also make locating to Cambridge a viable proposition for more than just the R&D subsidiaries of high-tech multinationals. The cluster would have a legitimate chance at being not only a technology hub but one with strengths in sales, marketing, and important corporate administrative functions. To make any of this feasible, national government will at the very minimum need to enact solutions to Cambridge's relative isolation and transportation bottlenecks. This would require actions like making Stansted an intercontinental international airport and overhauling Cambridge's road system, ideally adding efficient means of public transport such as light rail.

Breaking Cambridge's severe logistical constraints would still only offer a partial solution, however. Making it easier for people to access Cambridge would have to be complemented by new commercial and residential property development. The local political structure so far has made anything other than incremental, piecemeal improvements in these areas a legal impossibility. One possible solution can be found in a 1998 report concerning the future of the Phenomenon. Issued by a group of local leaders (notably including Hermann Hauser and Cambridge University Vice-Chancellor Alec Broers), the report made the far-reaching suggestion that the UK "government should extend the definition of 'Cambridge' by designating new development land as 'Cambridge High-Tech Development Zones'" and provide "incentives for companies to locate there."[264] As a way to sidestep local planning intransigence, the report recommended that these Cambridge High-Tech Development Zones (CHTDZ) be situated throughout the region as specially administered territories offering capital investment allowances, tax breaks, and fast-track planning approval for companies locating to them. Although providing no specifics, the proposers recommended that CHTDZ areas also would be constructed in a way as to meet "the housing, educational, health, and transport requirements of the people living and working in these areas."[265]

The report accurately reflects the sort of action national government will have to commit to if it is genuinely interested in seeing anything of greater economic substance arising from the Phenomenon. The CHTDZ concept does not represent the only feasible way forward but it does speak to the degree to which some major new direction in policy is necessary if Whitehall truly expects Silicon Fen to have any chance to compete head-to-head with Silicon Valley. Without some means to bypass the gridlock hampering the strategic planning and development of the region, the cluster will remain without substantial room for growth. Harold Wilson memorably came to power as Labour Prime

Minister in 1964 under the slogan of working to create a new Britain "forged in the white heat" of a "scientific revolution" led by science-based industries.[266] Some 40 years on, Silicon Fen has come to embody a tangible manifestation of that ideal. Yet without drastic changes to the constraints imposed by a lingering status quo, there is little likelihood that the Phenomenon will deliver to the nation substantively more in economic terms than what it already has.

Considering both the local and national issues facing the cluster, without hazarding a prediction, it can be safely said that for the foreseeable future the overall physical manifestations of the Cambridge Phenomenon are not going to alter perceptibly. With things as they currently are and are headed, the cluster is unlikely to develop tremendous density or become home to the campus of a once-small Phenomenon company that has been bred into a giant. The place to look for real progress within the cluster will be in its qualitative dimensions: increased interactivity, improved business facilitation, growing personal wealth, further refinements in its management strategies and innovation methods. Cambridge's biotech sector seems poised to expand to occupy an even larger proportion of the cluster's business base—an occurrence that will bring an interesting, though not particularly disruptive, change to the balance of the Phenomenon's industrial characteristics and capabilities. Whatever new directions the cluster takes, most of what will be transformed will probably occur beneath the radar screens of casual observers and political powers. The revolution "from within" will continue though probably running at a more moderate pace and being difficult to discern "from without." The innovative and the entrepreneurial who are able to make sense of the past and look beyond any misconceptions of the present will through their actions hew the contours of the Phenomenon's future.

# Epilogue: A Silicon World?　12

Is Silicon Valley indeed, as the trade press and other boosters claim, a modern Paradise? Or is it instead Paradise Lost, a thin, glittering surface of obsidian above a burning inferno ... There may be no more important question the modern industrial [world] can ask—because Silicon Valley is the future. One day we will all live in Silicon Valley, a coast-to-coast industrial park of concrete tilt-up buildings and manicured-grass berms; and then even the most remote citizen will know the meaning [of] this new electronic zeitgeist—intimately. Then there will be no turning back. Already there is a Silicon Gulch, a Silicon Mountain and Silicon Prairie. In time there will be a Silicon World.

Michael Malone, *The Big Score*[267]

What to make of Silicon Valley is, as Malone colorfully poses, a question of great significance to the modern world. How the planet's silicon landscapes and the enterprises that inhabit them are created, led, and the technologies and organizational models they generate are responded to, profoundly impacts the workings of our brave, New, Global economy.

The growing number of Siliconia around the planet lends support to the notion that, in time, there will be some form of "Silicon World." But if Silicon Valley is the future, that implies a world filled with knowledge-intensive, creatively dynamic clusters; something that is, fortunately, a far cry from a siliconized McWorld. To sustain locations like Silicon Valley and Silicon Fen requires valuing humans more than machines, critical thinking more than formulaic reasoning, individuality more than bureaucracy, action more than complacency. The spread of global Siliconia has yet to unleash a sterile, uniform, techno-centric culture. If anything, the forces of entrepreneurship and innovation that are at the heart of these clusters embolden an area's independent identity. Indeed, a location like Cambridge has already shown itself quite capable of halting the encroachment of those "concrete tilt-up buildings and manicured-grass berms" and continues to avoid most superficial trappings of the original Silicon Valley. If the Silicon Valleys of the world do provide glimpses of our long-term future, the view on offer is one of managerial insights, not of physical characteristics.

It thus remains unlikely that much of the planet will ever "look like" Silicon Valley, no matter how many locations slap the word "silicon" in front of some locally associated geographic feature. People will continue to be motivated by varying preferences in their choices and objectives in their actions. So long as human thinking and behavior remain diverse, so will the Siliconia of the world. Where a type of conversion will occur is in the way that other parts of the planet will awake increasingly to the opportunities for stimulating an area's indigenous capacity for innovation and entrepreneurship. As this happens, we witness the real spread—the sprawl beyond the sprawl—of Silicon Valley. Whether a location has as its economic mainstay the production of software or sausages, the task is not for other communities and enterprises to imitate those in Silicon Valley. Far more valuable is the opportunity to look beneath the surface of divergently successful clusters such as Silicon Valley and Silicon Fen to recognize how innovators and entrepreneurs have been responding to lengthy sequences of opportunities and challenges to bring about the creative destruction that drives these regions and their organizations forward. A holistic view of such clusters' virtues and shortcomings should also be taken in order to provide the observer with sufficient inspiration and warning. For lest it be forgotten: change is not inevitable. People can as easily shut out creative turbulence as they can uncritically succumb to it. It will be those that tend toward neither extreme but proactively manage the power of "new things" who will disproportionately benefit from the evolving Global/New Economy that the world's Siliconia so aptly represent.

# Endnotes

*A note about notes:* All direct quotes are sourced. Data that is a matter of general public record—for example, company earnings, stock prices, employment figures—are not sourced unless they are derived from a specially compiled listing or press item. Where appropriate, the uniform resource locator of an electronic source's website is listed along with the year in which it was accessed.

## FRONT MATTER

1   Aeschylus, "The Prometheus Bound," in Aeschylus, *The Suppliant Maidens, The Persians, The Seven Against Thebes, The Prometheus Bound*; trans. E. D. A. Morshead (London: Macmillan, 1908), 177.

## CHAPTER 1. INTRODUCTION: THE HIDDEN LESSONS OF "SILICONIA"

2   The roster of names can be found at Keith Dawson's "Tasty Bits from the Technology Front" located at tbtf.com/siliconia.html. The site claims to be "the definitive collection of *Siliconia* on the Web" and defines "Siliconia" as "appropriations of names beginning with 'Silicon' by areas outside Silicon Valley." The neologism "Siliconia" is tongue-in-cheek in origin but still useful shorthand for denoting regional economies that are associated with the output of advanced technology products or services. It is also worth noting that Dawson's compiled list goes beyond registering placenames that begin with "Silicon" and

includes locations with such nicknames as "The Dot Commonwealth" (Massachusetts), "Cyberabad" (Hyderabad, India), "Telecom Beach" (San Diego), and, a particularly curious twist in a non-siliconized name, "Philicon Valley" (Philadelphia).

3      Among the ten locales claiming the title of Silicon Prairie, associations representing two—Payne County in Oklahoma and greater Kansas City—are stirring up dust in a "legal tornado" (www.siliconprairie.org/legaltornado.htm, 2001).

4      Bob Metcalfe, "Asian Tour Provides Useful Insight on Silicon Valley's Worldwide Internet Edge," *Infoworld Electric*, 2 March 1998.

5      In academic circles, debates have already been raging although the orthodoxy as described here holds sway. For those interested in more academically oriented arguments against the two pillars of prevailing wisdom that *Clusters of Creativity* refutes, the home page by the University of Texas at Dallas' Stan Liebowitz, www.utdallas.edu/~liebowit/, and an article by the University of Minnesota's Ann Markusen, "Fuzzy Concepts, Scanty Evidence, Policy Distance: The Case for Rigour and Policy Relevance in Critical Regional Studies," *Regional Studies* 33, no. 9 (December 1999): 869–84; are excellent places to start.

6      Paul Krugman, *Geography and Trade* (Leuven/Cambridge, MA: Leuven University Press/MIT Press, 1991), 61.

7      Ibid., 62.

8      Ibid.

9      Ibid., 66–7.

10     A rallying cry for advocates of increasing returns and its tangential theory of path dependency is that "history matters." History is dead: it only appears alive when people elect, in the present, to perpetuate the legacies of the past. Against the background noise of shouts that "history matters," *Clusters of Creativity* retorts: "management matters." Management is the key to understanding a cluster. The way individuals uphold previously established patterns of behavior is but one of many factors that managers must in some manner address.

11     This book's explorations of the ways in which strategy and action determine the characteristics of a cluster contrast even more strongly with Krugman's contention that economic activity will somehow "self-organize"—as if a location itself is a sentient economic actor while its human constituency some passive mass of material. See *The Self-Organizing Economy* (Cambridge: Blackwell Publishers, 1996), a work that expands on the concepts advocated in *Geography and Trade*.

12     AnnaLee Saxenian, *Regional Advantage: Culture and Competition in Silicon Valley and Route 128* (Cambridge, MA: Harvard University Press, 1994).

13     Ibid., 37.

14     Ibid., 9.

15     Ibid.

16     Ibid., 130.

17     Ibid., 162.

18     Ibid., 133–59.

19     Another effect of the sort of logic encapsulated by *Regional Advantage* is the now popularly accepted notion that innovation is somehow by definition a collaborative rather than an individualistic undertaking. Collaboration can undeniably *facilitate* innovation in important ways. Until humans universally demonstrate powers of extrasensory perception, however, the wellsprings of innovation will remain lodged in the minds of individuals, not some imagined collective brain. Clusters like Silicon Valley thrive on the creative milieu to which the actors in these economic geographies have jointly contributed. Yet, at its core, innovation remains an intensely personal endeavor, one where individual choice and perseverance are still the ultimate determining factors.

20     Peter Swann and Martha Prevezer, "Introduction," in *The Dynamics of Industrial Clustering: International Comparisons in Computing and Biotechnology*, ed. G. M. Peter Swann *et al.* (Oxford: Oxford University Press, 1998), 3.

21     The full title of von Thünen's work is *Der isolierte Staat in Beziehung auf Landwirtschaft und Nationalökonomie (The Isolated State in Relation to Agriculture and Political Economy)*. It is available in an abridged English translation as *Von Thünen's Isolated State*, trans. Carla Wartenberg (Oxford: Pergamon Press, 1966).

22     Alfred Marshall, *Principles of Economics: An Introductory Volume*, 8th ed. (London: Macmillan, 1946; reprint, 1980). Marshall explores industrial districts in Book IV, Chapter X, "The Concentration of Specialized Industries in Particular Localities," 267–77.

23     Michael Porter, *The Competitive Advantage of Nations* (New York: Simon and Schuster, 1989).

24     Michael Porter, "Clusters and the New Economics of Competition," *Harvard Business Review*, November–December 1998: 78.

25     Joseph Schumpeter, "The Creative Response in Economic History," *Journal of Economic History*, November 1947; Joseph Schumpeter, *Essays on Entrepreneurs, Innovations, Business Cycles, and the Evolution of Capitalism*, ed. Richard Clemence (New Brunswick, NJ: Transaction Publishers,

1997; reprint, Cambridge, MA: Addison-Wesley, 1951), 222–3 (page references are according to the 1997 reprinted edition).

26    Karl Marx, *Theses on Feuerbach*, XI (1845), www.marxists.org/archive/ marx/works/1845/theses/theses.htm.

## SILICON VALLEY

## CHAPTER 2. INTRODUCTION

27    The percentage of residents who are foreign born is out of a total estimated population of 1.35m people living in the recognized boundaries of the Silicon Valley region (Joint Venture: Silicon Valley Network, *2001 Index of Silicon Valley*, 4).

28    The way in which the industrial fabric of Silicon Valley, although concentrated in Santa Clara and parts of neighboring counties, sprawls across a large territory in the Bay Area makes estimating the number of high-tech firms that legitimately function as part of the cluster difficult. The most comprehensive, reliable, and up-to-date accounting comes from Rich's Business Directories' annual *Rich's Guide to Silicon Valley/Northern California*, a compendium of high-tech firms whose listings are regularly verified by phone surveys. *Rich's 2001–2002 Guide* lists some 8,300 high-tech firms operating in Santa Clara, Contra Costa, Alameda, San Francisco, and San Mateo counties—this compares to other recent compilations that list Silicon Valley as home to anywhere from 7,000 to 10,000 high-tech firms. (The product codes used by *Rich's Guide* are available at www.norcalcompanies.com/prodcode.html.)

29    Joint Venture: Silicon Valley Network, *2002 Index of Silicon Valley*, 9. It is worth noting that JVSVN's tally of Silicon Valley's core workforce is limited in geographic scale to "Santa Clara County plus adjacent parts of San Mateo, Alameda and Santa Cruz counties." At the same time, it is enlarged in terms of its sectoral employment measure as this counts not only those working in the purely high-tech sectors of software, innovation services, semiconductors and equipment, computers and communications, bioscience, and defense and aerospace, but also the more peripheral professional services sector. (Ibid., 2.)

30    Joint Venture: Silicon Valley Network, *2001 Index of Silicon Valley*, 15.

31    Bay Area Economic Forum, *The Bay Area: Winning in the New Global Economy*, September 1999, 1.

32    Joint Venture: Silicon Valley Network, *2001 Index of Silicon Valley*, 7.

33    Bay Area Economic Forum, *The Bay Area*, 1.

34    Marty Kady, "No Doubt About It: Valley is Prince of Technology," Silicon Valley/San Jose *Business Journal*, 25 August 2000.

35    AnnaLee Saxenian, *Regional Advantage: Culture and Competition in Silicon Valley and Route 128* (Cambridge, MA: Harvard University Press, 1994), 61.


## CHAPTER 3. FROM SEMI-DESERT TO SILICON VALLEY

36    David Kaplan, *The Silicon Boys and Their Valley of Dreams* (New York: William Morrow, 1999), 18.

37    Data on daily earnings from Rodman Paul, *California Gold: The Beginning of Mining in the Far West* (Cambridge, MA: Harvard University Press, 1947), 120; quoted in Maureen Jung, "Capitalism Comes to the Diggings: From Gold-Rush Adventure to Corporate Enterprise," in *A Golden State: Mining and Economic Development in Gold Rush California*, ed. James Rawls and Richard Orsi (Berkeley: University of California Press, 1999), 59. 2000 dollar value based on multiple derived by Robert Sahr, "Inflation Conversion Factors for Dollars 1700 to Estimated 2010," www.orst.edu/Dept/pol_sci/fac/sahr/sahr.htm, 2001.

38    See Ronald Limbaugh, "Making Old Tools Work Better: Pragmatic Adaptation and Innovation in Gold-Rush Technology," and David St. Clair "The Gold Rush and the Beginnings of California Industry," in *A Golden State*, ed. Rawls and Orsi.

39    Arthur McEwen quoted in Oscar Lewis, *The Big Four: The Story of Huntington, Stanford, Hopkins, and Crocker and the Building of the Central Pacific* (New York: Alfred Knopf, 1938), 156–7.

40    Stanford University, *Stanford University: The Founding Grant with Amendments, Legislation, and Court Decrees* (Stanford, CA: Stanford University Press, 1971), 4.

41    Susan Wels, *Stanford: Portrait of a University* (Stanford, CA: Stanford Alumni Association, 1999), 9.

42    Hugh Aitken, *The Continuous Wave: Technology and the American Radio, 1900–1932* (Princeton, NJ: Princeton University Press, 1985), 238.

43    James Hijiya, *Lee de Forest and the Fatherhood of Radio* (Bethlehem, PA: Lehigh University Press, 1992), 90.

44    Books by Silicon Valley-based authors that celebrate de Forest as having

"invented" the "Age of Electronics" at Federal in Palo Alto include Jane Morgan's *Electronics in the West: The First Fifty Years* (Palo Alto, CA: National Press Books, 1967; see pp. 53–5) and Michael Malone's *The Big Score: The Billion Dollar Story of Silicon Valley* (New York: Doubleday, 1985; pp. 14–15). In his later years Hewlett-Packard co-founder Bill Hewlett went so far as to credit the importance of de Forest and his work as having triggered the "supernova" birth of industrial activity that created Silicon Valley. (See Carolyn Tajnai, "Links Between Stanford University and Industry," http://www-forum.stanford.edu/About/History/links.html.) As Hewlett's comments indicate, some among later generations of Valley entrepreneurs were no doubt inspired by de Forest's work. Yet it is incorrect to attribute either discovery of the regenerative circuit to de Forest or to attribute his work as having culminated in the Silicon Valley cluster of today. For the record, in contrast to the Silicon Valley accolades heaped on de Forest's work and the court ruling that found in his favor, bodies like the Institute of Radio Engineers, the Franklin Institute, and the American Institute of Electrical Engineers all recognize the original filer of the patent, Columbia University student E. Howard Armstrong, as the true inventor of regenerative circuitry. Detailed investigations by scholars furthermore confirm that de Forest and his team in Palo Alto fundamentally ignored the significance of what they stumbled upon in 1912. See, for example, Aitken, *The Continuous Wave*, 238–245; Hijiya, *Lee de Forest*, 89–90; and Tom Lewis, *Empire of the Air: The Men Who Made Radio* (New York: HarperPerennial, 1991), 192–204. The dearth of any major enterprises to emerge in the Valley on the heels of de Forest's research efforts provides the clearest testament that, apart from a "feel-good factor" and publicity value, de Forest's real impact on the specific characteristics of today's Silicon Valley are minimal to nonexistent.

45   James Williams, *Energy and the Making of Modern California* (Akron, OH: University of Akron Press, 1997), 193.

46   This section describing Stanford's operations during the Depression era draws extensively from Rebecca Lowen, *Creating the Cold War University: The Transformation of Stanford* (Berkeley: University of California Press, 1997).

47   Memo from David Webster to Frederick Terman, 2 May 1939, Frederick Emmons Terman Papers, Box 2/4/15, quoted in Lowen, *Creating the Cold War University*, 30.

48   Frederick Terman, "Frederick Emmons Terman," interviews conducted

by Arthur Norberg, Charles Susskind, and Roger Hanh" (Berkeley, CA: Bancroft Library, 1984), 9.

49    Ibid., 13.

50    Ibid., 29.

51    It is worth noting that the reasons for Bloch's opposition to government involvement in science differed from the Hoover-style ideological conservatism that pervaded administrative thinking at Stanford. Bloch, a Swiss national of Jewish heritage, was compelled to leave behind what had been a promising career at the University of Leipzig in Germany after the Nazis took power. He joined the faculty of Stanford in 1934. His fear of national government involvement in university research was from an altogether different experience with its consequences.

52    Frederick Terman, "Dean's Report, School of Engineering, 1946–47," Stanford University Archives, S. E. Wallace Sterling Papers, Box 39; quoted in Stuart Leslie, "How the West Was Won: The Military and the Making of Silicon Valley," in *Technological Competitiveness: Contemporary and Historical Perspectives on the Electrical, Electronics, and Computer Industries*, ed. William Aspray (Piscataway, NJ: IEEE Press, 1993), 77.

53    Ibid.

54    James Williams, "Frederick E. Terman and the Rise of Silicon Valley," in *Technology in America: A History of Individuals and Ideas*, ed. Carroll Pursell (Cambridge, MA: MIT Press, 1996), 287.

55    David Packard, *The HP Way: How Bill Hewlett and I Built Our Company* (New York: Harper Business, 1995), 34.

56    Frederick Terman, "Frederick Emmons Terman," 187.

57    Ibid., 192.

58    Ibid., 193.

59    Joan Hamilton, "David Packard: Silicon Valley's Class Act," *Business Week*, 8 April 1996.

60    Within a matter of months, another figure important to Silicon Valley's development, Intel co-founder Gordon Moore, exceeded Hewlett's donation by $200m through gifting $600m to his *alma mater*, the California Institute of Technology, in Los Angeles. Although Moore's munificence benefits a university community based outside the Silicon Valley cluster, it still demonstrates the incredibly strong ethos of support for academia that has been fostered in the Valley.

61    David Jacobson, "Founding Fathers," *Stanford Magazine*, July–August 1998.

62    Silicon Valley Manufacturing Group, www.svmg.org, 2002. Packard

was, undeniably, through his efforts at building cooperation among companies, helping create important business networks within Silicon Valley. But these and the Valley's other much-storied networks never became so powerful as to overtake the importance of autonomous decision-making among individuals and within firms. (More on this point will be elaborated in later sections.) What is obvious is that the tightly synergistic relationships that have sprung up in the Valley have lowered transaction costs and generally made doing business easier. By providing increased access to resources and support, networks have, when effectively used, in fact empowered individuals and strengthened the integrity of firms.

63    San Jose *Mercury News* "Silicon Valley 150," 16 April 2001.

64    HP corporate website, www.hp.com, 2001.

65    *Fortune 500*, July 2001, www.fortune.com.

66    San Jose *Mercury News* "Silicon Valley 150," 16 April 2001.

67    Diane Coyle, "Where It's At," *Analysis*, BBC Radio 4 broadcast, 7 December 2000.

68    Don Hoefler, "Silicon Valley—U. S. A.," *Electronic News*, 11 January 1971, 1.

69    Details on Shockley's life and how he came to establish his company in Silicon Valley are chronicled in Michael Riordan and Lillian Hoddeson, *Crystal Fire: The Birth of the Information Age* (New York: W.W. Norton, 1997).

70    Moore publicly laid down his famous law in an article: "Cramming More Components onto Integrated Circuits," *Electronics* 38, no. 8 (1965). Apart from being slightly off in terms of the time interval he estimated—it has actually taken an average of around 18 or more months for semiconductor capacity to double—over the years Moore's prediction has proven uncannily accurate. Its logic has been used to explain a wide variety of phenomena in the way high-tech electronics advance. In general, Moore's Law has been adopted by many as explanation for the extraordinarily fast rate of learning curves and economies of scale that apply to modern Information Technology sectors.

71    Tim Jackson, *Inside Intel: The Unauthorized History of the World's Most Successful Chip Company* (London: HarperCollins, 1997), 6 and 27.

72    Andrew Grove, *Only the Paranoid Survive: How to Exploit the Crisis Points that Challenge Every Company* (New York: Random House, 1996), 88.

73    Ibid., 95, 88, and 86.

74    Ibid., 89 and 93.

75    Saxenian, *Regional Advantage*, 118. See pp. 117–25 passim for the outlines of the supposedly proper Silicon Valley model of semiconductor production.

76    Market share statistics are according to Mercury Research and quoted in Dean Takahashi, "Limping Giant," *Red Herring*, 2 January 2001. (Takahashi's article provides an excellent perspective on some of the management problems that face Intel as the company moves to making the next generation of microprocessors. David Hamilton also provides an insightful account on the same topic in "Intel Gambles It Can Move Beyond the PC with New Microprocessor," *Wall Street Journal*, 29 May 2001. Intel's challenges in its transition once again demonstrate that past success is no guarantee of future accomplishment. How Intel resolves the issues confronting it will determine if it is able to maintain its lead in the global semiconductor industry.

77    Employment and sales figures per the "Silicon Valley 150," San Jose *Mercury News*, 16 April 2001.

78    David Eakins, ed., *Businessmen and Municipal Reform* (San Jose, CA: Sourisseau, 1976), 15; quoted in Philip Trounstine and Terry Christensen, *Movers and Shakers: The Study of Community Power* (New York: St. Martin's Press, 1982), 83.

79    Trounstine and Christensen, *Movers and Shakers*, 89–92.

80    Ibid., 92.

81    Dennis Taylor, "Cradle of Venture Capital," Silicon Valley/San Jose *Business Journal*, 16 April 1999.

82    Neal Douglas quoted in Clifford Carlsen, "Sand Hill Road Still the Address of Choice for VCs," San Francisco *Business Times*, 7 May 1999.

## CHAPTER 4. VALLEY DYNAMISM

83    Steve Jurvetson, "Changing Everything: The Internet Revolution and Silicon Valley," in *The Silicon Valley Edge: A Habitat for Innovation and Entrepreneurship*, ed. Chong-Moon Lee, William Miller, Marguerite Gong Hancock, and Henry Rowen (Stanford, CA: Stanford University Press, 2000), 124.

84    The proposer of this super-hardened telecommunications network was Paul Baran, a computer scientist employed at the Los Angeles think tank, RAND. It is described in Baran's paper: "On Distributed Communications," Rand Corporation Memorandum RM-3420-PR,

August 1964, available at www.rand.org/publications/RM/RM3420/. Baran's design was, despite its clear merits for national defense and strong support from the US Air Force, squelched as a proposal in 1965 because of intransigence from AT&T—a powerful example of how government-protected technology monopolies can thwart high-potential innovations.

85    Katie Hafner and Matthew Lyon, *Where Wizards Stay Up Late: The Origins of the Internet* (New York: Touchstone, 1998), 72.

86    Ibid., 78.

87    Company statistics and rankings according to San Jose *Mercury News* "Silicon Valley 150," 16 April 2001.

88    Scott Thurm, "Even as Rivals Began to Stumble, Cisco Believed Itself to Be Immune," *Wall Street Journal*, 18 April 2001.

89    San Jose *Mercury News* "Silicon Valley 150," 16 April 2001.

90    Alex Markels, "The Wisdom of Chairman Ko," *Fast Company*, November 1999; Bill Roberts, "CEO of the Year: Koichi Nishimura, Contract Manufacturing Visionary," *Electronic Business*, December 1999.

91    In December 2001, SCI and the Silicon Valley-based electronic manufacturing services company Sanmina merged. Even with Sanmina-SCI's combined fiscal year 2001 net sales of $12b, Solectron's $19b of sales volume reported (for its fiscal year ending in August 2001) still makes it the dominant player in the industry.

92    Solectron has done so well with its quality control and human resource strategies that, like HP, Japanese commentators now laud it for integrating the best practices of Japan's collectivistic and the US's individualistic management styles. A regional Japanese industrial group, for example, celebrates Solectron as a model business that explains "the secret of success in Silicon Valley" in a book by the same name: 清成忠男監修「シリコンバレーで成功する秘訣」(東京：八朔社、1998). (Japanese accolades heaped on HP can be found in books such as Menjou Hiroshi and Honjou Juuji's *For Japanese Companies that have Forgotten Japanese Style Management: Lessons from Hewlett-Packard, a Start-up with 90,000 Employees* [Tokyo: Diamond, 1995]: 校條浩、本荘修「日本的経営を忘れた日本企業へ―9万人のベンチャー企業。ヒューレット・パッカード」ダイヤモンド社、1995].) Throughout the 1980s and well into the 1990s, Silicon Valley, and American high-technology sectors in general, were in both awe and fear of "Japan Inc." Japan's collaborative, network-centric approach to business management was seen as superior until the pathological aspects of Japan's corporate collecti-

vism became more readily apparent after Japanese businesses fell into the quagmire of shared misery and denial that they have been enduring since the early 1990s. The major distinguishing factor between successful "Japanese-style" Silicon Valley firms and many of their counterparts in Japan is the degree to which individual empowerment (in everything from corporate governance structures to shop-floor responsibilities) sustains the vitality of the Silicon Valley companies.

93    Don Hoefler, "Silicon Valley—U. S. A.," Part II, *Electronic News*, 18 January 1971.

94    Ibid.

95    John Cassidy, "The Force of an Idea," *The New Yorker*, 10 January 1998.

96    James Daly, "The Robin Hood of the Rich," *Wired*, 5 August 1997.

97    In 2000, Reback resigned from Wilson Sonsini to join a local start-up— one of many indications of how successful Valley professionals, such as lawyers and venture capitalists, will easily transition from their more rarified positions into the nuts and bolts of firm formation and management.

98    Ranking according to gross revenue (which in 2000 was $450m for Wilson Sonsini with profits per partner at $930,000) as listed in "The Am Law 100" compiled by *The American Lawyer*, July 2001. See also Renee Deger, "Bay Area Firms Rocket Up Annual Am Law 100," *The Recorder*, 5 July 2001. Wilson Sonsini's state-wide ranking is an especially noteworthy feat in terms of economic geography because top positions in California's legal rankings have traditionally been the province of practices from Los Angeles.

99    Larry Sonsini, author's interview, 10 August 2000.

100   Ibid.

101   Mark Suchman, "On Advice of Council: Law Firms and Venture Capital Funds as Information Intermediaries in the Structuration of Silicon Valley" (Ph. D. diss., Stanford University, 1994), 95.

102   Larry Sonsini, 10 August 2000.

103   Suchman, "On Advice of Council," 109.

104   Scott McNealy, "Silicon Valley Doesn't Need a Reality Check," New York *Times*, 5 July 1999.

105   Luc Hatlestad, "I'm Gonna Sue Your Ass!", *Red Herring*, May 1999.

106   Suchman, "On Advice of Council," 43.

107   Doerr, one of the most vocal spokespeople for Silicon Valley, has for many years commented on the deeper meanings of the cluster. His stock quotes are repeated with usually only slight variations in phrasing

and are recounted in many sources. Here his direct quote comes from *Red Herring*, "It's a Wonderful Life," February 1997. It should be noted that after the market meltdown was in full swing, even the unflinching pitchman Doerr found himself in mid-2001 offering "something of an apology" for stoking Internet hype. (Silvia Cavallini, "Venture Capital: Sorry Returns," *The Industry Standard*, July 2001.)

108    In a slightly simplified formulation, "Metcalfe's Law" first appeared in a 1993 article by Valley technology pundit George Gilder. Gilder wrote of "Metcalfe's law of the telecosm" which demonstrated "the magic of interconnections: connect any number, '$n$,' of machines—whether computers, phones or even cars—and you get '$n$' squared potential value." (George Gilder, "Metcalfe's Law and Legacy," *Forbes ASAP*, 13 September 1993.)

109    Rafe Needleman, "Venturing Under the Influence," redherring.com, 7 September 1999.

110    *Business Week*, introduction to "Silicon Valley: How It Really Works," 25 August 1997, available at www.businessweek.com/1997/34/970825.htm, 2001. Research by the San Jose *Mercury News* indicates that the statistic is slightly misstated: it was not "a Valley" company that "went public every five days ..." but rather a company within the entire Bay Area—a territory that notably included areas like San Francisco's concentration of dotcoms. See Michelle Quinn and Jennifer Lafleur, "A Hard Look at Silicon Valley's Boom," San Jose *Mercury News*, www.siliconvalley.com, posted 27 December 1999.

111    Michael Lewis, *The New New Thing: A Silicon Valley Story* (New York: W.W. Norton, 2000), 13. Lewis has some experience in observing the casino mentality that can consume hallowed bastions of capitalist finance. In an earlier book, *Liars Poker*, he related his work as a bond trader in the 1980s as having placed him "somewhere in the middle of a modern gold rush. Never before have so many unskilled twenty-four-year-olds made so much money in so little time as we did in this decade in New York and London." (Michael Lewis, *Liar's Poker* [London: Coronet Books, 1989], 11.) Replace the words "New York and London" with "Silicon Valley" and visualize 20-something dotcom entrepreneurs instead of 24-year-old bond traders, and you have essentially the same scenario.

112    Rafe Needleman, "Reality Check Returned: Insufficient Funds," redherring.com, 28 February 2000.

113    Geoffrey Moore, foreword to *Silicon Gold Rush: The Next Generation of*

*High-tech Stars Rewrites the Rules of Business*, by Karen Southwick (New York: John Wiley and Sons, 1999), vii–viii.

114    Ibid., v.

115    Margaret Steen, "Job Loss Hit Valley Workers Hard, Fast," San Jose *Mercury News*, 23 February 2002. Quoted in the same article, Stephen Levy, Director of the Palo Alto-based Center for Continuing Study of the California Economy, observed that the job losses were "Something that two or three decades ago might have been strung out over a couple of years happened all at once." Levy notes that the rapid increase in unemployment figures indicates that local companies have become increasingly capable of quick reaction to changes in market conditions, a perverse demonstration of the regional economy's growing resilience.

116    John Wilson, *The New Venturers: Inside the High-Stakes World of Venture Capital* (Reading, MA: Addison-Wesley, 1985), 34.

117    Owen Edwards, "Legends: Arthur Rock," *Forbes ASAP*, 1 June 1998.

118    Wilson, *The New Venturers*, 36.

119    Randy Komisar, *The Monk and the Riddle: The Education of a Silicon Valley Entrepreneur* (Boston: Harvard Business School Press, 2000), 81–2.

120    William Bygrave and Jeffry Timmons, *Venture Capital at the Crossroads* (Boston: Harvard Business School Press, 1992), 31.

121    Gene Bylinski, "Who Will Feed the Startups?" *Fortune*, 26 June 1995.

122    The redirection of the company from Internet hosting to software appears to be the first viable move to get the firm to profitability. Further reflecting the changed environment, technology sector observers have lauded the transformation. See, for example, Ronni Colville and Donna Scott, "Loudcloud Wisely Changes Focus From Hosting to Software," *Gartner News Analysis*, 24 June 2002.

123    "Frontier," *Businessweek Online*, 5 February 2001.

## CHAPTER 5. VALLEY INNOVATORS

124    Joseph Schumpeter, "The Creative Response in Economic History," *Journal of Economic History*, November 1947; Joseph Schumpeter, *Essays on Entrepreneurs, Innovations, Business Cycles, and the Evolution of Capitalism*, ed. Richard Clemence (New Brunswick, NJ: Transaction Publishers, 1997; reprint, Cambridge, MA: Addison-Wesley, 1951), 223.

125    Data are per Accenture's *Annual Report, 2001* and "Company Information" provided by its website at www.accenture.com, 2001.

126    www.accenture.com.

127    Hughes, author's interview, 8 August 2000.

128    John Kao, author's interview, 16 August 2000.

129    Ethan Watters, "Kao's Theory," *Business 2.0*, September 1999.

130    John Kao, 16 August 2000.

131    Federico Faggin, interview with Rob Walker, 3 March 1995, in *Silicon Genesis: Oral History Interviews with Semiconductor Industry Pioneers*, hosted by Rob Walker, www-sul.stanford.edu/depts/hasrg/histsci/ siligen.html, 2001.

132    Federico Faggin, 3 March 1995.

133    Tim Jackson, *Inside Intel: The Unauthorized History of the World's Most Successful Chip Company* (London: HarperCollins, 1998), 57.

134    Joint Venture: Silicon Valley Network, *2001 Index of Silicon Valley*, 4.

135    Federico Faggin, author's interview, 2 August 2000.

136    Ibid.

137    Deborah Lohse, "Synaptics' Test of IPO Waters Goes Swimmingly," San Jose *Mercury News*, 29 January 2002.

138    Federico Faggin, 2 August 2000.

139    California Technology, Trade, and Commerce Agency, *Foreign Direct Investment in California*, and *California Export Factsheet—2000 Year-End Total*, www.commerce.ca.gov, 2001.

140    Sony deserves credit for setting up its PARC-style laboratory in 1990, far in advance of when most Japanese firms realized the shift away from routinized innovation.

141    Casio Research website, casioresearch.com/flash_index.html, 2002.

142    B. J. Fogg, author's interview, 28 July 2000.

143    Ibid.

144    Probably the best known of Valley companies employing the methodology is IDEO Product Development in Palo Alto, an "innovation services" firm established in 1978 by its CEO and Stanford product design professor, David Kelley.

145    Claudia Deutsch, "Xerox, Fading Copier King, Hasn't Used Its Innovations Well," New York *Times*, 19 October 2000.

146    Rich Gold, "Some Graphical Proverbs Plus Projects," www.parc.xerox. com/red, 2001.

147    Rich Gold, "PAIR: The Xerox PARC Artist-in-Residence Program," in *Art and Innovation: The Xerox PARC Artist-in-Residence Program*, ed. Craig Harris (Cambridge, MA: The MIT Press, 1999), 18. See also Gold's homepage at www.parc.xerox.com/red.

148    Gold, "PAIR," *Art and Innovation*, 13. The PAIR principles can largely be found online as a mixed graphic-literary document by Gold called "Eight Three-Dimensional Objects of Unknown Origin Presented in Sixty Four Known Pairings," www.parc.xerox.com/red.

## CHAPTER 6. POST-SILICON SILICON VALLEY

149    Nancy Vogel, "How State's Consumers Lost With Electricity Deregulation," Los Angeles *Times*, 9 December 2000.

150    Silicon Valley Manufacturing Group, *Projections 2000* (San Francisco: Association of Bay Area Governments, 2000), 31.

151    Jennifer Bjorhus, "Growing Valley Guzzling Power at High Speeds," San Jose *Mercury News*, 11 February 2001.

152    Ibid.

153    K. Oanh Ha, "Janitors Campaign Seeks to Shame Valley's Big Tech Firms," San Jose *Mercury News*, 29 May 2000.

154    Center for Economic Competitiveness, SRI International, *Joint Venture: Silicon Valley, An Economy At Risk: The Phase I Diagnostic Report* (Menlo Park, CA: SRI International, 1992), i.

155    Michelle Quinn and Jennifer Lafleur, "A Hard Look at Silicon Valley's Boom," San Jose *Mercury News*, posted 27 December 1999, www. siliconvalley.com.

156    Ibid.

## EUROPE'S SILICON FEN

## CHAPTER 7. INTRODUCTION

157    Geoffrey Wansell, "The Heart of New Britain," *The Business* (*Financial Times* weekend magazine), 4 March 2000.

158    Tony Blair, speech delivered at the St. John's Innovation Centre, Cambridge, 13 September 1999.

159    Cambridge City Council, *Cambridge Local Plan* (Cambridge: Cambridge City Council, 1997), 112.

160    Segal Quince Wicksteed, *The Cambridge Phenomenon Revisited* (Histon, UK: Segal Quince Wicksteed, 2000), part 1, 9. SQW's percentages apply

to those high-tech firms lying within the demarcated boundaries of the Phenomenon (see Figure 7.2).

161    Research Group, Economic & Community Development Unit, Cambridgeshire County Council, *Employment in the Hi-tech 'Community' in Cambridge* (Cambridge: Cambridge County Council, 2000), 3–4. Note that the Research Group of the Cambridgeshire County Council tallies firms in all of Cambridgeshire, a geography larger than the recognized boundaries of the Phenomenon. County Council figures register about 200 more firms and 8,000 more employees than SQW's data. A cluster's growth tends to spread beyond its recognized geography. In the case of Silicon Fen in particular, growth is suppressed by the government authorities of Cambridge City and South Cambridgeshire (the main political jurisdictions of the cluster), thereby directing it further away from the cluster's center. Thus, the more encompassing County Council company and employment figures are used here. Note that, unlike records on Silicon Valley's employment statistics maintained by Joint Venture: Silicon Valley Network, Cambridgeshire County Council figures do not include those for peripheral industries, such as professional services, that support Cambridge's high-technology community.

162    Le Parc de Sophia Antipolis website, www.sophia-antipolis.org.

163    The derivation of these statistics for Silicon Valley is explained in footnotes 28 and 29.

164    Whittle abandoned his intentions to develop his company, Power Jets, after leaders of established aircraft engine manufacturers convinced the government's Gas Turbine Technical Advisory and Coordinating Committee in 1945 to side with their view that "it should be no part of [Power Jets'] function to design and even prototype engines, and that there must be no competition with industry whatsoever." (John Golley, *Genesis of the Jet: Frank Whittle and the Invention of the Jet Engine* [Shrewsbury, UK: Airlife Publishing, 1996], 225.) Stripped of the right to operate Power Jets as anything more than an organization for basic research, Whittle (and later key members of his staff) left the firm and shortly thereafter it ceased to function beyond the level of a shell company with a portfolio of patents to its name. Power Jets was not Cambridge-based but had operations around Leicester some 60 miles away, a distance easily accommodated in a cluster and greater region the size of Silicon Valley's (see Figure 2.1). If Whittle had been allowed to grow Power Jets as he saw fit, it is impossible to speculate what the net effect would have been for Cambridge's high-tech development. As an

indication of the government's and entrenched industry's antagonism to entrepreneurs coming out of Cambridge at the time, however, the squashing of the initiative behind Power Jets is highly significant.

165    Joseph Schumpeter, *Capitalism, Socialism, and Democracy* (New York: Harper Torchbooks, 1976; reprint, New York: Harper & Brothers, 1942), 83.


## CHAPTER 8. THE PHENOMENON OF CAMBRIDGE

166    *Merriam-Webster's Collegiate Dictionary*, Electronic Edition, Version 1.5.

167    Acts of the Privy Council, New Series XII (1896), 68–9; quoted in H. C. Darby, *The Draining of the Fens*, 2nd ed. (Cambridge: Cambridge University Press, 1956), 16.

168    A note about terms: the word "entrepreneur," which comes from the Old French *entreprendre*—"one who undertakes"—did not actually enter the English language until around the middle of the 19th century. When we speak of an entrepreneur in English we are in fact meaning an "undertaker" in this original sense of the word.

169    Ross Clark, *Cambridgeshire* (London: Pimlico, 1996), 30–1.

170    Michael White, *Isaac Newton: The Last Sorcerer* (London: Fourth Estate, 1997), 221.

171    As it so happens, Petty's phrase comes from an early study by him on economic geography: *Another Essay in Political Arithmetick Concerning the Growth of the City of London: with the Measures, Periods, Causes, and Consequences Thereof, 1682* (London: Mark Pardoe, 1683).

172    Sheldon Rothblatt, *The Revolution of the Dons: Cambridge and Society in Victorian England* (Cambridge: Cambridge University Press, 1968), 273.

173    Martin Wiener, *English Culture and the Decline of the Industrial Spirit, 1850–1980* (London: Penguin Books, 1992; reprint, Cambridge: Cambridge University Press, 1981), 22–4.

174    Egon Larsen, *The Cavendish Laboratory: Nursery of Genius* (London: Edmund Ward, 1962), 13.

175    Hugh Kearney, *Origins of the Scientific Revolution* (London: Longmans, Green, 1964), 151.

176    Robert D. Friedel, *Lines and Waves: An Exhibit by the IEEE History Center* (1981), www.ieee.org.

177    M. Cattermole and A. Wolfe, *Horace Darwin's Shop: A History of the*

*Cambridge Scientific Instrument Company, 1878 to 1968* (Bristol: Adam Hilger, 1987), 3 and 42.

178   "Shaking Awake a Darwin Giant," Cambridge *Evening News*, 14 December 1967.

179   Graham Dowson quoted by Christopher Gwinner, "The Battle for Cambridge Instrument," *Financial Times*, 24 May 1968.

180   The issues precipitating Celltech's founding are detailed in Mark Dodgson's excellent study: *The Management of Technological Learning: Lessons from a Biotechnology Company*, de Gruyter Studies in Organization (Berlin: Walter de Gruyter, 1991), see especially pp. 25–35. Another well-written work that deals with the formation of Celltech and more broadly explores the issues of high-technology risk finance in Britain is Chris Lonsdale's *The UK Equity Gap: The Failure of Government Policy Since 1945* (Aldershot, UK: Ashgate, 1997). Lonsdale derives conclusions that support state intervention in the UK's venture capital market—a stance that takes the lessons of instances like Celltech's 1979 formation too far. Nevertheless, his treatment of Britain's perennially debated "equity gap" provides valuable information on the topic overall.

181   Gerard Fairtlough, author's interview, 14 November 1999.

182   Fairtlough describes his conceptualization and implementation of this organizational structure in his book, *Creative Compartments: A Design for Future Organizations* (London: Adamantine Press, 1994), see especially pp. 75–109.

183   A. Spinks, *Biotechnology: Report of a Joint Working Party* (London: HMSO, 1980), 41; quoted in Dodgson, *The Management of Technological Learning*, 29.

184   The merger produced a combined market capitalization of £696m. Another Golden Triangle acquisition, of Medeva, in 2000 provided Celltech with a new market capitalization of £1.3b and entered it into the FTSE 100. The company now has four main locations—Slough and Cambridge in the UK and Rochester and Seattle in the US—with the Cambridge site primarily focused on R&D.

185   Cambridgeshire County Council, *Employment in the Hi-tech Community*, 61 and 3.

186   Matthew Bullock, author's interview, 5 July 2000.

187   Segal Quince Wicksteed, *The Cambridge Phenomenon: The Growth of High Technology Industry in a University Town* (Swavesey, UK: Segal Quince Wicksteed, 1985; reprint, 1990), 15–16 and 19.

188   Ibid., 16 and 19.

189 Ibid., 15.

190 Cambridgeshire County Council, *Employment in the Hi-tech Community*, 3.

191 Segal Quince Wicksteed, *The Cambridge Phenomenon Revisited* (Histon, UK: Segal Quince Wicksteed), Part 1, 9.

192 Cambridgeshire County Council, *Employment in the Hi-tech Community*, 51.

193 Sarah Byles, "Acorn Rise 'Encouraging Little Story'—Minister," Cambridge *Evening News*, 6 July 1984.

194 Melanie Warner, "Cool Companies 1998," *Fortune*, 6 July 1998.

195 Lynch says he actually remarked words to the effect that if Silicon Valley is symbolized by Larry Ellison's jet, Cambridge is symbolized by a seagull; a smart seagull would try to work with the pilot of the jet rather than try to compete against it. (Mike Lynch, author's interview, 23 August 2000.)

## CHAPTER 9. CAMBRIDGE DYNAMICS

196 Charles Kingsley quoted in Richard Breen, *Cambridge Oddfellows & Funny Tales* (London: Penny Publishing, 1997), 2.

197 Greater Cambridge Partnership, *Congestion Ahead—Which Way to Turn* (Cambridge: Greater Cambridge Partnership, 1999), 7.

198 Department of the Environment, Transport and the Regions, *DETR Roads Review*, cited in Segal Quince Wicksteed, *The Cambridge Phenomenon Revisited*, Part 2, 89.

199 Suzy Jagger, "Wellcome Eyes Foreign Sites," *Daily Telegraph*, 9 September 1999.

200 John Halfpenny, "New Metropolis Would be Oppressive," Cambridge *Evening News*, 13 October 2000.

201 Gus Jeevar, "Time to Stand Up for Queen and Countryside," Cambridge *Evening News*, 26 October 2000.

202 William Holford and H. Myles Wright, *Cambridge Planning Proposals: A Report to the Town and Country Planning Committee of the Cambridgeshire County Council* (Cambridge: Cambridge University Press, 1950), 3 and 35.

203 Ibid., 47 and 81.

204 Ibid., 35 and 48.

205 Ibid., 48–9.

206 Ibid., 49.

207 Ibid., 50.

208 Ibid., 48–9.

209 Ibid., 50.

210 Ibid.

211 Ibid., 50 and 48.

212 Though gradually modified over time, the aftermath of *Holford* is immediately apparent. The report estimated a population of around 86,000 in Cambridge in 1948. Accepting that some organic expansion would be inevitable, the report set a population target of 100,000 as the limit that "would keep nearly all the present advantages and qualities of the town and its surroundings" (pp. 35 and 48). By 1981, when the Cambridge Phenomenon was entering its first major growth spurt, the population stood at 100,500. Increasing growth pressures, coupled with limited easing of restrictions, has since ruptured Holford's population ceiling but the excess has been slight. Population estimates for 1999 measure an increase of only 10,000 residents over 1981. (Cambridgeshire County Council, Research Group, "Mid Year Population Estimates: Parishes/Wards in Local Authority Districts, Cambridge City," www.camcnty.gov.uk.)

213 Holford, *Cambridge Planning Proposals*, 50.

214 University of Cambridge, Sub-Committee of the Sites and Town Planning Committee of the Financial Board (Mott Committee), "Relationship Between the University and Science-Based Industry: Notice by the Council of the Senate," *Cambridge University Reporter*, vol. C, no. 7 (22 October 1969), 373–4.

215 Ibid., 374.

216 Ibid., 373.

217 Quoted in David Wighton, "Mandelson Plans a Microchip off the Old Block," *Financial Times*, 23 October 1998.

218 British Venture Capital Association, *Report on Investment Activity, 1999* (London: British Venture Capital Association, 2000).

219 Bank of England, *The Financing of Technology-based Small Firms* (London: Bank of England, 1996), 19.

220 Danny Chapchal, interview on silicon.com, 27 July 1999.

221 British Venture Capital Association, *1999 Report on Investment Activity*, 33.

222 Department of Trade and Industry, Innovation Unit, *Private Investors: Improving Share Liquidity for Smaller Quoted Companies* (London: Department of Trade and Industry, 1999), 3.

223 Nigel Brown, author's interview, 7 September 2000.

224    Victor Keegan, "Can Acorn Become an Oak Tree Overnight?" *Guardian*, 16 June 1981. Hauser's "£100" refers to his half of the start-up capital invested.

225    Brown, 7 September 2000.

226    James Watson, *The Double Helix* (London: Penguin Books, 1999; originally London: Weidenfeld & Nicolson, 1968), 24–5.

227    Eastern Region Biotechnology Initiative, *Biobusiness Trends '99* (Cambridge: Deloitte & Touche, 1999), 17.

228    Ibid. SQW conducted the survey between November 1998 and February 1999 and received 156 responses, what the researchers believe approaches "half of the total number of relevant organizations in the region" (Ibid., 8).

229    Susan Ablett *et al.*, *The Cambridge Telecoms Phenomenon* (Cambridge: Analysys Publications, 1996), 2.

230    Jonathan Rauch, "The British Disease," *Reason Online*, July 1996.

231    Stephen Haseler, *The End of the House of Windsor: Birth of a British Republic* (London: I. B. Tauris, 1993), 73.

232    S. Ringen, "The Open Society and the Closed Mind," *Times Literary Supplement*, 24 January 1997, 6; quoted in David Cannadine, *Class in Britain* (London: Penguin Books, 2000; reprint, New Haven, CT: Yale University Press, 1998), ix.

233    Walter Herriot, author's interview, 29 June 2000.

234    Ibid.

235    International Center for Commercial Law, *Legal 500* (2000 edition), www.icclaw.com.

236    Rob Arnold, author's interview, 16 August 2000.

237    Ibid. The more lenient listing requirements are comprised in what is today known as FSA Chapter 20.

238    Nigel Brown, 7 September 2000.

239    Ibid.

240    Hermann Hauser, author's interview, 19 September 2000.

241    Ibid.

## CHAPTER 10. PHENOMENALLY INNOVATIVE

242    ARM, *2000 Annual Report*, 21.

243    Brian Groom, "ARM Muscles in on World Market for Digital Consumer Goods," *Financial Times*, 2 November 1999.

244 Rodney Dale, *From Ram Yard to Milton Hilton: A History of Cambridge Consultants* (Cambridge, Cambridge Consultants Limited, 1983), 4.

245 Lucy Rowbotham, author's interview, 21 August 2000.

246 Ibid.

247 Lucy Rowbotham and Nils Bohlin, "Structured Idea Management as a Value-Adding Process," *Prism*, 2 (1996): 79.

248 Gordon Edge, author's interview, 22 August 2000.

249 Ibid.

250 Gordon Edge, author's interview, 23 August 2000.

251 The Generics Group, *1999 Annual Review*.

252 Gordon Edge, 22 August 2000.

253 Gordon Edge, 23 August 2000.

254 The Generics Group, *Beyond Rationality: Reviving Inspiration in Management* (Harston, UK: The Generics Group, 1999), 7/02.

255 The Generics Group, *1999 Annual Review*.

256 An account of Absolute Sensors' background and management issues is presented in a Harvard Business School case study by Chad Ellis and Walter Keummerle, "Absolute Sensors," 15 January 1999 (N9-899-075).

257 Gerald Avison, author's interview, 18 July 2000.

258 Ibid.

259 Gerald Avison, author's interview, 18 September 2000.

260 Ibid.

261 Ibid.

## CHAPTER 11. THE FUTURE OF THE PHENOMENON

262 Segal Quince Wicksteed, *The Cambridge Phenomenon: The Growth of High Technology Industry in a University Town* (Swavesey, UK: Segal Quince Wicksteed, 1985; reprint, 1990), xi.

263 According to a college alumnus' tracking of prizes, Trinity scholars have racked up 31 Nobel prizes (26 in the sciences); France has produced nearly 50 Nobel laureates. To Trinity's immense credit, it publicly debunks the legend about its alleged Nobel prize "victory" on the college's website, www.damtp.cam.ac.uk/user/smb1001/trin/nobel.htm. Despite such public denials, the urban legend surrounding Trinity's Nobel prize tally persists.

264 Susan Ablett *et al.*, *Cambridge 2020: Meeting the Challenge of Growth* (Cambridge: Analysys Publications, 1998), 59.

265     Ibid.

266     Wilson's famous words were first uttered at the Labour Party Conference held in Scarborough on 1 October 1963. Though they continue to echo in debates about the technological advancement of British society, the context in which they are interpreted has changed dramatically. Unlike the inspiration for today's "Third Way" Labour leader, Tony Blair, Wilson was not inspired by the technological progress of the United States but by what he saw as the scientific might and socio-economic accomplishments of the Soviet Union. Wilson's revolution had little room for free enterprise which he perceived as providing profits to the elite but offering little benefit to the working masses. Wilson saw the "white heat" of a technocratic revolution as a means for Britain to "re-define and restate" a socialistic agenda while doing away with the amateurism viewed to be a by-product of the country's decidedly un-scientific class system. (For an exploration of the ideology underpinning "white heat" see Ben Pimlott, *Harold Wilson* [London: HarperCollins, 1992].) The current wave of dominant political thinking, on the other hand, looks to free-market competition as a vehicle for developing Britain's "capabilities in skills, science, and entrepreneurship." See the Department of Trade and Industry whitepaper: *Our Competitive Future: Building the Knowledge-Driven Economy*, 1998, www.dti.gov.uk/comp/ competitive/main.htm.

## CHAPTER 12. EPILOGUE: A SILICON WORLD?

267     Michael Malone, *The Big Score: The Billion-Dollar Story of Silicon Valley* (Garden City, NY: Doubleday & Company, 1985), 9.

# Index